Love, Rōshi

Love, Rōshi

Robert Baker Aitken
and His Distant Correspondents

HELEN J. BARONI

COVER ART courtesy of iStockphoto / image of Zen-like paper background / contributor: wepix and stack of old letters / contributor: bgwalker

All quotations from Robert Aitken's published and unpublished materials are protected by copyright and are used with permission of the Estate of Robert Aitken.

Published by State University of New York Press, Albany

© 2012 State University of New York

All rights reserved

Printed in the United States of America

No part of this book may be used or reproduced in any manner whatsoever without written permission. No part of this book may be stored in a retrieval system or transmitted in any form or by any means including electronic, electrostatic, magnetic tape, mechanical, photocopying, recording, or otherwise without the prior permission in writing of the publisher.

For information, contact State University of New York Press, Albany, NY
www.sunypress.edu

Production by Diane Ganeles
Marketing by Fran Keneston

Library of Congress Cataloging-in-Publication Data
Baroni, Helen Josephine.
Love, Rōshi : Robert Baker Aitken and his distant correspondents / Helen J. Baroni.
    pages cm
Includes bibliographical references and index.
ISBN 978-1-4384-4377-5 (hc : alk. paper)—978-1-4384-4378-2 (pbk : alk. paper)
1. Aitken, Robert, 1917–2010—Correspondence. 2. Zen Buddhists—United States—Correspondence. I. Title.
BQ940.I85B37 2012
294.3'927092—dc22

2011048284

10 9 8 7 6 5 4 3 2 1

In memory of Robert Baker Aitken
(1917–2010)

Contents

List of Tables	ix
Acknowledgments	xi
Preface	xiii

Preliminary Matters

Introduction	3
Chapter 1. Setting the Stage: Aitken and the Context of Zen in America	23

Part I: Distant Correspondents Write to the Rōshi

Chapter 2. Why People Write	47
Chapter 3. Patterns of Zen Practice among the Distant Correspondents	67
Chapter 4. Areas of Special Concern Raised by Distant Correspondents	81
Chapter 5. Special Constituencies within the Distant Correspondents	115

Part II:
The Rōshi Responds

Chapter 6. Robert Aitken's Zen Ministry by Mail   137

Chapter 7. These Words Are Your Words:
    Patterns in Aitken's Responses to his Distant Correspondents   149

Conclusion   171

Notes   179

Bibliography   187

Index   191

Tables

1. Distribution of Letters through Time 10
2. Age at First Contact 11
3. Geographical Distribution in the United States 13
4. Establishment of Zen Institutions in the United States 39
5. Zen Institutions by Affiliation 40
6. Reasons for Writing 48
7. Types of Advice Sought 51
8. Practice Data 70
9. Other Practice Information 70
10. Recommendations for Specific Teachers 157

Acknowledgments

I must begin by thanking Robert Aitken and the members of the Honolulu Diamond Sangha for inviting me to participate in the Robert Baker Aitken Papers project that got everything started and made this research possible. I enjoyed working with and getting to know everyone who volunteered. I would especially like to thank Nelson Foster and Michael Kieran for talking with me and clarifying many matters related to HDS and Aitken Rōshi's work. Kathie Ratliff and Ginger Ikenberry made me welcome and provided me with their perspectives on the archive, HDS history and Aitken Rōshi's commitment to his distant correspondents.

Nancy Ellegate, Senior Acquisitions Editor at SUNY Press, shepherded the manuscript through peer review and provided her own keen observations for improvement. I cannot thank her enough for her steady support. I would also like to thank the anonymous readers who commented on the manuscript, making constructive suggestions for improvements.

The research began during a sabbatical leave from the Department of Religion at the University of Hawaii at Manoa, and I would like to thank the College of Arts and Humanities for providing that support. Many colleagues and students at UHM have offered help and encouragement in preparing the project. Three friends and colleagues, Nick Franchini, Kathie Kane and Christine Walters, read through the entire first draft of the manuscript and made many valuable suggestions. Kathie continued to offer her encouragement and insightful ideas throughout the writing process. Christine's brainstorming for methods to study Buddhist sympathizers probably inspired the initial idea for the project. Michel Mohr read portions of the manuscript and helped with ideas for restructuring it. Tom Hilgers reminisced with me about the heady days of exploring Asia and Asian religions in the 1960s and 1970s, and along the way provided me with some much needed perspective. Lynn Davis, Librarian and Head of Preservation at Hamilton Library made the research possible in the most basic sense. She gave me access to the archive while her staff was still processing it, provided me with a comfortable workspace and cheered me on as I made my way through all the boxes. A group of talented graduate students Jessica Friedman, Takashi Miura, Justin Stein, and Christine Walters helped me to thrash out my ideas in the early stages of the writing. They pushed back in the most collegial manner possible. My thanks to all of you.

Finally, as always, my gratitude to Rod, Lena, and Philip.

Preface

Starting sometime during the Spring of 2002, I became involved with the Robert Baker Aitken Papers project, which culminated in creating an archive now housed as a Special Collection at the University of Hawaii at Manoa's Hamilton Library. Robert Aitken's assistant called me from his home in Kaimu, on the Big Island of Hawaii. She explained the purpose of the archive project and conveyed to me Honolulu Diamond Sangha's (HDS) invitation that I participate as the designated Humanities' scholar. Robert Aitken, founder of Honolulu Diamond Sangha, decided to donate his correspondence files and other written materials to the University. In consultation with him, members of Honolulu Diamond Sangha were already preparing the materials for submission. In order to defray the costs of the project, they planned to apply for a Preservation and Access Grant sponsored by the Hawaii Council for the Humanities. The grant application required that HDS secure the participation of a humanities scholar who could assess and report on the likely scholarly value of the materials. I later learned that a former graduate student of mine, an active member of HDS, recommended me as a possible candidate. I enjoy opportunities to work with local religious groups, especially Zen communities, so I readily agreed.

After the Hawaii Council for the Humanities approved the grant, I was in regular contact with Aitken's assistant as we negotiated my planned visit to the Big Island and other aspects of my role in the project. In addition to traveling to Kaimu to review the contents of the archive, they were hoping that I would take the lead in the public program that would introduce the project to the local community, another required element for the grant. Later they would also ask me to devise a plan for the formal public announcement of the archive via print media to the scholarly audience and to other Buddhist organizations. First, however, we needed to work out plans for me to visit Aitken on the Big Island.

The assistant explained that they wanted me to come for several days, so that Aitken could get to know me and I would have ample time to become acquainted with the archive materials. In that moment, I was torn. I wanted to go, but I had been imagining a day trip, overnight at most. My younger child was still breastfeeding, and even four days away posed something of an obstacle. At the time, pressure remained strong at the university that professional women not openly discuss their family obligations. I hesitated on the phone, trying to imagine how to bring up breastfeeding and still sound like a professional consultant. I muttered something vague about family issues. She immediately became enthusiastic; she too was a working mother. She asked me about my children, their ages and gender and names, and how I managed to juggle career and family. As we chatted, I felt comfortable confessing my dilemma. We considered options. Then I heard a voice in the background—a man's voice asking if there was a problem. His solution came loud and clear across the room and the phone connection: "Tell her to bring the whole family!" And so my family visited Kaimu in October 2002.

We stayed with Tom Aitken, the Rōshi's son, who lived just across the street. Aitken's home at the time was a lovely Japanese structure, inspired by Zen temple architecture. It sits perched atop a recent lava flow, overlooking the ocean. We took our meals with Aitken, his staff and his son, and we all accompanied Aitken on his daily walks. Aitken adores children, and he made the most of these interactions, endearing himself to me with his obvious affection for my children. He would speak firmly to my son during meals to quiet him down, and then hoot with laughter when his mock stern tone did the trick.

Aitken made time each morning to visit with me, before getting down to his daily writing sessions. In retirement, he maintained a "writing program" whenever his health permitted. Although I made a concerted effort to interview him, I was well aware that he was actively returning the favor. The experience was unlike any fieldwork I have ever done. Our discussions were intense and intellectually stimulating. He quickly ascertained that I had been raised in a devout Catholic family and that my childhood heroes included Dorothy Day and the Berrigan brothers. I was profoundly impressed by Aitken's commitment to social justice and delighted by his sense of humor. He had an infectious laugh, that emerged loud and all of a sudden. The visit transformed my relationship with Aitken and HDS from a strictly professional arrangement to one more akin to friendship. For many years after that visit, my children referred to Aitken as "Uncle Rōshi," following the island custom to refer to adults as "auntie" or "uncle." And I feel that many HDS members have accepted me as something more than an outside scholar, although they understand that I hope to write about HDS in the future.

When I began the present project in spring 2008, I was very much taken by the idea that I could use the archive materials as a means to study Zen sympathizers, although I was not yet deeply interested in the subject itself. On the contrary, I was already thinking ahead to my larger project related to HDS. I didn't plan to invest much time or energy in the Distant Correspondent project. I thought it would be a nice warm up exercise for the real focus of my sabbatical leave. I would collect some data, write a short paper, and move on to my larger plans to complete the archive research for a monograph about HDS. After a few weeks working in the archive, however, I realized that my attitude was shifting. I was writing far more extensive notes than I could possibly need or use for a paper.

From early on in the process, the letters came to represent more than just research data, they told people's stories. I couldn't resist reading more of them and recording my ever-lengthening notes. More than once, an exchange of letters brought me to tears or made me laugh out loud. I found the stories so compelling that I related them to friends over lunch or to my family at dinner. By the time I reached the halfway mark in the files, I had long since abandoned my plan to stop taking notes on the Distant Correspondents after collecting a preset number of cases. I was hooked. I continued to read and record notes to the end, reading through all 48 archive boxes of general correspondence.

When I began to write up the research, I once again determined to constrain myself to the limits of a relatively short research paper. I hoped to the let the voices of the Distant Correspondents bring the material to life, rather than presenting a dry analysis of the data, but I was still committed to adhere to my planned research agenda. Before I knew it, the project got away from me once again. I felt compelled to tell more of the stories, and relatively minor categories of Distant Correspondents such as the Walking Wounded (individuals wounded by their dealings with other

Zen teachers) and the prison inmates, seemed to demand a place in the project. Once again, I let myself get carried away by the flow of my interest, and a monograph began to take shape. I abandoned my other research plans for the time being, and kept writing. The present book is the result of that happy period of obsession, writing to suit my own interest, and rather than staying on track, generating a new path.

The title "Love, Rōshi" first came to me in 2004, when I spent the summer systematically reading through the archive for the first time. I sampled approximately one third of the correspondences files that summer, on a reconnaissance mission to determine realistically what types of projects this extraordinary resource could inspire and support. Most of the correspondence in the files is between Aitken and his students, family members and friends. In letters to students, he often signed the letters "Love, Bob" or "Love, Rōshi," and the latter came to sound like a refrain as I read. The effect was no doubt amplified by the fact that at the time, I concentrated almost exclusively on reading Aitken's side of the correspondence.

Since I anticipated writing about Aitken's life and teachings, I hoped that the teaching style represented in his letters would prove to be a possible topic. I kept extensive notes on biographical details, elements of teaching style, as well as information relevant to several other possible topics of interest. In addition to these practical concerns, I was dealing with an emotional response that never came up doing historical research on individuals long deceased. I felt no qualms at all reading Aitken's letters, since he had donated the archive and intended it for public use. I felt far less comfortable when I read the letters addressed to him, composed by people who did not necessarily know that their letters would be made available in this manner. Indeed, I soon realized that I knew a number of the correspondents both from my dealings with Honolulu Diamond Sangha and from my interactions with colleagues in the field.

In 2004, I had not yet decided what ethical parameters I should follow in reading other people's letters preserved in the archive, so I avoided the issue as much as possible by not reading them, especially when the individual was known to me. When I returned to the archive in 2008 to collect data on the Distant Correspondents, I knew that I would be collecting specific kinds of data that would be used primarily in the aggregate, so that issues of privacy would be minimized as would my need to read the letters of most HDS members, some of whom I now regard as friends.

In January 2008, when I proposed an early version of this study for presentation at the annual conference of the American Academy of Religion, I decided to use the "Love, Rōshi" refrain as its title. At the time, I didn't yet know that Aitken did not typically sign his letters to strangers in that fashion. Once I began working in the archive, I soon understood that he was far likelier to sign off with "Cheers" or "Gassho," and I conscientiously changed the proposed title of the monograph to the more accurate, if less appealing "Gassho, Rōshi." Friends and editors have since convinced me that the original title would serve much better. As one friend (and long-time student of Aitken) maintained, the original title was true in spirit if not accurate in fact. I agree. Robert Aitken displayed a remarkable ability to fill his letters with affection and genuine concern, whether he was addressing complete strangers or beloved friends. So with apologies to Rōshi for taking liberties with his words, I changed the title back.

Preliminary Matters

Introduction

> I remember reading in the memoirs of Walter De La Mare how impressed he was on looking over what he had written forty years earlier: "What a clever fellow I was!" he exclaimed. Well I don't have that response when I read my old writings.... I write about the Buddha Dharma. My early writings might have interest for a scholar pursuing a history of North American Zen, but my purpose in publishing this collection is not simply to resurrect my archives, but to set forth Zen in the truest way I can at this present moment.
> —Robert Aitken, *The Morning Star: New and Selected Zen Writings*

An oncologist rises early to squeeze in thirty minutes of meditation before showering and dressing for work. The dean of a large state university law school strives to apply Buddhist principles and values in her daily decisions at work. At the end of a long day, a mother relaxes before bed reading a book of Buddhist reflections after tucking her children in for the night (she hopes). A young Vietnamese American scientist stays connected with Buddhist friends online and discusses Buddhist themes in his weekly blog. These individuals and others like them are what Thomas Tweed calls Buddhist sympathizers.[1] If asked about their religious preference on a survey, some of them would self-identify as Buddhist, while others would not. All over America, individuals such as these practice Buddhist meditation and follow the Buddha's teachings as they understand them without the benefit of membership in a Zen center or a Buddhist temple. When scholars map out the growth of Buddhism in the United States in the last hundred years or seek to gage its influence on American culture, sympathizers remain largely invisible.

The present study makes use of the correspondence between Robert Baker Aitken (1917–2010), Zen teacher, author and the founder of Honolulu Diamond Sangha (hereafter HDS)[2] and his "distant correspondents" as a window to view the beliefs and practices of these Buddhist sympathizers and solo practitioners, the least studied segment of the Western Buddhist community.[3] Robert Baker Aitken is well known within the world of Buddhism in the West as one of the pioneers of twentieth-century Zen that trained in Asia with Japanese teachers, received full designation as a Zen teacher[4] and founded a Buddhist community in the United States. Like many of his Distant Correspondents, Aitken came to the study of Zen through books, in his case translations of Zen classics by R. H. Blyth, while confined in a prisoner of war camp in Japan during the Second World War. In turn, Aitken's own books, especially *Taking the Path of Zen* and *The Mind of Clover*, brought many readers to the practice of Zen.

The categories of Buddhist sympathizer and solo practitioner include individuals introduced to Zen through various means, most often through Zen literature and university classes that are not directly affiliated with a Zen center or monastery. In most cases, they have had little direct experience meditating with a practicing Zen community or direct access to guidance from a teacher. The study also includes individuals that previously practiced at a Zen center, in some cases with a teacher, who no longer actively maintain those ties and nevertheless continue to practice Zen on their own. It explores the concerns that these individuals bring to bear in their letters written to a recognized American Zen teacher, the understanding of Zen practice and the image of the "Zen master" implicit in their letters, and the responses the letters elicit from Aitken himself.

The letters used in the study were written over a thirty-year period, roughly from 1970 to 2000. They represent one small part of the Robert Baker Aitken Papers, an archive housed at the Hamilton Library at the University of Hawaii. The full collection comprises all written materials saved by Aitken over several decades, including extensive personal and professional correspondence, HDS records from his tenure as director and teacher, HDS newsletters, drafts of Aitken's unpublished sermons and talks, as well as copies of his published materials. Excluded from the present study are Aitken's extensive correspondence with family, personal friends, other Zen teachers, and active members of HDS, ripe fodder for future studies. The remainder of Aitken's correspondents includes hundreds of "distant correspondents," the majority of whom wrote to Aitken as complete strangers.

The letters composed by the Distant Correspondents represent a remarkable resource for scholars seeking to understand the manner in which Buddhism has influenced American culture as well as the styles of belief and practice that are taking shape in the United States beyond the confines of organized Buddhist communities. Since the 1970s, scholars have studied various institutional forms of Buddhism that were established in the United States during the latter half of the twentieth century. Nevertheless, these studies only tell a part of the story of Buddhism in America. They cannot bridge the gap between Americans who join Buddhist communities and the relatively large percentage that self identify as Buddhist and yet choose not to affiliate with an established religious institution.

The number of Americans who self identified as Buddhist increased dramatically in the final decades of the twentieth century, more than doubling between 1990 and 2001 alone from 401,000 to 1,082,000.[5] Nevertheless, the overall percentage of the population remains extremely small, representing only 0.5 percent of the adult population in 2001. The ARIS report published in 2001 estimated that only about 28 percent of self identified adult Buddhists in America were affiliated with a community at that time.[6] This means that more than two thirds of Americans who regard themselves as Buddhist fall outside the purview of existing studies. Nor can existing studies give accurate accounts of the influence that Buddhist teachings have on Americans who sympathize with the tradition without identifying themselves as Buddhist. The present study of Distant Correspondents provides the first glimpse of unaffiliated American Buddhists and Buddhist sympathizers, based on their own words.

Zen Letters

There are, of course, precedents familiar to scholars of Chan and Zen in China and Japan of teachers corresponding with lay and monastic disciples. Letters composed by better-known Zen monks sometimes appear in very limited numbers in published collections of their writings. Looking at the published letters of two early modern Zen teachers, Ōbaku monk Tetsugen Dōkō (1630–1682) and Rinzai master Hakuin Ekaku (1686–1769), for example, one finds a small corpus of letters that share some basic features. First, the letters were selected and then edited for publication, either by the teacher himself or posthumously by his disciples. In some cases, it appears that the letters were originally composed with wider distribution in mind, such as circulation within the extended household of a lord and his retainers or a nun and her religious community. At least portions of a letter from a famous teacher would be read aloud for the instruction of other members of the household or monastic community.

Both Tetsugen and Hakuin made use of letters as teaching devises, and it seems likely that the letters included in published volumes were selected precisely because of the pedagogical value of the contents. In the case of Tetsugen, some of his letters take a form nearly indistinguishable from the Dharma lessons that he composed for individual disciples. In other cases, when Tetsugen composed a letter for a particular purpose, such as to raise funds for his publishing project or for famine relief, he nonetheless made use of the opportunity to express his understanding of how the situation related to appropriate Buddhist practice.[7]

Hakuin made somewhat more extensive use of letters as a means to instruct his monastic and lay disciples. Several of his letters were collected and published during his lifetime, while others appeared in posthumous collections. Hakuin's letters served a wide variety of pedagogical purposes, and displayed his ability to craft his lessons in language and style appropriate to his immediate audience. To high-ranking samurai, for example, Hakuin typically couched his lessons in terms of Confucian ethical norms, which would have been familiar to all educated members of the samurai class. In letters to monks and nuns, Hakuin more often made use of Buddhist texts, but again those specifically appropriate to his correspondent. To a Nichiren nun, for example, he writes about the Lotus Sutra, while quoting from Zen sources only for Zen practitioners.[8]

In most cases, the published letters of Tetsugen and Hakuin were addressed not to strangers, but to individuals with whom they had already established a relationship. The recipients were typically either monastic disciples living elsewhere, or wealthy patrons who likewise practiced as lay practitioners under their guidance. It should be noted that such recipients numbered among the educated elite. Although literacy rates rose rapidly during the early modern period in Japan, letter writing remained rare among less educated classes of Japanese. Finally, in no case does the published collection include letters from the correspondents.

The letters in the Aitken archive differ considerably from the patterns just noted. The letters form an extensive corpus of unpublished materials that include more letters from the Distant Correspondents than responses from Aitken. Although Aitken's letter writing represents a form of ministry, Aitken did not compose his responses to the Distant Correspondents for purposes of broader circulation or for future publication. Nor did he regard them as a primary vehicle for his teaching. The letters served other purposes, discussed in chapters 6 and 7, while Aitken, an accomplished author, used his extensive published works as his primary means of teaching individuals outside the HDS community.

Finally, the letters in the Aitken archive have not been edited, with the exception that some letters related to kōan practice were removed before the archive was transferred to the university. Aitken explained to me in the early stages of the archive project that he planned to remove certain materials that amounted to written forms of *dokusan* exchanges (private encounters between teacher and student). Within the Zen tradition, what happens in *dokusan* is generally regarded as private, not to be divulged by either the teacher or the student. Aitken was especially concerned that some of this material could present a potential hazard for other practitioners who may one day read through the archive. In particular, he was unwilling to make public exchanges that led to either an acknowledgment of *kenshō* (an initial enlightenment experience) in a beginning student or represented progress in the kōan curriculum for more advanced students.[9] Despite this minor form of censorship, both in its extent and its unedited nature, the Aitken corpus represents an extraordinary new resource for the academic study of Zen in the West. The general correspondence section alone comprises forty-eight archive boxes of material, and this excludes Aitken's family correspondence. I know of no other comparable archive that is currently publicly available, and anticipate that it will prove to be a treasure trove for scholars studying Zen in the United States and other societies outside of Asia in the twentieth century.

Aitken regarded his published writings, much of which came out of his immediate work with HDS, as an important aspect of his teaching outreach. He maintained that the aim in all of his writings was to spread the Dharma, and of course he was well aware that many of his students came to Zen through encounters with Zen literature just as he did himself. In many of his publications, Aitken included an invitation to his readers to write to him with questions, complete with his mailing address. He invited their letters and as shall be seen throughout this text, proved a dedicated correspondent throughout his teaching career and into retirement. I will argue that the more private corpus of his writings, his extensive correspondence with students and strangers alike, represents a separate but critical aspect of his "ministry" to promote Zen in the West.

Preliminary Methodology: Identifying the Distant Correspondents

Correspondence preserved in the Aitken archive is arranged alphabetically, with a file or files labeled for each individual correspondent. Files typically contain the original letters composed by an individual, carbon copies of Aitken's responses, and occasionally other items sent via mail, such as postcards, holiday cards, newspaper clippings, original art work, and poetry. The category of general correspondence is broad, comprising letters Aitken exchanged with his students, other Buddhist teachers, personal friends, as well as the Distant Correspondents who wrote as strangers. The archive thus preserves something of the original filing style established by Aitken and his secretarial staff. In preparing the archive for use by the public, however, the library staff attempted to arrange each individual file in chronological order, although not all the materials are dated. The staff likewise separated out Aitken's correspondence exchanged with his family, as well as his wife Anne Aitken's correspondence, which had previously been mixed with the rest. The present study made only limited use of the family files and no use of Anne Aitken's correspondence.

The process of identifying the Distant Correspondents required an initial reading through each file within the general correspondence to determine if the individual met the criteria for inclusion in the study. Since the majority of correspondents could be classified as personal friends, Aitken's students, or professional contacts, including other Buddhist teachers, most were excluded from the research group. For each of the cases identified as Distant Correspondents, a file number was assigned and data was collected, including basic demographic information (gender, age, and mailing address), number of letters in the file, the dates composed, and whether the individual had ever met Aitken or seen him speak.

More descriptive data and extensive quotations were collected under the following categories: familiarity with Zen, reasons for writing, questions asked, and requests made. Under the rubric "familiarity with Zen," I recorded various kinds of self-disclosed information related to how the individual first learned to meditate, what books he or she mentioned as critical to personal practice, how long the individual had been meditating, whether he or she had ever worked with a teacher or participated in a meditation group or attended a Zen center, and so forth.

For Aitken's responses, data was collected for the dates of replies, general tone of the letter(s), answers to questions, responses to requests, and salutation style. In many cases I likewise took notes on whether the letter was typed or handwritten, the style and content of marginal notes that Aitken made on the correspondent's letter, and whether the reply had been appended to a General Letter sent regularly to all individuals on the mailing list.

Distant Correspondents

The study identified 261 cases of Distant Correspondents, who wrote to Aitken between the years 1968 and 2002 (see table 1). For the purposes of this study, I defined "Distant Correspondents" to include individuals who practice Zen on their own or in small groups, often based exclusively on their reading of contemporary Zen literature, as well as Zen students and aspirants with only brief or indirect contact with Aitken. In other words, at the time they first wrote, these individuals are distant not only in geographical remove, but in terms of establishing any personal relationship with Aitken as a Zen teacher. In most cases, they seem to know of him only through his publications or public appearances. As a rule, the study does not include active members of HDS affiliate groups on the mainland of the United States, because those individuals had regular access to Aitken either when he visited their centers to lead *sesshin* or when they traveled to Hawaii to participate in *sesshin* or for longer periods of residential practice at HDS. A limited number of new members from international HDS affiliate groups, specifically those from Australia, New Zealand, and Germany, were included in the study, since these individuals wrote as virtual strangers before they had practiced directly with Aitken. It should be noted that in several cases, people included in the study initially wrote as strangers but eventually became students of Aitken and affiliated themselves with HDS and actively participated in *sangha* activities either in Hawaii or with an affiliated group.

Demographic information related to the Distant Correspondents, including gender, age at initial contact, occupation, and geographic location was collected when available in the letters and analyzed to gain a

Table 1. Distribution of Letters through Time

Years	No. Cases	Percentage
1968–1974	6	2%
1975–1979	30	11%
1980–1984	48	18%
1985–1989	69	26%
1990–1994	67	26%
1995–2002	31	12%
No date	7	3%

general sense of the study group. No attempt was made to determine other demographic patterns, such as ethnicity or socioeconomic status, given the limitations inherent in the sources. It should likewise be noted that, while the study makes use of this group to gain an understanding of the practice and belief patterns found among Zen sympathizers and solo practitioners more broadly, the study group cannot be regarded as a representative sample in the technical sense. In the first place, these Distant Correspondents took the initiative to write to a Zen teacher, which alone sets them apart in some way from other solo practitioners and sympathizers. Moreover, as will be discussed in more detail further on, many correspondents indicate specific reasons why they felt drawn to this particular Zen teacher, who was known for his practical advice about meditation and for his stress on ethical conduct as a basis for and an outgrowth of Zen practice. A similar study conducted with the correspondence of a different teacher could yield different results.

The demographic analysis of the study group revealed very few surprises, with the possible exception of the size of the imbalance in the gender profile. The ratio of men to women was greater than 3 to 1, a ratio that held steady through time. The study group included 189 individual men, sixty-one individual women, and five heterosexual couples; I had insufficient information to classify the remaining six cases.[10] Demographic data cited by Layman suggests that this ratio may have been typical for membership at Zen centers on the mainland of the United States during the early portion of the time period.[11] Tipton's work reports a more balanced ratio of men to women among the membership at San Francisco Zen Center in the 1970s.[12] While I do not have membership lists or demographic data for HDS membership, pictorial evidence suggests that like SFZC, HDS enjoyed a much more balanced gender profile throughout its history.[13] In passing remarks in a few of his responses, however, Aitken indicated that Maui Zendo experienced at least periods of gender imbalance among the resident population, those who visited for periods of intense practice, as opposed to regular members who lived nearby in the local community. In one such letter, dated January 16, 1970, Aitken indicated to a male correspondent that Maui Zendo was already at full capacity (at that time twelve residents plus the Aitkens), and that all the residents were men, leaving Anne as the only woman. He indicated that both he and Anne were unhappy with that imbalance.

The Distant Correspondents ranged in age from seventeen to eighty-four (see table 2). Data related to age is partial, of course, since only eighty-nine correspondents (or 34 percent of the study group) indicated age or date of birth. Viewed as a whole, the largest percentage of these correspondents are individuals in their twenties. When viewed diachronically, however, the data indicates a steady pattern of increase in the median age of the correspondents such that the median age rose from the early thirties during the 1970s to the late thirties in the 1980s and then to the early forties during the 1990s. This pattern mirrors the general aging pattern seen among the membership at HDS and at other Zen centers in the West over the same decades.

Table 2. Age at First Contact

Age	1970–1980	1981–1990	1991–2001	Total
17–19	1	2	1	4
20–24	3	6	2	11
25–29	3	7	6	16
30–34	3	6	—	9
35–39	1	6	2	9
40–44	3	2	6	11
45–49	1	5	3	9
50–54	—	1	5	6
55–59	—	—	2	2
60–64	1	—	1	2
65–69	—	—	1	1
70–74	—	—	—	—
75–79	—	—	—	—
80–84	—	1	—	1
Median	30–34	35–39	40–44	35–39

The geographic data, nearly complete, and carefully collected and analyzed, produced no unusual results. The group included 219 individuals living in the United States, seven Americans living overseas, and forty-two individuals living outside the United States who identified themselves as other than American citizens. The patterns for American correspondents (see table 3) appear to correlate to geographic factors such as proximity to Hawaii and areas of dense population, as well as to geographic patterns of religious affiliation in alternative religions noted by other research studies.[14] More than one fourth of the correspondents live in the Pacific region, which combines all of the previously mentioned factors, proximity, areas of dense population, and high levels of affiliation in and relative openness to alternative religions. The South Atlantic region, extending from Maryland and Delaware down to Florida, showed the lowest numbers, a mere 6 percent, in keeping with the region's low levels of affiliation in and relative intolerance of alternative religions. Among the forty-two individuals from other countries, more than a third (thirteen cases) were living in Australia. It should be noted that Zen enjoyed a rapid growth in both interest and membership in Australia in the 1980s and 1990s, and that Aitken regularly made annual visits to Australia during that period. Several Zen centers in Australia eventually affiliated with Diamond Sangha, and continue to be led by Aitken's Dharma heirs. Other nationalities with significant representation among the Distant Correspondents include England and Germany, each with six cases, and Canada with five.

The distribution of the letters through time, shown in table 1, reflects both changes in Robert Aitken's teaching and writing career as well as the general growth in the interest in Zen in America throughout the period. The letters begin to gradually increase after 1974, a critical year for Aitken. First, Aitken received his initial permission to teach independently from Yamada Kōun in that year, and subsequently began to function as a teacher within the Sanbōkyōdan lineage. He likewise published his essay "The Zen Buddhist Path of Self-realization" that year, in which he included his postal address and an invitation to readers to consult him by mail.[15]

The decade from 1985 to 1994 saw the greatest growth in letter writing. More than half of the Distant Correspondents wrote to Aitken during this time period, which also corresponds to the period of Aitken's growing success as an author. His most popular books, *Taking the Path of Zen* and *The Mind of Clover*, appeared in 1982 and 1984, respectively, raising his profile among a broader audience. In personal interviews, Aitken confirmed that during these years, especially the latter half, Honolulu Diamond Sangha likewise enjoyed its greatest period of growth in

Table 3. Geographical Distribution in the United States

Region	No. Cases	Percentage
Pacific	69	26%
Mountain	17	7%
North Central	29	11%
South Central	28	11%
New England & Mid-Atlantic	36	14%
South Atlantic	16	6%

membership.[16] At the same time, the United States was experiencing a period of the most rapid growth in the number of Zen centers throughout the country. It should be noted that active membership at HDS in the late 1980s and early 1990s rose to approximately 100, while 136 Distant Correspondents wrote during that same time period.

Finally, the number of letters begins to taper off rapidly after Aitken's retirement in 1996. At least as late as fall 2008, Aitken continued to receive and answer letters from new correspondents in his retirement, although the majority of this correspondence was conducted electronically. It is highly likely that the number of Distant Correspondents identified during the final time period, 1995 through 2002, does not accurately reflect the actual number of individuals who contacted Aitken during those years. By 1995, many individuals had already shifted from conventional mail to email, Aitken included. The archive does not as a rule include printouts of email exchanges. In addition, it is not known how many newer, active files Aitken chose to retain when he prepared his older correspondence files for inclusion in the archive.

Epistolary Relationships and Other Challenges

Archival letters provide scholars with firsthand accounts written by ordinary people, in this case Buddhist sympathizers and solo practitioners, thus allowing some access to their understanding of Buddhism and their practical concerns. Letters allow us to hear the voices of these individuals, to hear their stories in their own words, and to build a clearer picture of this so far largely "imagined" category of American Buddhists. Unfortunately, very little scholarly work has yet been done using archival letters as a resource for studying religious beliefs and practices, so that no standards yet exist for a methodology. The present study is therefore somewhat experimental in nature, combining standard historiographical practices for analyzing primary source material with certain sociological sensibilities. The letters were viewed chronologically, for example, in order to facilitate the identification of diachronic patterns. In addition, since one can presume that many of the correspondents are alive, ethical concerns related to preserving anonymity exist. Much of the data is therefore discussed in the aggregate, which poses no problem. Nevertheless, specific examples bring the study to life and are critical for grounding the data in the context of actual individuals' life and practice. I have therefore decided to preserve anonymity when discussing particular individuals and quoting from their letters, while providing some relevant information about gender, age, location, profession, and the like.

A thorough bibliographical search of the scholarly literature identified no works related to religion and archival letters. Work has been done with published letters written by ordinary believers, such as Robert Orsi's compelling study of St. Jude's devout, who wrote to voice their petitions and express their gratitude toward St. Jude.[17] Orsi reviewed all the letters published in two religious journals published by the National Shrine of St. Jude, and his analysis of these letters forms the basis for his description of the primary concerns, the hopeless causes that motivated the devout to turn to Jude for intercession. Orsi's basic approach to the material is similar to that which I have taken with the letters from the Aitken archive. Certain differences in the sources, however, should be noted. Orsi did not have access to an archive of all the letters sent to St. Jude's Shrine, only the items selected by the staff for publication. As Orsi notes, although the staff may not have significantly altered the letters when they were edited for publication, the selection process itself weeded out subjects deemed inappropriate according to official doctrine.[18]

Recent historical studies based on archival collections of European immigrants' letters written home as a means to better understand the immigrant experience in America provide some practical historiographical suggestions as well as some illuminating points of contrast for the present study.[19] First, one is well advised to recall that the Distant Correspondents may hope to positively impress Aitken, and therefore seek to present themselves in the best possible light, in much the same way that immigrants tended to present their life in America in rosier terms than was probably accurate. They may exaggerate their devotion to Zen practice, for example, and overestimate the regularity of their practice patterns. I have nonetheless decided to take the correspondents at their word when coding the data for further analysis. There is simply no practical method to fact-check the letters, and I regard the information to be at least as valid as data collected through survey instruments. Indeed, precisely because the correspondents are entering into an "epistolary relationship" with Aitken, rather than answering questions for an unknown researcher, their self-observations may be more honest.

The epistolary relationship between Aitken and his Distant Correspondents is a type of ethical discourse not unlike a conversation between a potential student and a teacher. Letter and response serve mutual needs and demonstrate mutual respect. The Distant Correspondents approach Aitken for assistance and guidance; they show respect for him as a qualified Zen teacher. It is not necessarily in their best interest to paint a picture of themselves as completely successful in their practice or satisfied with their current status, since that would undercut their role as suppliant.[20] As a teacher, Aitken needs to find students in order to promote the Dharma; he demonstrates his respect for his correspondents first and foremost by writing back to them, despite his busy schedule. In addition, his letters are peppered with words of affirmation and references to answering "your important questions" or "your urgent request."

In his work with immigrant letters, Gerber observes that there are few commonalities to be found in the corpus and that analysis risks imposing order where none exists. The same would perhaps be the case for an analysis of letters written by Aitken's students, who sought to maintain their relationship with him between visits via the written word. In the case of the letters written by Distant Correspondents, however, there are many commonalities of purpose. First and foremost, they write to establish a relationship with a Zen teacher, not to maintain one. On a secondary level, they write to create for themselves an identity as a Zen practitioner that they can present to Aitken.[21]

Establishing a Distant Relationship with a Teacher

In reviewing the letters from the Distant Correspondents, a basic pattern emerges that applies to the majority of them. They seek first to establish a relationship with Aitken, and then they make requests of him based upon their tentative status as "distant students." In order to establish the relationship, most Distant Correspondents undertake two fairly distinct steps in their (first) letter, which do not follow a strict order. They need first to indicate in some manner that they recognize Aitken as a valid Zen teacher, one they trust and with whom they may wish to practice. Second, they need to present themselves as sincere students, worthy of the teacher's attention.

Correspondents accomplish the first step in a variety of ways, but the most common is to comment favorably on Aitken's writings or to express gratitude for his published teachings. In all, 44 percent of the Distant Correspondents took this approach. In many cases, the correspondent states directly that he or she already regards Aitken as his or her teacher, based solely on his published works. One woman, writing from the island of Kauai, said that reading *Taking the Path of Zen* seemed to open up a path for her personally, and that she was filled with enthusiasm and questions. Then, when she read *The Mind of Clover*, she found in it "the voice of my inner teacher. I bow down to this teacher. There are no questions." An oncologist from New York wrote, "I have a strong affinity for your words in print. I hope to someday meet you and thank you for your teaching and patience. . . . With great respect to my rōshi, my teacher, I wish you health and long life."

Correspondents typically accomplish the second step, presenting themselves as sincere and worthy students, by discussing their religious history and/or current religious practice. It is in the context of the second step that the correspondents provide a wealth of information about their beliefs and patterns of practice that inform this study. It is likewise here that an outside observer may identify a secondary but related purpose, the creation of a self-identity as a Zen practitioner despite the realities of isolation from a teacher or a community. Individuals living beyond the reach of a Zen community typically have had no opportunity to publicly establish their identity as a Zen practitioner, a process that would naturally occur in the everyday context of communal interaction with a Zen group. They have not had the opportunity to learn how to be a Zen practitioner through observation and socialization and are thus left to their own devices to create such an identity based on their reading. In this sense, letter writing serves both as a bridge toward possible affiliation as well as the correspondent's first opportunity to "publicly" self-identify as Buddhist.

In many cases, Distant Correspondents describe their religious background and practice at some length, providing details that allow for further analysis. Based on their descriptions, a substantial portion of the Distant Correspondents may be accurately identified as solo practitioners, although many of them indicate that this pattern of practice no longer serves their perceived needs. They are therefore seeking a teacher or a community to support their Buddhist practice. Material related to patterns of practice is discussed in chapter 3.

Having established a tentative relationship with Aitken, most Distant Correspondents then get down to the business of making a request of him as a Zen teacher. The two most common categories of request include asking for advice about some aspect of Buddhist practice and asking for assistance in finding a teacher with whom to work or a community with which to practice, topics discussed in detail in chapter 2.

In his responses, Aitken encourages his Distant Correspondents to establish some kind of relationship with a trustworthy teacher and find a supportive practice community. He recommends a new pattern of affiliation for the many individuals that wish to practice as laypeople but live beyond the easy reach of an established Zen center. This pattern of affiliation, which I call Distant Membership, falls somewhere between full and active membership in a Zen *sangha* on the one hand and going it alone as a solo practitioner on the other. These and other topics related to Aitken's responses are discussed in chapters 6 and 7.

Armchair Buddhists, Night-Stand Buddhists, and Zafu Buddhists

Scholars who study American Buddhism have long understood that Buddhism in general, as well as Zen more specifically, appeals to a broader audience than just those individuals that self-identify as Buddhist on surveys or the even smaller number that are affiliated with an established religious community. Thomas Tweed has argued convincingly that scholars of American Buddhism need to regard the broader category of individuals drawn to Buddhism as an important part of the history of the development of American Buddhism. In his chapter "Night-Stand Buddhists and Other Creatures: Sympathizers, Adherents, and the Study of Religion," Tweed recommends the term "sympathizer" be applied to those individuals who are influenced by Buddhism, but do not become Buddhist adherents.[22] Unfortunately, most of these individuals remain invisible to scholarly methodologies, and therefore the category of sympathizer remains largely an "imagined community."

The present study allows us to gain at least a partial glimpse of individuals whom Tweed would classify as sympathizers. What emerges in the study is a broad spectrum of patterns of Buddhist influence, from sympathizers with reading knowledge only (armchair Buddhists), to those who dabble with self-taught meditation (Tweed's description of night-stand Buddhists), to a substantial number of individuals who develop regular patterns of daily practice. Based on the findings of this study, I would like to propose a more nuanced understanding of the very broad category of "sympathizers." I would like to distinguish between sympathizers (including the dabblers), who may do little more than read Buddhist texts and make a few attempts to sit in meditation, and solo practitioners, who practice daily for extended periods of time, self-taught or otherwise, without the benefit of a practicing community or a teacher to support their efforts. This latter group would more aptly be called Zafu Buddhists, since unlike "armchair scholars" or "night-stand Buddhists," whose practice consists primarily of reading Buddhist literature, these solo practitioners go far beyond reading to practice *zazen* on their cushions. (A *zafu* is a small, round pillow used for seated meditation. It is placed on top of a larger, square pillow known as a *zaniku*.)

In a strict sociological sense, the Distant Correspondents cannot be regarded as a representative sample of Buddhist sympathizers and solo practitioners. Rather they represent a subsection of sympathizers and solo practitioners who are drawn specifically to Zen practice (as opposed to Tibetan or Theravada Buddhism) and to a particular Zen teacher who inspired them. Based on the data I collected for this study, I conclude that what the Distant Correspondents found so inspiring in Aitken's writings as to compel them to take up their own pens was generally one or more of the following: Aitken's practical and straightforward advice about the process of meditation; his focus on *zazen* (as opposed to doctrinal or philosophical concerns) as the heart of Zen; and his insistence on ethical behavior and engagement in the world as a critical basis for meditation and Buddhist practice. In particular, Aitken's *Taking the Path of Zen* was one of the first and most readily accessible guidebooks for individuals interested in undertaking the practice of Zen.

When *Taking the Path* first appeared on library and bookstore shelves in 1982, the burgeoning area of Zen publications had already attracted a broad reading audience of Americans. Yet only a handful of publications provided practical advice and instructions for individuals interested in undertaking the practice of *zazen*. Only Kapleau's *The Three Pillars of Zen* was widely available. The first edition, originally published in 1965,[23] included a small section of illustrations of *zazen* postures at the back, while the revised and expanded version published in 1980[24] included a much longer section of questions and answers for meditators. Other practical guidebooks existed, such as John Daishin Buksbazen's *To Forget the Self*[25] and Gudō Nishijima's *How to Practice Zazen*,[26] but enjoyed a more narrow circulation. Aitken's work filled a need felt by a portion of the broader Zen reading audience who wanted more than translations, historical studies, and philosophical discussions of Zen could provide to support their practice.

Members of the Baby Boomer generation, who comprised the majority of the American Buddhist reading audience, had witnessed and in many cases participated in the civil rights and antiwar movements of the 1960s and 1970s. Aitken's active participation in these and other social justice movements may have appealed to many of them. And as Buddhist adherents and sympathizers struggled to make sense of the scandals that rocked the various practice centers throughout the country in the 1980s and 1990s, Aitken's clear stress on grounding one's practice in the precepts, as exemplified by his third book, *The Mind of Clover: Essays in Zen Buddhist Ethics*, may have struck a welcome cord.

In addition to individuals who would find Aitken's approach to Buddhism congenial, there exist several other types of Buddhist sympathizers and solo practitioners with alternative views of Buddhism or differing preferences for practice that I assume would never consider writing to Aitken. Individuals who regard Buddhism primarily as a philosophical system, for example, may regard reading and study as personally satisfying and sufficient for their needs, and never feel motivated to write to any Buddhist teacher. Others who are drawn more intensely to Theravada thought and practice or those favoring the esoteric approach of Vajrayana Buddhism would perhaps contact teachers associated with those branches of the Buddhist tradition rather than a Zen teacher. Even among Zen sympathizers and solo practitioners, those who feel a stronger affinity to *shikantaza* as opposed to kōan practice may be less inclined to write to Aitken. A few such individuals may be numbered among Aitken's Distant Correspondents, but they are largely absent. The act of writing necessarily entails a clear process of self-selection. Despite this very real limitation, the letters composed by the Distant Correspondents provide a unique glimpse at the manner in which Zen sympathizers and solo practitioners view their practice, how they regard the role of a teacher, and what challenges they face in their own words.

The next chapter sets the context for the later substantive chapters by providing both a biographical sketch of Robert Baker Aitken and an overview of the growth of Buddhism in the West during the last three decades of the twentieth century. The remaining chapters are divided into two main sections, patterned after the exchange between a correspondent and a teacher. The first section, chapters 2 through 5, deals with the letters that Distant Correspondents addressed to Robert Aitken. The second section, chapters 6 and 7, analyzes the patterns found in Aitken's replies. The balance struck between the two sections reflects several factors. First, in sheer volume, there are many more letters written by Distant Correspondents than there are responses. As discussed in chapter 6, the archive does not preserve all the responses that Aitken actually composed, nor did he respond one for one to all the letters he received. Second, Aitken's responses, written by a single individual, manifest far greater consistency in content and style than the letters written by his numerous Distant Correspondents. It was therefore possible to identify the relevant patterns with relative brevity. Finally, the Distant Correspondents remain the primary focus of this study, since their letters provide the window to view the beliefs and practices of Buddhist sympathizers and solo practitioners who have previously remained invisible to scholars of American Buddhism.

Chapter 2 discusses the reasons for writing to Aitken that the Distant Correspondents themselves invoked in their letters. The primary reasons include expressing gratitude or appreciation for Aitken's writings, requesting advice of various kinds, and requesting help in finding a Zen teacher or a *sangha* with which to practice. Reasons raised by smaller numbers of individuals, including writing to challenge the *rōshi*, asking confirmation for an "enlightenment experience," and requesting personal counseling are also addressed.

The Distant Correspondents routinely describe their practice histories and current patterns of practice. Chapter 3 provides analysis of the data collected regarding these patterns, especially how many correspondents report practicing *zazen* on their own, how many practice with a group or a Zen center, and how they say they were introduced to Zen. Chapter 4 addresses particular issues raised by significant numbers of the Distant Correspondents, since these represent widespread concerns among Zen solo practitioners and sympathizers. These include: social justice and ethics for Zen Buddhists, isolation from a qualified Zen teacher or a Zen *sangha*, whether or not a teacher is necessary for Zen practice, monastic versus lay practice options, resistance to joining a group, and issues related to Zen ritual. Chapter 5 concludes the section on the correspondents' letters by identifying several subcategories represented among the Distant Correspondents, including the "Walking

Wounded," individuals hurt by their experiences practicing with other teachers or Zen groups; "Seekers and Dabblers," who indicate either that they have practiced other alternative religions or that they have not undertaken the practice of Zen with consistency; Long-term Correspondents; and prison inmates.

Chapter 6 introduces the responses that Aitken wrote to Distant Correspondents by contextualizing his letter-writing program within his overall teaching ministry. It likewise reviews the general procedures for correspondence that Aitken established. Chapter 7 describes the typical patterns found in Aitken's letters, including his efforts to place individuals with qualified teachers, his advice regarding solo practice and meditating with a group, his recommendations for reading and otherwise enhancing his correspondents' practice, and his use of "silence" or non-response.

CHAPTER 1

Setting the Stage

Aitken and the Context of Zen in America

It began when an acquaintance remarked that my writings reminded him of Oriental poetry. I borrowed translations of Japanese and Chinese literature from the library, and met Basho and Po Chu-i.
—Robert Aitken, *Taking the Path of Zen*

Robert Baker Aitken is often referred to as the dean of American Zen, one of the first generation of American Zen teachers who trained in Japan and sought to establish a viable form of Zen practice for Americans. He is perhaps best known for his extensive writings, which include more than twelve books and numerous other publications. He and his wife Anne together founded Honolulu Diamond Sangha, which is now in its third generation of teachers and has grown to include a number of affiliated Zen centers throughout the United States and Oceania. I have come to regard HDS as one of several pivotal Buddhist organizations critical to the development of Zen in America and other Western countries. As the founder and director of HDS, Aitken sponsored several Japanese teachers of Zen to instruct his fledgling community. Some prominent teachers came to lead periodic *sesshin*, while other less prominent individuals served HDS for longer periods of time as resident advisors. Throughout the first two formative decades, Aitken likewise pursued his own Zen training in Japan with several teachers, including Nakagawa Sōen, Yasutani Hakuun, and Yamada Kōun. HDS thus served as a meeting ground for American practitioners, Japanese teachers, and a Japan-trained American teacher.

A teacher of Aitken's stature and the community that he founded are certainly worthy subjects for an extensive case study. This is not the objective of the present study, which focuses on Aitken's relationship with Distant Correspondents. For this purpose, a brief biographical account of Aitken's life and works will have to suffice to set the stage for the chapters that follow. The chapter will likewise situate HDS into the larger context of the growth of Zen communities in the United States in the latter half of the twentieth century.

Robert Aitken and Honolulu Diamond Sangha

Several short biographical and autobiographical sketches of Aitken already exist, and the following section is based upon them along with additional materials derived from personal interviews, Aitken's other publications, and letters from the Aitken archive. Aitken composed the autobiographical essay "Willy-Nilly Zen" in November 1971, at the behest of Yamada Kōun after confirmation of his *kenshō* or first breakthrough experience. The essay appears as an appendix in *Taking the Path of Zen*.[1] It fits the pattern of an extended testimonial, or *kenshōki*, which Sanbōkyōdan teachers encouraged their students to write.[2] Aitken composed an additional autobiographical summary that appears on the University of Hawaii Special Collections page as part of the Robert Baker Aitken Papers.[3] Finally, Helen Tworkov included a biographical essay of Aitken in her *Zen in America: Profiles of Five Teachers*.[4]

Robert Baker Aitken was born in Philadelphia, Pennsylvania on June 19, 1917 to Gladys B. and Robert T. Aitken. His father, an ethnologist, moved the family to Honolulu in 1922, when he accepted a position at the Bishop Museum. Robin, as he was addressed in his youth, was then five years old. He grew up in Honolulu, interspersed with periods of time living with his grandparents in California, and acquired most of his primary and secondary education in Hawaii schools. As he told the story, his first encounter with Buddhism occurred when he was a boy exploring the city riding about on his bicycle. He would sometimes stop to admire the art at the Honolulu Academy of Arts, and found himself much taken by a statue of Guanyin dating from the Northern Song Dynasty (c. 1025), still prominently displayed at the museum today. He would sit and contemplate the statue, sensing the compassion and serenity of the bodhisattva without yet understanding its provenance.[5]

After graduating from high school, Aitken attended the University of Hawaii for two and a half years without much interest or success. After dropping out of college in 1940, he spent a year doing construction work on Midway Island, located at the far northwestern end of the Hawaiian archipelago, returning to Honolulu at the end of his contract. Despite the obvious signs of approaching war in the summer of 1941, he signed up for a second contract, this time for work on Guam. The Japanese captured the island almost immediately after the attack on Pearl Harbor on December 8, 1941, and Aitken was transported to Kobe, Japan, where he spent the remainder of the war as a civilian internee.

Due to their civilian status, Aitken and the other enemy foreign nationals held in Japan were not forced to engage in manual labor. Aitken has commented that many of the other men found it an emotionally debilitating experience to pass the long days of detention without gainful employment. Aitken, on the other hand, found ways to make the idle period serve his purposes. Since detainees had ready access to reading and study materials, Aitken devised his own regimen of productive activity. He spent his internment reading and studying language with more enthusiasm than he had previously shown in his formal education. In his letters home, he reported that he made significant progress with French, German, and Japanese, and that he read history, philosophy, and literature as widely as was possible.

Aitken did not seem to regret his years of confinement, viewing them as an opportunity to settle himself through reflection and study. In a letter dated December 8, 1944, addressed to his mother, he wrote,

> I have not changed any attitude, merely developed one, and shed a few abstractions. This internment is a stepping-stone rather than a Slough of Despond. I have actually, honestly learned to study, and to read. I finished Spengler a few months ago and it strongly influenced me and steadied my ideas. I do look forward to reunion, aside from the real reasons, to talk to you all for the first time.

His letters maintain a cheerful tone throughout the war, assuring his family of his good health and emotional well-being. The former claims were certainly an exaggeration maintained for the sake of his mother, since he later reported that he suffered long bouts of asthma and respiratory illness during his confinement. The latter claims relating to his positive emotional state appear to have been more accurate. He has continued to write and speak about his time in the internment camp as a period of personal growth that was critical for his development.

While in the internment camp, Aitken was introduced to Zen teachings through his reading. One of the Japanese guards, aware of Aitken's interest in Japanese literature, loaned him a copy of R.H. Blyth's newly published *Zen in English Literature and Oriental Classics*. Aitken describes reading it as transformative for him.

> I must have read that book ten times, finishing it and starting it again. I would have experiences at various places in the book. . . . Everything was transformed for me by those experiences, and to this day I am motivated by that book. All my writing springs from its style and intention. All my work comes from the profound vow that was made for me on reading it: that I would devote my life to Zen Buddhism, no matter what the difficulty.[6]

Not long after, Aitken had the opportunity to meet and study with Blyth himself when the Japanese consolidated all of the civilian internee camps in the Kobe area. During the fourteen months they were interned together, Aitken studied Japanese language, poetry, and Zen literature with Blyth as his mentor.

At the end of the war, badly malnourished from his period of confinement, Aitken was repatriated and returned to Honolulu. He reapplied to the University of Hawaii, and this time relished his studies, completing a degree in English literature in 1947. The same year, he married his first wife Mary Laune, and the couple moved to Berkeley, where Aitken began graduate work in Japanese studies at the University of California. During a visit to Los Angeles over a winter break, Aitken sought out the acquaintance of the Zen teacher Senzaki Nyogen.[7] Senzaki became his first Zen teacher, and Aitken began to practice *zazen* under his guidance. As a result, Aitken shifted his studies to UCLA, and he and his wife moved to Pasadena to be nearer Senzaki.

Mary Aitken grew unhappy in Southern California, and the Aitkens moved yet again, returning to Honolulu in 1949. Aitken returned to the University of Hawaii and there completed his master's degree in Japanese Studies in 1950. His first book, *A Zen Wave*, is based on his graduate thesis. After graduation, Aitken received a fellowship to study both *haiku* and Zen in Japan. This time he traveled alone, leaving Mary and their newborn son Thomas in Honolulu. In Japan, he experienced his first introduction to Zen monastic practice, including the intensive periods of meditation known as *sesshin*.

Aitken attended his first *sesshin* at Engakuji in Kamakura under the direction of the abbot Asahina Beppō Sōgen. Uncomfortable with the ritual bowing required of him and the austere practice conditions, he left Engakuji and sought out Nakagawa Sōen,[8] a friend of his teacher Senzaki, who spoke good English and was himself a creative poet and student of Japanese literature. With Sōen's introduction, Aitken entered Ryūtakuji, a Rinzai Zen temple in Mishima, Shizuoka prefecture, where he spent seven months practicing with the abbot Yamamoto Genpō.

Aitken was among the first Westerners to enter a Japanese monastery in the postwar period, and the Zen teachers he encountered made little effort to accommodate him. He continued to experience problems with the sparse diet and the long hours of *zazen* using the traditional *zafu*, and his chronic respiratory problems recurred. In California, Senzaki had greatly altered the practice to suit his American students. They generally sat *zazen* using Western-style chairs, for example, and they did not prostrate themselves before Buddhist images. Aitken found his health once again compromised and he returned to Honolulu in 1952 without having made great progress in his meditation.

Aitken describes the next five years as a Dark Night. His marriage with Mary had been severely strained by his absence, and they divorced two years after his return from Japan. In 1953, he returned to Southern California to practice once again with Senzaki. Stress from the divorce and separation from his son combined with the lingering effects of physical strain from his years in Japan eventually led to hospitalization for respiratory problems, followed by many dreary months of slow recuperation. In 1956, life began to improve. Aitken secured a teaching position at Happy Valley School in Ojai, where he met Anne Hopkins. The couple married in February 1957 and at the end of the school year traveled to Japan for their honeymoon. During this trip, Aitken met and sat his first *sesshin* with Yasutani Hakuun, the founder of Sanbōkyōdan.

Up until this time, Aitken had been practicing with Zen teachers within Rinzai lineages. The Sanbōkyōdan lineage is distinct from both Rinzai and Sōtō Zen and represents a hybrid form of Zen practice that adopts elements from both Rinzai and Sōtō. Its founder Yasutani Hakuun (1885–1973) was ordained within the Sōtō tradition and practiced with and received Dharma transmission from Harada Daiun Sogaku

(1871–1961), likewise an ordained Sōtō priest, who made use of kōan. The use of kōan as a focus for meditation is more often associated with Rinzai Zen, while Sōtō practitioners generally prefer *shikan taza*. Like Harada, Yasutani felt that monastic Zen had become ossified in Japan, and Yasutani chose to concentrate his teaching efforts on lay practitioners.

In 1954, Yasutani established Sanbōkyōdan as an independent lay school of Zen, based on Harada's style of teaching. Although Yasutani accepted ordained students, he did not function within the Sōtō monastic system and the majority of Sanbōkyōdan members have always been laypeople. Not only did Yasutani develop his form of meditation practice specifically for laypeople, most of the teachers within the lineage after him are not ordained. Unlike most Zen teachers in Japan, Yasutani welcomed Western students, and the Aitkens were among the first to practice with him. After learning the basics of *zazen*, Sanbōkyōdan students typically undertake kōan practice, beginning with the Mu kōan. Since this is the norm in most Rinzai lineages, the practice would have been familiar in general terms to Aitken. One minor observable difference is that Sanbōkyōdan practitioners sit facing the wall, in typical Sōtō fashion, while Rinzai practitioners usually face inward, toward their fellow meditators. It should be noted that since its founding, Sanbōkyōdan holds a relatively marginal status within the world of Japanese Zen, especially compared to the larger Zen denominations,[9] and it remains considerably smaller than Rinzai, Sōtō, or Ōbaku. As shall be seen, it plays a much more dominant role in the spread of Zen to America.

After their honeymoon, Anne and Robert Aitken returned to California and taught one more year at Happy Valley School. In 1958, they relocated to Honolulu so that Aitken could be closer to his son Tom. Together he and Anne opened a secondhand bookstore in Chinatown that specialized in Asian religions and Hawaiiana. They began to keep a list of the names and addresses of all their customers with an interest in Buddhism, and they later used this list as the basis for establishing a small meditation group that would meet in their home, starting in October 1959.

At the beginning, Robert and Anne acted as "first among equals," or in Aitken's own words, "elder sister and brother" for HDS, hosting meditation sessions in their living room twice each week. Beginning in 1960, they arranged for the first in a series of Zen teachers from Japan to visit HDS. Over the years, less prominent individuals served as resident advisors and generally stayed for extended periods of time, while more prominent teachers such as Nakagawa Sōen and Yasutani Hakuun typically came to lead a single *sesshin*, usually while in transit between Japan and the U.S. mainland.

The first long-term resident advisor for HDS was Eidō Shimano, known to the Aitkens and other members of the HDS community as Tai San. Robert and Anne first met Tai San in Japan while staying at Ryūtakuji on their honeymoon. At that time, he made a positive impression on them, and they promised to assist him in fulfilling his desire to teach in the United States. Later, when Sōen Rōshi agreed to allow Eidō to move to Honolulu to serve as resident advisor for the fledgling HDS community, Robert and Anne served as legal sponsors for his visa. Eidō remained at HDS for four years, from 1960 to 1964, living with the Aitkens at Koko An.

Aitken has written very little in his published works about the disastrous results caused by Eidō Shimano during his tenure as resident advisor. Aitken wrote more openly to friends about events, and the archive letters contain numerous references to the time period. In later years, Aitken became more willing to speak out publically about the damaging effects that Eidō's inappropriate sexual behavior had on the HDS community, especially the two female members who were abused, and his own feelings of complicity in remaining silent. Vladimir Keremidschieff and Stuart Lachs discussed the events related to the Eidō debacle at some length in an online article,[10] and a large collection of material from the Aitken archive is posted online as part of the Shimano Archive.[11]

In 1964, two female members of HDS were hospitalized for psychiatric care as a result of sexual abuse. Aitken eventually learned of Eidō's alleged misconduct from hospital staff. With two of his *sangha* members hospitalized, Aitken began volunteering at the mental health facility, and Eidō sometimes accompanied him. Eventually a staff member at the hospital requested that Aitken stop bringing Eidō, since he was implicated in the women's reports of abuse. Aghast at what he heard, Aitken sought confirmation of the allegation from the psychiatrists treating the women and requested a written statement that he could take with him to Japan.

Aitken's visit to Japan proved unsuccessful in resolving the problem, and it permanently damaged his relationship with his teacher Sōen Rōshi. Neither Sōen nor Yasutani, who around this time assumed teaching responsibility for both Eidō and Aitken, took the allegations seriously. They regarded such sexual misconduct as "rascal" behavior that would naturally diminish once Eidō was married and settled down. Aitken flew back to Honolulu, frustrated by their apparent lack of concern and uncertain how to proceed.

On his return, Aitken found Eidō poised to leave for New York, angered that Aitken had spoken with his superiors in Japan without first confronting him with the allegations. In letters to friends and colleagues, Aitken described the events that followed at HDS as "a great collapse"[12] that split the small *sangha*. At the time, most members were unaware of Eidō's misconduct, and some of them blamed Aitken for driving away their teacher. Aitken felt obliged to remain silent for many years both for the sake of the women involved as well as to preserve the strained relations with his teachers in Japan. At the time, Aitken accepted the blame for causing Eidō to depart and struggled to heal the fracture in his community. He continued to feel the weight of his visa sponsorship for Eidō, and made efforts to sever that relationship as quickly as possible.[13]

Much more could be said about Aitken's relations with Eidō throughout the rest of his career, more than is appropriate for this project. Suffice it to say that Eidō's conduct while in residence at Koko An influenced Aitken's work in many ways, as did his disappointment in his Japanese teachers' lack of adequate response. Evidence of this will become apparent in his dealings with Distant Correspondents. The events and the desire to set things right remained critical to Aitken until the end of his life. At the advice of publishers, he never wrote openly about what had transpired, but he did not maintain his initial silence.[14] By the early 1970s, Aitken openly discussed events with his senior students at HDS, so that it was common knowledge at Maui Zendo and Koko An.[15] During the early 1980s, he began boycotting teachers' meetings and public events at which he would feel obliged to pretend that he regarded Eidō as a colleague and encouraged colleagues to do the same. Toward the end of his life, he allowed for the release of the portion of his archive related to Eidō that had previously been sealed from the public.

The second resident advisor, Sekida Katsuki, proved to be a more stable influence for the HDS community. He remained with HDS from 1965 until approximately 1971, making the move to Maui to assist Robert and Anne in establishing Maui Zendo. Aitken spoke well of Sekida as a teacher. In a letter dated May 31, 1968 to a Distant Correspondent, for example, he wrote, "[Sekida] is an excellent teacher, and I have learned much more from him than I have from any Rōshi, in fact from all of them put together." In addition to Sekida's guidance, HDS welcomed prominent teachers from Japan to lead *sesshin* both at Koko An in Honolulu and in the newly established Maui Zendo. From 1961 until 1969, Yasutani Hakuun came regularly to Hawaii to lead *sesshin*, and other teachers including Nakagawa Sōen came on occasion. Aitken thus had resources to support and maintain his own practice in Hawaii throughout these difficult years. In addition to his regular practice in Hawaii, Aitken likewise pursued Zen training in Japan, where he and Anne annually took an extended visit starting in 1961. During most of these visits, Aitken worked with Yasutani.

Throughout the first decade of HDS's history, Aitken earned his living working for the University of Hawaii, while acting as director for the fledgling HDS community in his spare time. In 1969, he retired from the university and relocated to Maui, where he and Anne established Maui Zendo. From that time on, HDS maintained two sites, Koko An in Honolulu and Maui Zendo in Haiku, Maui. Koko An continued to serve a core group of members who lived in the neighboring community as well as a few residents who traveled to Hawaii either for *sesshin* or an extended practice visit. Maui Zendo served as a residential program, with anywhere from twelve to twenty practitioners in residence.

At about the same time that he retired, Aitken began to make progress in his practice, and he started working his way through the Sanbōkyōdan kōan curriculum. In 1971, he and Anne accepted Yamada Kōun as their new teacher, and Aitken went on to complete the kōan curriculum in fairly rapid order under Yamada's guidance. In 1974, Aitken received permission to teach independently from Yamada Kōun, who by then had assumed the leadership of Sanbōkyōdan as Yasutani's successor. Within Sanbōkyōdan, this meant that Aitken had attained the status of Junshike or Associate Zen Master and was qualified to accept students, offer *dokusan*, authorize *kenshō*, and start students on the kōan curriculum.[16] Aitken readily admitted that he was not initially comfortable with his new authority, and that he turned to his friend and Dharma brother Maezumi Taizan for guidance in his new role as teacher.[17]

With a resident teacher of its own, HDS no longer needed to rely upon teachers from Japan, and the community was able to stabilize under Aitken's leadership. Not surprisingly, Aitken's early doubts gave way to growing confidence as he gained in experience.[18] For the next twenty years, HDS continued to serve as an official branch center for Sanbōkyōdan. In addition to traveling between the Koko An and Maui Zendo communities to lead *sesshin*, Aitken soon began to travel regularly to lead *sesshin* for smaller Zen communities on the West coast of the United States as well as in Australia and New Zealand, thus establishing what would become the extended network of HDS affiliated centers.

In 1983, Aitken and Anne decided to return permanently to Oahu and concentrate their efforts on the Koko An community. Their departure eventually led to the Maui Zendo being closed and sold in 1986.[19] On Oahu, the HDS community began to make plans and raise funds to build a larger facility that would accommodate the needs of both a residential program, designed for practitioners "who are born to be monks or nuns,"[20] and the growing local membership. In 1987, they broke ground for the new temple, located in the lush Palolo Valley of Honolulu. The new temple, called Palolo Zen Center, opened its doors in 1989.

In 1985, Aitken received full designation as Yamada's Dharma heir. In Sanbōkyōdan parlance, he became a Shōshike (Authentic Zen Master), the first and only such designation that Yamada conferred on a non-Japanese teacher. Aitken thereby formally became the head teacher for HDS, qualified to independently designate his own Dharma heirs within the Sanbōkyōdan lineage. Aitken's status as a full Dharma heir came under challenge after Yamada's death in 1989. The new Sanbōkyōdan leadership began to restrict the independence of all non-Japanese teachers that had been appointed by Yamada.[21] This and other issues led to a parting of the ways for HDS and Sanbōkyōdan.

HDS remained affiliated with Sanbōkyōdan until 1995, when it formally split and became an independent American Zen lineage. Aitken has called this split an "amicable divorce," but he sometimes wrote confidentially to friends about his reservations about the involvement of Sanbōkyōdan leaders in Japanese big business and their general "lack of connection with society." While concerns about the leadership restricting his status as an independent Dharma heir certainly precipitated the break, Aitken's underlying concerns about the relationship between Zen teachings and social activism likewise informed his decision.

In June 1994, Anne Aitken was taken ill with flu-like symptoms and eventually hospitalized. She died a few days later on June 13, with Aitken, her stepson Tom, and a few close friends at her bedside. Aitken and Anne had enjoyed a long, happy, and loving marriage, and they worked together as partners from the beginning in nurturing the development of HDS. When dealing with new members and other strangers, Anne's social skills balanced his awkwardness. In addition to her strong emotional support, Aitken relied upon her for a wide variety of other forms of day-to-day collaboration, especially as HDS grew, his publishing career blossomed, and his calendar grew ever fuller. She sorted and prioritized his mail, acted as a buffer when publishing deadlines loomed, and provided him with a trusted sounding board. He felt her loss keenly.

Aitken retired as head teacher of HDS in 1996, having designated Nelson Foster as his sole candidate to succeed him as the teacher for HDS two or three years earlier. The sangha then made the final decision to appoint Foster as their teacher in a process that Aitken called sangha transmission. In 1997, Aitken moved to the Kaimu district on the Big Island to be closer to his son Tom, building a lovely house perched atop a recent lava flow, overlooking the sea. At about that time, Aitken was diagnosed with Hodgkin's lymphoma and underwent both chemotherapy and radiation treatments that led to a full remission. Throughout his years in Kaimu, Aitken continued to lead a small community of students who met weekly for meditation and to guide a few of his longtime students in their practice. He directed most of his other students and all newcomers to work with Nelson Foster or another of his Dharma heirs.

In 2004, Aitken returned to live on Oahu. After a brief stint in an assisted living facility, he returned home to the teacher's quarters at the Palolo Zen Center, where members of the HDS community participated in his care until his death. In the last few years, in addition to his regular practice of answering mail, now mostly in the form of email, from Distant Correspondents, he undertook a new venture, writing a blog to extend his outreach to a new audience of Zen sympathizers. Until just before his death, he continued to write and to participate in *sangha* events whenever his health and strength allowed. He died on August 5, 2010 at age 93. The HDS community is now led by Michael Kieran, Nelson Foster's Dharma heir.

HDS has affiliate Zen centers throughout the western region of the United States and overseas in Australia, New Zealand, and Germany. Aitken has recognized the following Dharma heirs:

- **Nelson Foster (1988)**, at the Ring of Bone Zendo in Nevada City, California
- **John Tarrant (1988)**, at Pacific Zen Institute in Santa Rosa, California and Desert Lotus Zen Sangha in Phoenix, Arizona
- **Patrick Hawk (1988)**, at Zen Desert Sangha in Tucson, Arizona
- **Augusto Alcalde (1988)**, at Shobo An Zendo in Cordoba, Argentina

- **Rolf Drosden** (**1996**), at Wolken-und-Mond-Sangha in Leverkusen, Germany
- **Pia Gyger** (**1996**), named Affiliate Master, no longer teaching with HDS
- **Subhana Barzaghi** (with John Tarrant, 1996), at Sydney Zen Center in Sydney, Australia
- **Ross Bolleter** (with John Tarrant, 1997), at Zen Group of Western Australia in Perth, Australia
- **Jack Duffy** (**1997**), at Three Treasures Sangha in Seattle, Washington
- **Joseph Bobrow** (**1997**), at Deep Streams Zen Institute in San Francisco, California

Aitken's recognition as a Zen teacher spread widely with the success of his publishing career. Two of his early books had the greatest impact both on his reputation as a writer and teacher and on the readers who would become his Distant Correspondents. His second major book, *Taking the Path of Zen*, appeared in 1982, and quickly became popular among Zen students and sympathizers alike. Two years later, *The Mind of Clover* established his reputation as a Zen teacher deeply concerned with ethics, as a proponent for everyday engagement with the world as a Buddhist, and an advocate for social justice. Aitken subsequently published numerous other books, which further extended his influence and standing as one of the leading American Zen teachers. He likewise traveled widely, visiting other Zen communities, speaking publicly at bookstores and universities, and participating in social justice activities. Nevertheless, *Taking the Path of Zen* and *The Mind of Clover* proved to be most influential for the Distant Correspondents and deserve some attention here.

Taking the Path of Zen was designed as "a manual that may be used, chapter by chapter, as a program of instruction over the first few weeks of Zen training" as well as a reference for more advanced practitioners (p. xi). Aitken based the book on the orientation talks that he gave at HDS, starting in 1972. As Aitken explains, students typically receive little instruction in the mechanics of *zazen* in traditional Japanese Zen monasteries; they are expected to learn by observation, imitation, and trial and error. Traditional manuals for *zazen* have existed for centuries in China and Japan,[22] but not a structured process of orientation such as one finds at most Western Zen centers.[23] The idea for student orientation sessions did not originate in the United States. Harada Daiun broke with Japanese tradition when he instituted a series of introductory talks for his students, and Yasutani Hakuun continued the practice within the Sanbōkyōdan lineage, from which Aitken gained the inspiration for his orientation talks (p. xi).

By way of defining Zen and the goals of its practice, the first chapter of *Taking the Path of Zen* presents a brief account of the historical Buddha's practice of meditation and awakening. Aitken holds out the Buddha's experience as the model for the new student to emulate. "The Zen path is devoted to clearing away these obstructions and seeing into true nature. This can be your path. . . . It also involves application of such realization in the daily life of family, job, and community service" (p. 6). One sees, even here in this brief definitional section of Zen practice and attainment, Aitken's emphasis on living the tradition outside the meditation hall.

The second chapter introduces the basic mechanics of sitting in meditation and breath counting for the beginner. Aitken not only describes the posture for arms, legs, torso, and eyes, he explains the purpose for each element of the preferred positions. He maintains the traditional recommendation that meditating in the full lotus posture is ideal, as well as providing stretching exercises to make that physical goal more attainable, but warns the beginner to proceed with caution. One sees here his flexibility, as he introduces alternative postures and the basic recommendation to not push the body too far.

Throughout the book, Aitken provides pragmatic advice for setting intermediate goals that reduce a sense of failure as one makes progress along the path.

> All of us fear failure, to one degree or another, and prefer not to try something that seems too difficult. This device of adjusting your goal to your present capacity is one by which you can avoid unnecessary frustration at the outset of your practice. However, it is important to understand that Zen training is also a matter of coping with failure. Everyone fails at first, just as Shakyamuni Buddha did. (pp. 27–28)

Aitken offers many words of encouragement that the practitioner accept him or herself, observing that self-hatred undermines the process. "[I]f you reject yourself, you are rejecting the agent of realization" (p. 9).

While the book is quite slender and could easily be read in a few sittings, Aitken clearly meant for it to be read and applied more gradually.

Each chapter introduces a new pattern for meditation, particularly variant patterns for breath counting, to be applied in one's daily meditation over a period of time, perhaps a week for each new pattern. In this way the book mirrors the series of orientation lectures that used to be required by Sanbōkyōdan for new members. Indeed, for some time *Taking the Path of Zen* was required reading for people planning to come to Maui or Honolulu to attend a *sesshin* at HDS.

While *Taking the Path of Zen* clearly lends itself to serve as a how-to guide for the solo practitioner, Aitken wrote it with the assumption that in the normal course of events, the student would join a community, meet a teacher, and begin attending *sesshin*. He prepares the beginner for all of this, describing normal procedures at HDS and noting that other centers may handle matters somewhat differently. He concludes the book with a chapter on the Mu kōan that reads like a *teishō* (Zen talk) that would be given by the teacher on the first evening of *sesshin*. At HDS the opening *teishō* is always related to Mu, since most students participating will be working on it. Aitken's overall agenda in *Taking the Path of Zen* is very much in keeping with his overall purpose in personally responding to the Distant Correspondents; he invites his reader to begin or persevere in the practice of *zazen* and seeks to guide her or him toward as full participation in Zen practice as possible. His letters are peppered with the same basic advice that appears within its pages, often using identical language.

In *The Mind of Clover*, Aitken continues in his role as Zen teacher to "clarify [the Buddhist precepts] for Western students of Buddhism as a way to help make Buddhism a daily practice" (p. 3). He presents his understanding of the Ten Grave Precepts, which he translates as Not Killing, Not Stealing, Not Misusing Sex, Not Lying, Not Giving or Taking Drugs, Not Discussing Faults of Others, Not Praising Yourself While Abusing Others, Not Sparing the Dharma Assets, Not Indulging in Anger, and Not Defaming the Three Treasures, taking them up one per chapter. Aitken originally composed the chapters as lectures and essays for his students at HDS, and the format retains the flavor of a teacher instructing and exhorting his own *sangha*. Aitken makes it clear that the practice of Zen for the individual necessarily entails the application of realization gained on one's cushions to life outside the *zendo* (meditation hall). He likewise expresses his strong preference that the *sangha* act as a community in organizing acts of community service and social activism.

While Aitken admitted that it is not traditional for Zen teachers to focus on the precepts as the subject of Zen talks (*teishō*) and commentaries, he firmly believed it was his responsibility as a Zen teacher to do so (p. 5). He suggested that reticence in publically teaching and discussing the precepts arose from fears that the teaching "could be misunderstood to mean that one has license to do anything, so long as one does it forgetfully" (p. 5). Indeed, Westerners often associate Zen with antinomian attitudes and behavior, and it is not uncommon to hear just such sentiments expressed by Zen practitioners. Aitken often met with resistance from his students because of his emphasis on ethics. Anticipating resistance from those readers who would immediately reject external norms as foreign to the Zen tradition, he suggested that the precepts would best be understood not as "commandments engraved in stone," but as archetypes that inspire a Buddhist life, "skillful means" for Zen practitioners "to use in guiding our engagement in the world" (p. 15).

For Aitken, Zen ethics begin on one's cushion and extend ever outward to encompass one's dealings within the *sangha*, with one's family and friends, and within the community and the natural world. He rejected a perfectionism that recommends waiting for self-realization before beginning the practice of compassion, since there is no end to the process. He likewise rejected the notion that politics is inimical to the religious life. "Politics in our day of nuclear overkill is a matter of ignoring the First Grave Precept [of Not Killing] or acting upon it" (p. 20). Many of his readers found inspiration in his attitude that social activism should be grounded in religious practice and that Zen practice naturally entails this kind of engagement in the world. This was one of Aitken's distinguishing features as a Zen teacher, and it had a significant impact on what sort of Buddhist—adherent, sympathizer, or solo practitioner—was attracted to him as a potential teacher.

Overview of Buddhism in America from 1970 to 2000

Many authors have already written the story of the transmission of Zen to the United States from various perspectives,[24] and it is not my intention to repeat their efforts here. Rather, I will offer some observations about the establishment and growth of Zen centers throughout the country during the twentieth century, especially the final three decades, a pattern that provides concrete evidence for the rapid growth in American interest in learning about and practicing Zen. This institutional aspect of the story, rather than a discussion of individual teachers who contributed to the same process, directly impacts the experiences of the Distant Correspondents, since many of them found themselves outside the easy reach of a center or meditation group, despite indisputable evidence of institutional growth.

First, it should be noted that Zen as we know it today in the United States represents the combined influences of teachers and styles of practice originating in China, Japan, Korea, and Vietnam, although the strongest influence derives from Japanese Zen. In addition, the transmission of Zen to the United States has likewise been the joint effort of Asian teachers who visited or settled in the United States and Americans who visited or lived in Asia for extended periods of time to acquire training. The pattern is quite familiar to scholars of Japanese religion, since similarly combined efforts of exchange between Chinese and Japanese Buddhist monks led to the establishment of Zen in Japan in the twelfth to fourteenth centuries.

Japanese Buddhist missionaries from the Sōtō denomination of Zen established the first permanent and lasting Zen institutions in the United States and its territories early in the twentieth century. The Reverend Hōsen Isobe, representing the Sōtō mission, established Betsuin Shōbōji in Honolulu in 1913, Zenshūji in Los Angeles in 1922, and Sōkōji in San Francisco in 1934. The Japanese priests subsequently assigned to these temples served the religious needs of the local Japanese and Japanese American communities living in Hawaii and California, and simultaneously began outreach programs to introduce Buddhism to other Americans. The critical role played by these so-called ethnic temples is sometimes lost in the telling of Zen history in America, since primary focus typically falls on institutions established to serve the non-Japanese, largely Euro-American community.

The data provided in table 4 were derived primarily from Morreale's *The Complete Guide to Buddhist America*, which includes self-reported information from Buddhist centers throughout the United States. Centers were invited to provide various kinds of information, including affiliation and an establishment date, both of which are used here when provided. It should be noted that the listing includes only those groups that voluntarily participated. No attempt was made to account for groups that failed to respond, nor to account for groups that passed out of existence before the guide was published in 1998. In addition, very few of the so-called ethnic Buddhist temples, those that serve first-generation Asian immigrants and their Asian American descendents, provided profiles, and are therefore largely invisible despite the rapid growth of ethnic temples reported else-

Table 4. Establishment of Zen Institutions in the United States

Years	New Sites	Percentage	Cumulative Totals
1910–1949	6	3%	6
1950–1959	4	2%	10
1960–1964	4	2%	14
1965–1969	8	4%	22
1970–1974	31	14%	53
1975–1979	22	10%	75
1980–1984	28	13%	103
1985–1989	40	18%	143
1990–1994	51	24%	194
1995–1997	23	11%	217

where for the same time period.[25] The data necessarily remains incomplete as a resource to accurately track the growth of Buddhist groups. Nevertheless, it offers a rudimentary indication of growth patterns for the appropriate decades. Where possible, I supplemented the relevant information regarding ethnic temples such as Zenshūji and Sōkōji, which played a significant role in the early development of Zen in America.

Before 1960, the vast majority of Zen institutions established in the United States were ethnic Japanese and Chinese Zen temples, mostly located in Hawaii and California. All but one of the early Zen sites included in table 4 were founded by Japanese teachers; six of the ten were founded by Japanese missionaries specifically seeking a non-Japanese audience for their teachings. Honolulu Diamond Sangha, founded by Robert and Anne Aitken, represents the sole exception to this pattern, although HDS likewise relied upon guidance from Japanese teachers when they were available.

As the data in table 4 demonstrates, the final three decades of the twentieth century saw rapid growth in the number of Zen centers throughout the United States. This pattern of growth closely mirrors the numbers of letters composed by Distant Correspondents over the same time period, as seen in table 1. Throughout the period, Sōtō Zen continued to dominate the scene, representing nearly one third of all the centers that provided information about their affiliation (see table 5). Included among the thirty-six centers with an affiliation to Sanbōkyōdan, sometimes known as the Harada-Yasutani lineage, are centers that specifically

Table 5. Zen Institutions by Affiliation

Affiliation	No. Sites	Percentage
Sōtō	94	29%
Korean	39	12%
Rinzai	36	11%
Sanbōkyōdan*	36	11%
HDS	13	4%
Vietnamese	11	3%
Mindfulness	94	29%
TOTALS	323	100%

*Includes various lineages, such as White Plum, HDS, and Rochester Zen Center.

listed Sanbōkyōdan as their affiliation as well as centers that indicated an affiliation with HDS, White Plum, and the Rochester Zen Center. This lineage group represents a relatively large presence in the United States, equal in numbers to Rinzai-affiliated groups. This is especially noteworthy given the marginal status of Sanbōkyōdan in Japan.[26]

The growth pattern of Zen centers in table 4 would appear even more dramatic if it were possible to include the ninety-four Mindfulness groups that base their practice on the teachings of the Vietnamese Zen teacher Thich Nhat Hanh. Unfortunately, very few of these groups independently provided information for the guidebook, and therefore establishment dates are known for only a handful. Mindfulness centers in the United States are part of a larger international network; the majority of the centers included in the guide are listed as affiliated with the Community of Mindful Living, headquartered in Berkeley, California, established in 1983.

Throughout the final twenty years of the twentieth century, the growing number of American-born Dharma heirs designated as qualified Zen teachers helped to fuel the growth of Zen centers throughout the country. Although the majority of the centers are still located in the Pacific region, especially California, the guide lists Zen centers located in forty-five states and the District of Columbia. Over these same decades, leadership at leading Zen centers shifted from the initial group of American-born teachers to second- and third-generation Dharma heirs. By all reports, the membership at Zen centers has aged over the same time period, and it is not yet clear whether or not sufficient numbers of younger Americans will become attracted to Zen practice to preserve the existing network of Zen centers through the twenty-first century.

Common Zen Terminology

Terminology used in discussing Zen within an American context can appear confusing for individuals unfamiliar with the tradition's historical roots in East Asia and the current diversity of practicing Zen communities in the United States and other Western countries. As a relatively new religious tradition in the West, the Zen community continues to employ a host of terms derived from either the Japanese or Chinese sources of the tradition, and to a lesser extent terminology derived from Korean and Vietnamese forms of practice. In some cases, terms have been translated into English, but without any standardization between one community and another, or between authors. For this reason, I have included the following section to introduce some of the terminology associated with Zen that is employed throughout the rest of the book. The intention here is to introduce the terminology as it is commonly employed by American Zen practitioners, rather than to provide exhaustive word studies of usage in classical Zen literature. Readers familiar with Zen history and practice can easily skip this section.

The first term that requires clarification is Zen itself. The word Zen represents the Japanese pronunciation for a Chinese character, pronounced *Chan* in Mandarin Chinese. The word means meditation or concentration, and was originally adopted in Chinese as the standard translation in Buddhist texts for the Pāli term *jhyāna*, rendered *channa* in Chinese. The term Chan eventually was adopted as the name for a school of Buddhism that emerged in China sometime during the Tang dynasty (618–907 CE). Chan eventually spread throughout East Asia to Korea (where the same Chinese character is pronounced *Son*), Japan (where it is pronounced *Zen*) and to culturally related areas such as Vietnam (where it is pronounced *Thien*).

As noted earlier, American Zen includes a broad spectrum of influences from teachers and communities from Japan, China, Korea, and Vietnam. While some religious communities and practitioners continue to employ the Chinese, Korean, or Vietnamese pronunciation of the name, most communities and individuals in the English-speaking world have adopted the Japanese pronunciation. The use of a common nomenclature clarifies the relationship that these various communities share as claimants to be modern descendents of the Chan lineages that originally emerged in China. In addition, the term Zen enjoys widespread familiarity and cultural collateral among English speakers.

The term *sangha*, commonly used today to refer to Buddhist communities from all denominations of Buddhism, derives from Sanskrit.[27] Among many Western Buddhist communities, the term is understood to refer to the traditional "four-fold community" established by the historical Buddha that includes male and female monastic practitioners as well as male and female lay practitioners. For this reason, the term is sometimes used as a general term for all Buddhists, regardless of denominational affiliation or style of practice. In other contexts, however, the term is used to refer to smaller practicing communities, including Zen centers and Zen meditation groups. It should be noted that ordained Buddhist clergy from the Japanese American Buddhist communities more often employ the term to refer exclusively to ordained Buddhists, the monastic community, or religious professionals, as opposed to lay practitioners.

Zen communities use a variety of terms to address their clergy and teachers. At Japanese American temples, ordained clergy are typically addressed as reverend. In non-ethnic settings, the most commonly used title is the Japanese word *rōshi*, which can be translated as "venerable teacher." Robert Aitken and other recognized Zen teachers are commonly addressed as Rōshi, although some Zen teachers prefer other, less formal, forms of address. At HDS, for example, when a member refers to "the Rōshi," they invariably mean Aitken, rather than the current head teacher, Michael Kieran, who to my knowledge does not (yet) wish to be addressed in that fashion. In direct address, HDS members generally call Kieran "Michael," and refer to him indirectly as "my teacher" or "our teacher." In other communities, practitioners may call their teacher "sensei," the most general term for teacher in Japanese.

Terminology for various forms of Zen practice is perhaps more standardized, with many of the Japanese terms appearing in English dictionaries. Most Zen communities, for example, use *zazen* and its English translation "seated meditation" interchangeably. Two basic styles of *zazen* practice, kōan and *shikan taza* ("just sitting"), are associated respectively with Rinzai and Sōtō communities. Kōan, which refers to stories (also known as encounter dialogues) usually derived from classical Zen literature, are commonly used by Zen practitioners from Rinzai and Sanbōkyōdan lineages as a focal point for meditation. Rinzai and Sanbōkyōdan lineages likewise each use their own standardized curriculum of kōan cases as the basis for training new teachers. *Shikan taza*, which can be variously translated, typifies practice within Sōtō communities.

Most Zen centers in the United States that have a teacher in residence offer retreats, periods of intensive meditation practice typically called *sesshin*. At most Western Zen centers, *sesshin* vary in length from three to seven days. Participants may include a combination of local members, distant members (discussed in chapter 7), and unaffiliated visitors who apply to attend the *sesshin*. During *sesshin*, participants have daily opportunities to meet privately with the resident teacher; these private interviews are called *dokusan* or *sanzen*. Some Zen centers have also introduced longer periods of intensive training, usually lasting three months, sometimes called *ango*, that are patterned after the traditional Buddhist monastic "rainy season retreat." Some centers limit full participation in these longer periods of practice to residential members, while others allow for local members to participate as their work and family obligations allow.

Finally, many Zen communities have developed a form of initiation ritual, known as *jukai*, in which members accept or receive the precepts from their teacher. These rituals vary significantly in meaning and form from community to community, and cannot be generalized here. In monastic forms of East Asian Buddhism, the term *jukai* usually refers to ordination ceremonies in which monks or nuns receive the initial Ten Precepts and join the monastic community. There also exists a long history in Chinese and Japanese Buddhism for lay precept ceremonies, in which lay practitioners affirm their commitment to Buddhism by accepting or receiving the Five Precepts of a lay Buddhist: Not to kill; not to steal; not to engage in sexual misconduct; not to lie; and not to drink liquor. In some communities, the *jukai* ceremony is referred to as a form of lay ordination. In HDS, the terminology of "confirmation" would perhaps be more accurate, although I have never heard it used by members, since individuals generally do not request to participate in the ritual at the beginning of their practice, but only after they have practiced for a significant period of time.

PART I

*Distant Correspondents
Write to the Rōshi*

CHAPTER 2

Why People Write

> When I was a classroom teacher I always felt there was more hope for the student who threw a piece of chalk at me when my back was turned than for the one who put his head down on his desk. That piece of chalk gave me a chance to do something, to say something. But what can one do if there is no response? In meeting with the rōshi, it is important that you speak up and show something.
>
> —Robert Aitken, *Taking the Path of Zen*

Etiquette demands that, when writing a letter to a stranger, one explain one's purpose. The Distant Correspondents largely complied with this dictum, making it relatively easy to create an initial list of reasons why individuals wrote for later coding and analysis (see table 6). On closer reading, however, I found that many letters that began by saying, for example, that the person was writing to express his or her thanks to Aitken for writing *Taking the Path of Zen*, went on to do other things, such as ask for advice or request information. I therefore adopted the assumption that correspondents could have multiple purposes, and did not seek to prioritize their purposes or limit my analysis exclusively to the reasons that they self-identified. As a result, most letters fall under two or more categories in the table. Moreover, I assigned some letters to a category such as "Seeking encouragement," which only a few writers made explicit, based on my reading of the letter.

For the majority of cases that involved one to three letters (80 percent of the study group), I included the reasons that I observed in all of the letters written by the correspondent. For long-term correspondents, I coded only the purposes expressed in the first few letters. After that, especially

Table 6. Reasons for Writing

Reason	No. Cases	Percentage
Comment on writing	114	44%
Ask advice	111	43%
Seek a teacher/sangha	86	33%
Information about HDS	51	20%
Want to join HDS	32	12%
Seek encouragement	21	8%
Counseling by mail	17	7%
Request interview	13	5%
Personal counseling	13	5%
Confirmation of an "experience"	12	5%
Information on rituals	11	4%
Challenge Aitken	10	4%
Request a place for retreat	6	2%

for correspondence that continued over several years, coding every letter was neither practical nor appropriate. Once the correspondent and Aitken had firmly established a relationship, whether student-teacher or friendship (and sometimes both), the nature of the exchanges changed, and later letters primarily serve to preserve the relationship.

Three reasons that motivated Distant Correspondents to write to Aitken stand out: to express their gratitude or admiration for one or more of Aitken's published works (44 percent), to request advice of some kind (43 percent), or to request help in finding a teacher or *sangha* with whom to practice (33 percent). These topics will be taken up at some length, as well as some of the less common reasons, such as seeking confirmation of an enlightenment experience and writing to challenge the *rōshi*, topics that are of particular interest in understanding how Distant Correspondents perceive the role of the Zen teacher.

Expressing Gratitude or Admiration

A substantial number of Distant Correspondents, 114 individuals, expressed thanks or admiration for one or more of Aitken's published works. Distant Correspondents felt drawn to his words, and many said that they felt compelled to write because they were deeply moved or inspired by them. As mentioned in the introduction, Distant Correspondents found Aitken's most compelling themes to be his practical advice about the mechanics of seated meditation, his primary focus on *zazen* as the heart of the Zen tradition, and his insistence on ethical conduct and social engagement with issues of justice and peace as critical aspects of Zen practice.

I was struck that in many cases, by opening their letters with sincere words of gratitude, the Distant Correspondents sought to establish a kind of long-distance relationship with a Zen teacher, thus laying a basis for the requests for advice or information that so regularly followed. The letters thus serve as much more than simple fan mail, while often retaining something of that flavor. Indeed, I found only fifteen letters that were written exclusively to express gratitude or admiration, the exceptions that prove the rule, if you will.

In the early years of Aitken's teaching career, the period extending from the earliest such letter in 1968 to approximately 1982, when *Taking the Path of Zen* appeared in print, people wrote to Aitken primarily based on personal recommendations received from other Zen practitioners, information acquired while visiting the Hawaiian islands, and information shared at other Zen centers. The number of cases from this fifteen-year span is a modest forty-nine, and slightly more than half fall into the word-of-mouth category. Nevertheless, even in the early period, seven people wrote in response to his early essay "The Zen Buddhist Path of Self-realization," published in John White's edited volume *What Is Meditation*.

Throughout the years, the most popular of Aitken's books remains *Taking the Path of Zen*. James Ishmael Ford, in his recent guide to American Zen, notes that it became "a classic and seminal to many starting the Zen way."[1] My research bears this out. More than one in four of the Distant Correspondents singled it out for mention, and not a few of these indicated that it served as the basic guide for their practice of meditation. One longtime British practitioner, an ordained Zen monk, wrote to Aitken that he found it to be "perhaps the best English language introduction to *zazen* I have seen." Another man called it his "finger pointing to the moon," and still a third said that he found answers there to questions he had grappled with for thirteen years, from the time he was twenty-three, and that the book "changed my life fundamentally."

The Mind of Clover, Aitken's commentary on the Ten Grave Precepts, in which he discusses applying Zen ethics in the Western context, came in a distant second in popularity among the works cited by the Distant Correspondents. Only twenty-seven individuals mentioned this book. Nevertheless, several found it to be the most critical guide for their practice. The dean of a law school at a large state university, for example, wrote to Aitken:

> I am writing just to thank you for all the help you've given me along the Buddhist path. I've read all of your books except the newest [*Encouraging Words*]. I keep your book of *gathas* by the bed and read selected ones to my husband at night (selected according to the kind of day we've had!) *Mind of Clover* is my favorite—I've read it twice. More than any other book I've read, it helps me apply the Buddha's teachings in my day to day interactions with people.

A musician from the Midwest wrote that "*Taking the Path of Zen* and *Mind of Clover* have been influential in resolving some of the problems and doubts I had with Zen Buddhism, especially as applied to life in the US. . . . I have been able to embrace the practice of Zen Buddhism wholeheartedly."

A number of these Buddhist sympathizers and solo practitioners unilaterally accepted Aitken as their teacher based solely upon his printed words. While sixteen correspondents explicitly mentioned this, numerous others implied it by indicating that they used his works as their guide not only for meditation but the broader practice of Zen. The woman from Kauai indicated that when she read *The Mind of Clover*, she found in it "the voice of my inner teacher. I bow down to this teacher." Not surprisingly, she later made direct contact with Aitken, became his student and an active member of HDS. A Colorado woman, who mentioned that her first introduction to Zen came in an English literature class at the University of Hawaii for which Aitken gave a guest lecture, wrote to him several years later after reading *A Zen Wave* and *Taking the Path of Zen*.

> Perhaps I am like the duckling that, as soon as its eyes are open, follows the first thing it sees as 'mother'—but much thought and considerable reading propels me in the direction of Maui and Koko An as spiritual 'home.' I am not of course talking about geography. In a sense, I feel I am already your student, in that

your two books, and the few *teisho* tapes that I have been able to hear, have meant a great deal to me—have drawn me.

A female convert to Islam, clearly seeking help in her spiritual quest, wrote from England to seek Aitken's advice. She began by saying she had read all of his books and, "There is no living person of whom I know that I would like to learn from as much as yourself." An oncologist, preparing to move from New York to a practice in the rural South where he would no longer have access to a Zen teacher and community, wrote, "I have a strong affinity for your words in print. I hope to someday meet you and thank you for your teaching and patience. . . . With great respect to my rōshi, my teacher, I wish you health and long life."

Requesting Advice about Meditation

A total of 111 Distant Correspondents explicitly requested advice from Aitken Rōshi. In order to gain a better understanding of the needs that they brought to their written interaction with him, I broke down the category of Requesting Advice into several subcategories (see table 7). Once again, those who asked for advice often asked for more than one kind of advice, and I coded them accordingly. It should be noted that I excluded from this category all requests for help in finding a teacher or *sangha*, however the request was phrased.

Table 7. Types of Advice Sought

Related to:	No. Cases	Percentage of 111
Zazen specifically	43	39%
Other aspect of practice	23	21%
Living Buddhist life	20	18%
"Counseling by mail"	17	15%
Personal counseling	13	13%
Practice in Japan	8	7%
Suggestions for reading	7	6%
Writing and translation	3	3%
Not specific	11	10%

Distant Correspondents most commonly sought advice related to the practice of *zazen*. This is no surprise, given the nature of Aitken's writings. The category includes a wide variety of issues, and a few of the more typical examples will have to suffice. It can be noted, however, that many of these requests were quite vague, especially those coming from beginners and the self-taught. Many correspondents indicated that they practiced as best they could on their own, and now needed the guidance of a teacher. A high school student, in the first of several letters written over a five-year period, formally requested permission from Aitken as his teacher to begin meditating based on *Taking the Path of Zen*. Aitken encouraged him to do so, reiterating advice found in the book.

A high school English teacher who had been sitting daily for eight weeks described an experience of "happy-warm-silence without thoughts or ego intrusions" achieved during meditation. He asked whether Aitken thought he was ready to begin with Mu, the first kōan given to Zen students within Aitken's tradition. Again, Aitken responded positively to the correspondent's reported progress; he assured the man that he should regard his experience as a breakthrough and a milestone in his practice. "I have no objection to your starting on Mu." Aitken then clarified that it was time to consider attending *sesshin* somewhere, supplying three specific options, including information about two mainland Zen centers as well as HDS. It was not at all unusual for Aitken to make the determination that an individual was ready to begin kōan practice, coupled with advice about working with a teacher. He regularly recommended teachers who were geographically closer to the correspondent with the understanding that few people could afford regular trips to Hawaii.

A correspondent who first wrote while still affiliated with one of Kapleau's groups reported that he was then sitting for four hours per day, counting his breath, but was having difficulty controlling his mind. Because his group practiced without a resident teacher, he had no one to consult with his concerns. He asked, "May I begin a koan? May I write to you again?" Aitken declined to give permission to another teacher's student to undertake kōan work, but nevertheless responded to his implicit question related to *zazen*. "You do not gain control of your thoughts by forcing. It is not possible to block thoughts. Those thoughts are you, so when you try to stop them, the battle will be between you and yourself.... Never mind the thoughts—just let them go by."

Some individuals wrote for advice and reassurance when they experienced *makyō*, unusual physical sensations or intense mental images that may arise during *zazen*. For example, an engineering student who managed to attend one orientation weekend at Maui Zendo described the physical sensations she had since experienced that worried her: sharp jerks, the sensation of heat, sometimes nausea and spinning. She asked, "Should I continue with my breath counting?" Aitken responded in a reassuring letter, "Your *zazen* sounds fine. It is natural that you go through certain *makyō* experiences. Please continue with your breath counting right through these experiences. Regard them simply as the context of your practice." Even longtime practitioners, including those still working with another teacher, sometimes asked Aitken for technical advice when they experienced special problems. One detailed example will suffice.

A female member of SFZC with eight years of meditation experience wrote for assistance with a problem she had been having for about a year: Whenever she sat down to meditate, her whole body would begin to shake violently. She indicated that the problem seemed to arise directly from the practice, and not to be emotional or medical in origin. She described her struggle to maintain regular practice, and her desire to continue daily sitting. She admitted that problems at SFZC made it difficult to get the guidance she needed from her teachers there. Her letter is dated 1983, the year that Baker Rōshi's sexual misconduct became public knowledge, and a time of great upheaval and internal strife within the SFZC community. Aitken's response is long and detailed. He called her problem a "dark night of the soul," an important phase of the true religious path. He recommended that she continue sitting as best she could, with frequent consultation with a trusted teacher. Even one *sesshin* with such a teacher could bring her to the other side. He suggested that she try different postures for meditation, Burmese style, or even a chair or lying down. "You are in process, so your posture doesn't matter that much." He suggested that she experiment with using a focus, such as breath counting, but admitted that he could not recommend this as a firm suggestion because they were not working face to face. He closed his reply with a warm invitation to come to Hawaii for a *sesshin*.

Seeking Advice for Living a Buddhist Life

Beginning with *The Mind of Clover*, Aitken's writings often address ethical issues and the manner in which Zen practitioners should conduct their lives in a Western context. Distant Correspondents therefore wrote to him about their concerns in these matters. While a few of them asked about engagement in the ecological movement or antinuclear/antiwar movements, more often correspondents enquired about the benefits of monastic as opposed to lay practice, how to balance regular practice with the demands of marriage and childrearing, or raised their concerns about understanding such Buddhist ethical concepts as Right Livelihood in the contemporary context.

Married individuals wrote to Aitken for advice about practicing as a couple and balancing their practice with the demands of family life. In other cases, Aitken made it a point to ask his correspondents questions about these concerns, anticipating that they would eventually arise. Does their spouse support them in their practice, or is it a source of friction in the relationship? Can they get away for a *sesshin* without putting an undue burden on their spouse and children? One woman wrote poignantly that no one seems to comment on the human failings of the Buddha, specifically that by leaving his wife and children, the Buddha "reveals a painful disparity between men and women and leads people to believe that the quest for personal enlightenment takes precedence over the struggle and fulfillment of human relationships." She plaintively continued,

> What we so desperately need now is a Buddha awakening through taking care of children (along with their diapers and quarrels), or a Christ knowing his or her essential nature through the good and difficult times of friendship. We especially need this story from a man, because women have been telling it since the beginning but don't know how to say it so that it resonates for men.

In his reply, Aitken pointed out that the Buddha not only abandoned his family, but he was hesitant to admit women to the *sangha*. Aitken assured her that despite this, there are plenty of words from the Buddha and his successors about equality. "In this case, we should do as they say, not as they did . . . I agree with you that one only matures through relationships, human and non-human, sentient and non-sentient."

At least seven Distant Correspondents wrote to Aitken to express their urge to undertake a monastic practice, in several cases despite being married men. Aitken was completely consistent in his replies to these individuals, stating his strong preference for lay practice for contemporary Americans. He strongly urged married practitioners to stay with their spouse and continue their practice as laypeople. One man, just returned to the United States after a four-month retreat at a Korean Zen monastery, admitted that he would have remained in the monastery if not for his wife. Aitken responded,

> Is the marriage state as such one of the delusions and attachments that Shakyamuni said keep us from seeing we have the wisdom and virtue of the Tathagata? I don't think so. Then why ask disciples to become celibate? The life of the householder makes too many demands on the attention of a serious student. The monastery can also be a place of distraction.

Aitken likewise advised against ordaining for most of the single individuals who expressed an interest in monastic options. To a real estate lawyer contemplating ordination, who admitted that he had consistently avoided intimacy because of his monastic inclinations, Aitken replied that he might be using his interest in religion as an excuse for not starting a family. "Forgive me if I am being presumptuous here. My own feeling is that wife and family enhance practice. I don't think that becoming a monk is a viable way for many people in our culture."

Several individuals sought advice about traveling to Japan to enter a monastery there, following in Aitken's path as it were. In these cases, Aitken not only encouraged them to forego ordination, but further recommended that they reconsider practicing in Japan. He writes to one such correspondent,

> I understand very well your drive for monastic practice, a drive I shared when I was exactly your age. . . . [However] it is almost impossible for a Westerner to fit into the monastic routine in Japan. Language and cultural barriers, and the insanely rigorous routine make it all just too difficult. I speak from personal experience, and also from observation of the experience of others. . . . I am convinced it is possible to pursue Zen practice as a layperson with a good teacher.

Aitken thus encouraged Distant Correspondents to seek a practice community closer to home, the real locus of Zen practice as he understood it.

During my initial review of the correspondence files, when I was reading to gain an overview of the archive's contents, I came away with the impression that large numbers of people wrote to Aitken for personal counseling in such matters as loss of a loved one, problems in their love lives, substance abuse, and career choices. In the course of this research, for which I systematically excluded Aitken's students from the study group, it became clear that very few strangers actually wrote to Aitken in that manner. Indeed, I only identified thirteen cases among the Distant Correspondents that seemed to fit into this category. On closer analysis of this group, it became apparent that all but two had experience practicing somewhere at a Zen center with a teacher; four of them had actually met Aitken in person and may have felt some personal connection to him from that experience. I therefore tentatively conclude that solo practitioners and Zen sympathizers with only indirect knowledge of Zen (typically acquired through books) do not regard the Zen teacher as a sort of minister to whom one goes for personal counseling. Instead, it is Zen practitioners that possess direct experience practicing at a center who seem to possess this view.

Seeking a Teacher and a *Sangha*

One third of all the Distant Correspondents (eighty-six cases) wrote explicitly to ask for help in finding a Zen teacher with whom to work or to ask for help in locating a Zen group to join. The majority of them (forty-nine cases) made it clear that they wished to work with a teacher in the United States, many indicating that they would appreciate a recommendation for the teacher or group geographically closest to them. Among this group, thirty-two individuals requested permission to come to Hawaii to join HDS or explicitly asked Aitken to accept them as his student. Only five requested assistance in locating a teacher or monastery in Japan.

Distant Correspondents often describe reaching a point in their solo practice where they feel the need for guidance from a teacher rather than a book. They may explain that they have previously met a teacher or visited a group, and that they were not satisfied. Several indicated that they would come to Hawaii if it were a practical option, but financial concerns or family responsibilities made this impractical. A few of these stories stand out. A beginner writing from Texas in 1990 explained that he regularly sat with a local group that used Kapleau's book (*The Three Pillars of Zen*) as a guide, but the group had no teacher. He no longer found this arrangement satisfactory, because he believed that "Zen is embodied in a living master." He tried attending a nearby Tibetan Buddhist center for a class on Mahayana Buddhism, but he realized that Tibetan Buddhism was not for him. He concluded, "I do not want a huckster or a New Age backwater, but the real thing. . . . You seem to have integrity so I thought you might be able to offer some good advice or helping hand in the matter. Specifically, is Diamond Sangha a possibility for me or should I seek elsewhere?" Aitken responded, "I think certainly the Diamond Sangha is a possibility for you." He then recommended that the correspondent start by visiting his Dharma heir Pat Hawk, whose Zen center was then geographically closest to him.

Another man began by explaining that he recently met Aitken at a book signing in Los Angeles.

> As you signed, you asked me, "Do you practice?", to which I replied, "Yes." You then asked, "Where?", to which I mumbled, probably incoherently. That has been on my mind ever since . . . my own kōan. I practice on my own. I have visited the Zen Center in Los Angeles. . . . I hesitate going there now that I have a wife and two small children. My family is my practice. Where do I practice? I should have answered, "I try to practice everywhere."

He concluded by asking if there is such a thing as an offshoot of the Diamond Sangha in Los Angeles. Clearly touched by the man's letter, Aitken responded, "You are part of a great shift in Buddhism as important as the rise of the Mahayana, to lay-family practice." Explaining that there was no group affiliated with HDS in Los Angeles, he sent along brochures for the affiliated groups in other parts of California, Ring of Bone and California Diamond Sangha. "Or you could come here for *sesshin*. I also enclose a 1995 *sesshin* schedule."

Seeking Confirmation for an "Experience"

Among the 261 Distant Correspondents, I identified twelve individuals who explicitly sought confirmation of an enlightenment experience (identified by some correspondents as *kenshō* or *satori*). These individuals either presented an experience in writing for Aitken's response, or indicated that they wished to "request an interview to have my spiritual experience of awakening confirmed" or to "bring my realization of Zen to a *rōshi* and be near a *sangha*." In several other cases, letters suggested an implicit request for confirmation. In many cases, the description of the individual's spiritual experience(s) takes up several pages of text, recounting a full spiritual autobiography. In some cases, Aitken affirmed that the experience was in some way authentic, and then recommended that the person seek out a teacher with whom to practice face to face. Occasionally, Aitken asked "checking questions" that a Zen teacher would normally ask face to face in *dokusan*. A teacher may employ a checking question as a follow-up to a student's response to a kōan in order to determine whether or not a student has attained some understanding.

In 1991, an oncologist described his progress over a nine-month period as a solo practitioner that began with reading books about Zen, "including *Taking the Path of Zen* and *Mind of Clover* three times each." Eventually, he began to meditate each morning, and then he undertook Mu, until reaching his present practice of sitting daily for fifty minutes using Mu as his focus. He described how he came to see his experience as a cancer doctor, "officiating over the death of sentient beings," as related to his experiences in meditation. "Life seems to literally flow and pass through my fingers and hands, 'empty' hands." Aitken responded with encouragement regarding his realization and asked a checking question, "Can you point to Mu?" The archive preserves no answer from the correspondent to Aitken's questions. A "successful" response may have been removed from the archive, although there is no definitive indication that any answer was received.

In another case, dating from 1985, a priest who had practiced Zen for sixteen years wrote to "outline several powerful experiences" he had, and specifically requested Aitken's response to his account.[2] Aitken's reaction appears enthusiastic, "Your experience of Mu sounds authentic. I wish we could sit in *sesshin* somewhere." He provided his schedule for the next few months, in hopes that they could arrange to meet. He went on to recommend two Catholic Zen teachers, Willigis Jager and Joan Rieck, with whom the correspondent might prefer to work, and provided their contact information. Aitken concluded, "Years ago, Yamada Rōshi predicted that Zen practice would become a stream within the Catholic Church. . . . It is not yet clear just where the movement of Zen for Catholics is headed, but one thing is clear, it is promising and important. I hope that you will join up!"

I include here one more example, perhaps more instructive for Aitken's response than for the description of the experience. The correspondent, a psychiatrist and psychoanalyst from New York City, wrote to Aitken after reading a piece Aitken penned about *makyō*.[3] The doctor recounted to Aitken a dream he had, one he identified as a Death of Self Dream, which precipitated a major shift in his Zen practice. "Since you have presented yourself as a sympathetic (if distant) ear, I will presume to tell you about it." In the dream, he came upon his own dead body in the street. The affect of the dream was transformational and he experienced a heightened state of awareness that lasted for several days. Before the dream, he described his practice as "halfhearted." Afterward, he began to practice *zazen* in a completely new way, much more seriously than before. He eventually worked with Tetsugen Glassman and passed the Mu kōan under his guidance. Aitken responded that the dream was definitely a *makyō*. "I deplore the misunderstanding of *makyō* which can be found even among Zen teachers. They consider it something to be disregarded. Well, it is true that it is not realization, and to treat it as such is a grave mistake, but nonetheless it is an important milestone on the path, and sometimes leads directly into a resolution of Mu. I always instruct my students to report their *makyō* to me."

Challenging the *Rōshi*

Ten Distant Correspondents wrote to challenge Aitken, somewhat in the manner one would find in classical Chan and Zen literature recounting encounter dialogues between teachers and students. Several of these cases are worthy of detailed description, because they raise some important issues faced by the American Zen community as a whole. First, let me provide some general observations. All of the correspondents who wrote to challenge Aitken were male. It is interesting to note that six of them appear to have had significant experience working with other teachers, while three appear to be solo practitioners without such experience. In the final case, there is insufficient information to make even a tentative guess. The type of practice experience they had seemed to affect the tone that these men took with Aitken. Two of the solo practitioners assumed a harsh tone, apparently mimicking *mondo* (question and answer) exchanges one finds in the classical Chan corpus. Those who had previously worked with teachers took either a gentle approach to their challenge, reflecting their obvious respect for Aitken as a teacher, or assumed an angry tone because they were defending their own teacher.

The earliest challenger, who wrote five letters from late 1981 through 1982, provided little information about his own practice, but appears to have been self-taught. In his initial letters he quoted extensively from the Chan masters and posed harshly stated challenges to Aitken's understanding of Zen. In response to these letters, Aitken recommended that the correspondent undertake simple breath counting and suggested that he attend *sesshin* with a teacher. Aitken provided contact information for two teachers on the mainland and extended an invitation to come to HDS. He concluded with a warning that Zen practice is not for the "autodidact." Aitken appears to reserve this particular term as a derogatory expression for the small minority of practitioners who place themselves in grave danger by refusing to consult a teacher. I found no cases in which he used it to describe the self-taught solo practitioners who wrote to him for guidance. In this set of exchanges, Aitken assumed a stern "voice," one rarely encountered in the archive letters. It reminded me of the tone that I heard him assume at public events when challenged in a similar manner, which I dubbed Aitken's "teacher voice."

In one of his later letters, the same challenger railed quite vehemently against Aitken's use of Japanese forms within the context of American Zen. In response to this, a complaint likewise expressed by other challengers, Aitken explained, "We are in the first generation and until we can fabricate our own vessel, we need the old vases from the Orient. I, for one, am not wise enough to be able to fabricate a strictly western form at this time."

A solo practitioner, who explained that he had practiced Zen on his own for twenty years using books as his teachers, reported that he heard a *teishō* of Aitken's and found it deeply upsetting.[4] He therefore asked Aitken as a "'certified' or 'inka-fied' Rōshi about this: Cards be put on the table, face up please. What is Buddha-hood, anyway? Is it mostly myth, archetype . . ." Aitken responded briefly, "I wish never to speak. . . . Mea culpa."

The first challenge to take a gentle approach was penned by a gay man in response to reading *The Mind of Clover*. While he found "the section on sexual orientation on p. 42 [to be] open and beautiful," he was disappointed that Aitken limited his discussion of marriage relationships to heterosexual marriages. He "senses this is important to you because of the union of vastly different psyches (yin and yang). How vastly different are male and female psyches?" His second issue related to Aiken's understanding of fairy tales—he agreed that they don't teach children to crunch on their parents' bones, but insisted that they do teach a set of hurtful values by promoting a "preoccupation with physical beauty and ugliness, and the all consuming importance of a 'perfect' heterosexual partnership."

Aitken responded to this correspondent with an equally gentle tone. He began by acknowledging "that my words in the chapter on 'Misusing Sex' were not inclusive enough." He explained that he had only recently acquired some insight into gay orientation, so he regarded "the letter as a very helpful corrective." About the fairy tales, however, he begged to differ, maintaining that the magical thinking in fairy tales relates to personal power, rather than the power of others. "It may be that environmental factors, particularly family factors, created misunderstandings for you."

A district attorney, who referred to himself as a "serious zen practitioner," likewise wrote in response to *The Mind of Clover*, which he said was "the best discussion of precepts I have seen in writing." He asked Aitken about his comments on Takuan—what should he have taught? In *The Mind of Clover*, in his discussion of the first precept, not to kill, Aitken criticized Takuan Sōhō (1573–1645), a Japanese Rinzai Zen teacher from the early Tokugawa period. Takuan made frequent use of images drawn from the martial arts in his letters to contemporary samurai who numbered among his lay students. Aitken commented that Takuan failed to live up to his responsibility as a Zen teacher to properly explicate the precepts to his students.[5] The correspondent likewise mentioned that he had a policeman friend and asked, "Can he be a Buddhist? Is it right livelihood?" Aitken responded that were he in Takuan's position, he hoped he would have set up a hostel for samurai widows and orphans. "As for the police sergeant, I bow nine times. Police work in the service of maintaining the peace can be right livelihood."

The third gentle challenge came from a psychotherapist who worked with abused children. In his third letter, he asked if Aitken had personally struggled with kindness. He noted that while Aitken's teaching style is always kind, what he himself found attractive in Zen is the harshness and directness that he thought "translates as honesty." Aitken's response, unfortunately partially obscured and illegible, reads, "You are very insightful. The dark side is doubtful and passive. I use it as best I can in trust that you, all of [you?] will come forth."

A student of Sasaki Rōshi,[6] angered by something he heard Aitken say at a book signing, wrote, "Zen is young in this country, don't ya think, old man? What is more important at this point, a bunch of new procedures and new translations and books, and bunches of students, or depth of understanding and experience?" Aitken called this letter "a good salutary splash of cold water. I am glad that the old teacher has such a loyal student to remind the rest of us that Zen is inclusive after all. But you know, if you are familiar with my work, you know that my approach and his (S.R.) are very different. Perhaps you were testing my tolerance. Well, I flunked, I guess."

Another angry student, this time a longtime member of SFZC who said that he had "worked with [former SFZC teacher] Baker Rōshi for twenty years, and with [SFZC founder] Suzuki Shunryu for ten years before that," read an interview with Aitken. He accused Aitken of making "repressive use of Precept and Commandments" as well as taking a "wrongly positive view of Christianity." He further accused him of grandstanding in relation to Baker, apparently assuming that Aitken's comments about inappropriate behavior by Zen teachers referred to Baker. Aitken's tone sounds tight when he responded that since the criticism lacked specificity, he would quote chapter and verse from his own writings in response. He explained that his words about abuse in *The Mind of Clover* were made in reference to Eidō Rōshi, and not Baker. He elaborated that he was Eidō's first visa sponsor when Eidō served as the resident teacher at Koko An, and that as a result of Eidō's sexual misconduct with students, two women ended up hospitalized.[7]

One challenge appears rather oddly in a letter that the correspondent presented as and appears to sincerely intend to be an apology for having precipitously left *sesshin*. He begins, "I owe you and the *Sangha* a long overdue apology for leaving Rohatsu early without talking to anyone first last November. I'm sorry for the break in rhythm I must have caused the group . . ." In his application to attend the Rohatsu *sesshin*, the same correspondent stated that he had previous experience sitting a number of *sesshin* with Maezumi at ZCLA and one with Sasaki, noting that he generally preferred to practice *shikantaza*. In the same letter, he requested to receive *jukai* from Aitken, during what would be his first meeting with Aitken and his first *sesshin* at HDS. Aitken welcomed him to attend *sesshin*, but cautioned him against requesting to take *jukai* so soon. He encouraged him instead to get acquainted with HDS and to be certain that this was the lineage he wanted to make his home before undertaking the ritual.

In the letter apologizing for leaving *sesshin* in a disruptive manner, the correspondent admits that he "missed an opportunity to confront some demons" and did not handle himself properly, but he cannot resist offering a challenge.

> I'd love to dispute the structure and methodology of your approach, but obviously now is not the time for that and who am I to question the strategies of the old masters? Nevertheless, I can't resist one irreverent question, which I'm sure you've been asked a million times before. Where does oriental culturalism leave off from the actual practice or are the two inseparable? Is it truly necessary to adopt pseudo militant attitudes during *sesshin* or is this just the way the Japanese have practiced?

Apparently catching himself, he concludes, "What began as an apology is now taking shape as a manifesto, so I'll shut up."

Aitken's response is warm and cordial, accepting the apology, saying, "I am glad to have your reconsiderations. You would be welcome to give *sesshin* another go." He then responds directly to the challenge:

> Pseudo military attitudes are your own projection. We practice *zazen* rigorously—that's all. Our practice uses forms that come down to us through India, China and Japan. At each step they acculturated. Here they are in the first generation of acculturating again. Give the process a chance!

Aitken indicates elsewhere in his letters that the style of practice he encouraged at HDS moderates to a significant degree the stricter forms he himself experienced at Zen temples in Japan, which he found to be too harsh for most American practitioners.

A final challenge came from a German man seeking clarification about certain passages from the German translation of *The Mind of Clover*. He rejected Aitken's apparent endorsement of teachers who abuse drugs or alcohol. He averred that "although an addict may be able to experience something like enlightenment and solve kōan, it is certain that a drug addict, no matter if he or she uses caffeine, nicotine, alcohol or pot, etc., has not overcome his or her craving for a substance and consequently, cannot be considered to be a liberated person and is unable to guide other people to freedom." Aitken responded first by providing the relevant passage from the original English text, which reads,

> This is not to say that you cannot learn from a drunk. You can, and not merely by negative example. A Zen *teacher* who drinks excessively or gets stoned on *grass* can still be a *teacher*. However, the students of such teachers are placed in the awkward position of acknowledging their teacher's apparent violation of the precepts while accepting his or her guidance in other aspects of the practice. (Emphasis added.)[8]

Aitken indicated two subtle changes in the German translation that alter the tenor of the original statement. First, where Aitken wrote "teacher," the German reads "master," and second, the generic word "drugs" was substituted for his own mention of "grass." Aitken then went on to explain cultural factors that complicated the matter. He identified the teacher in the passage as Maezumi Rōshi of ZCLA. (By the time this letter was written in 1992, Maezumi Rōshi had long since publicly acknowledged his drinking problem.) Aitken explained that Maezumi remained unaware of his addiction for quite some time, in part because there is no term for alcoholism in Japanese.[9] He further explained that there existed a keen awareness of the dangers of addiction in the United States.

In explaining why they write, some of the correspondents discuss what they hope to accomplish through the practice of Zen, and in so doing reveal something about how they understand the tradition. An Australian from New South Wales first wrote to Aitken in 1983 because there were "no teachers in OZ." He could not afford to travel to Hawaii, nor did he think he had the personality to teach himself how to meditate, so he wrote to Aitken for advice. He described what he wanted to get from Zen practice: "mental discipline, peace, a faith not based on mere dogma, something to aspire to, and a way of tidying up my room." Many Zen sympathizers share his understanding that Zen practice can help one achieve peace of mind. In the first class period of my undergraduate seminar on Zen, I always ask students to write down, using words or pictures, three images that best describe Zen. Peace of mind is consistently high on the list. The notion that the correspondent expresses that Zen appeals because it does not require blind faith or the emphasis on dogma likewise typifies the modern Western understanding of the tradition.

What surprisingly few correspondents express directly is a desire to attain awakening, or enlightenment, as the term *satori* is more often translated. Perhaps the correspondents regard this as so obvious it can go unsaid, since nearly all descriptions of Zen practice discuss awakening as its primary goal. One correspondent, however, set enlightenment as her goal in the clearest possible terms: "My hopeful aim is [*sic*] attain enlightenment within this lifetime. Please tell me what I should do to accomplish this aim. What form of zazen should I practice?" A highly educated housewife and mother of two from Massachusetts, she wrote to Aitken in 1980 to ask for his advice. She assured him that she had "plenty of time to devote to my quest for Truth." Her own experiences with clinical depression made her "determined to find an answer to suffering." She had previously experimented with other forms of meditation and recently having read *Three Pillars of Zen*, began practicing "my interpretation of zazen."

The reasons that motivated the Distant Correspondents to write reveal some of their attitudes toward Aitken as a teacher based upon their reading of his published works, as well as certain implicit images of what characterizes a qualified "Zen master" derived from other forms of Zen literature. It is clear first of all that the correspondents typically viewed Aitken as an expert in meditation practice, largely based on their reading of *Taking the Path of Zen*. Nearly two thirds of the correspondents that requested his advice specifically asked for assistance either with *zazen* or some other aspect of Zen practice. One third of the study group relied upon his expertise to identify an appropriate teacher or community on their behalf. A significant number likewise regarded him as an expert on living a Buddhist life, especially as a lay practitioner, or in interpreting the Buddhist precepts in the contemporary American context, based largely on their reading of *The Mind of Clover*. Approximately 20 percent requesting his advice addressed him in that capacity.

Smaller proportions of the Distant Correspondents appear to have written Aitken for more stereotypical purposes based on popular images of Zen masters, especially the interaction between a master and a disciple, derived from Zen literature, including translations of kōan collections and the recorded saying of famous teachers that include encounter dialogues. Some of the individuals that wrote to challenge Aitken or to seek confirmation of an enlightenment experience appear to approach Aitken in this more stereotypical fashion. These individuals represent only a tiny minority in the study group, although other correspondents may have shared similar perceptions of Zen masters.

Two of the challengers raise important concerns about the use of Asian forms and procedures as opposed to forms more in keeping with American culture and sensibilities. Many other correspondents and many members of the broader American Zen community share similar concerns, and most of the older Zen centers have modified their styles of practice to some extent over the decades. For example, Aitken sometimes expressed concern that use of the warning staff (*kyōsaku*), even within a community such as HDS where the practitioner's consent is required before it is used, could cause trauma for anyone who had experienced child abuse or spousal abuse. Michael Kieran confirms that he and other HDS practitioners experienced much more yelling in the meditation hall and hitting with the warning staff during the early period when they followed much more closely the practice styles established by Harada and Yasutani. Use of the stick and yelling reduced steadily over time at HDS.[10]

In some cases, American Zen practitioners experience feelings of distaste when required to behave according to a foreign, Asian custom, such as bowing or prostrating oneself before an image or a teacher. Aitken encountered this himself during his first monastic experience in Japan. In other cases, the resistance seems to arise not so much from offended cultural sensibilities as an assumption about what Zen is or should be. Many Americans first encountered Zen through the writings of D. T. Suzuki. Suzuki presented Zen as pure experience, unencumbered by the accoutrements of culture or social context. It would perhaps be easier to maintain the assumption, I would say the illusion, of this if one's encounter with the practice of Zen were dressed up in familiar American forms. The Asian forms of robes, bows, chanting, and offering incense appear glaringly as the product of a cultural context, precisely because they are foreign. More familiar Western forms would perhaps register as nearly invisible, and therefore appropriately "formless."

This chapter provided an overview of the reasons Distant Correspondents had for writing to Aitken, starting with the reasons that they identified within their letters. The following two chapters delve into these reasons in more depth and seek to portray how the Distant Correspondents practice Zen, exploring the practice histories and current patterns of practice that they describe, identifying special concerns that they raise within their letters, and distinguishing some distinctive subcategories or constituencies among the Distant Correspondents.

CHAPTER 3

Patterns of Zen Practice among the Distant Correspondents

> The *rōshi* will ask you why you wish to do zazen. This is an important question and you should be prepared in advance to answer it. . . . He or she will ask you your age, marital status, occupation, and so on, by way of getting acquainted. But the main question is, "What brings you here?"
> —Robert Aitken, *Taking the Path of Zen*

"What Brings You Here?"—Establishing Contact

Many Distant Correspondents appear to be answering precisely the type of questions they would anticipate hearing at a first interview with the teacher, called *shōken* in HDS, as Aitken described it in the aforementioned quotation. In *Taking the Path of Zen*, Aitken provides this very brief description of *shōken* as it was conducted at HDS at that time. I believe this passage may explain the manner in which so many Distant Correspondents introduce themselves, providing in the process a wealth of demographic and practice-related data.

When Distant Correspondents relay to Aitken the present status of their practice, sometimes describing it in great detail, they appear to be offering him evidence of their sincerity of purpose in approaching him as a Zen teacher. One graduating college senior wrote, for example,

> This is rather an odd way of asking acceptance into a community, but I have absolutely no knowledge of the workings of a modern Zen monastery, if that's what one calls it nowadays. Perhaps I

need to come and bang on the gates in the middle of the night and cut off my arm or something to convince you of my sincerity in this, but for now I'll leave you with this letter.

Like the majority of her fellow Distant Correspondents, she had read Zen literature, but never before approached a living teacher. It is not uncommon for a correspondent to apologize for his or her ignorance of the proper protocol and to request that Aitken provide some parameters or guidelines.

I am well aware that individuals writing to a Zen teacher may be motivated to present themselves in the best possible light. They are writing to establish some sort of epistolary relationship with Aitken, one that may later develop into a direct relationship with him as student and teacher. In their effort to impress the teacher, they may exaggerate certain details, such as the regularity with which they sit or the length of time they devote to practice each day. I have nevertheless chosen to accept the Distant Correspondents at their word. In practical terms, the researcher has no way to verify the statements made by individuals about themselves. This limitation on the reliability of data likewise holds true for data collected using surveys or even personal interviews. On the other hand, there may be some natural limits inherent in the process of writing to a recognized teacher that help minimize the problem.

First, the Distant Correspondents approach Aitken with an attitude of respect, and this respect may well mitigate against unethical behavior such as exaggeration and lying. Many Zen enthusiasts credit Zen teachers with having attained extraordinary levels of awakening and perception. They may therefore believe that the teacher can see through a lie or an exaggeration, and therefore reject their overture toward establishing a relationship should he detect insincerity or deceit. Second, Zen practitioners routinely regard an inability to maintain a regular practice schedule, or the gap between their aspiration and accomplishment, as the very kind of problem to bring to the teacher.

As a part of their effort to establish a student-teacher relationship with Aitken, Distant Correspondents routinely describe their current style of Zen practice, as well as providing their history of experience with Zen meditation and other forms of religious practice (see table 7). Their letters therefore provide a wealth of data related to patterns of Zen practice for collection and analysis. Not everyone provides the same level of detail, of course, and some letters are so vague on the subject as to defy reliable interpretation. Nevertheless, the most significant observation to be made from the data is that over 75 percent of the Distant Correspondents, 198 individuals out of the study group of 261, claim to practice some form of meditation, and 190 indicate that they practice *zazen*. The actual number is no doubt higher, since I erred on the side of caution and coded only the cases that were sufficiently explicit. Only nineteen individuals, a modest 10 percent, made it clear that they possessed only a reading knowledge of Zen and/or that they had never meditated. In the remaining forty-four cases, the Distant Correspondent either did not mention practice at all or left the matter too vague for classification.

Solo Practitioners

Among the group of Distant Correspondents that specifically indicated that they practice *zazen*, 150 individuals provided sufficient information to make further determinations about their patterns of practice. The largest percentage indicate that they practice on their own (ninety-five cases), representing fully 36 percent of the entire study group and 50 percent of those indicating that they practice *zazen* (see table 8). The remaining cases are divided between those who say they currently practice at a Zen center (that is, an organization with a recognized Zen teacher) and those who indicate that they sit with a smaller meditation group. In addition, forty-nine individuals indicated that they previously sat *zazen* at a Zen center in some manner, ranging from regular active membership to occasional attendance at *zazenkai*, or a single *sesshin* or orientation weekend, although it was no longer their current style of practice.

Many Distant Correspondents provided additional pieces of information relevant to their current practice of *zazen*, such as frequency and duration, whether they typically followed breath counting, kōan, *shikantaza*, among others. Unfortunately, these mentions were provided so sporadically that they defy meaningful analysis. One cannot conclude, for example, how many individuals who indicated that they meditate do so on a daily, weekly, or less regular basis, since less than forty people mentioned frequency at all. The data are nevertheless included in table 9 as a matter of interest.

A substantial number of the Distant Correspondents in the study group explain that they not only practice alone, they are likewise self-taught, most typically based on their reading of Zen literature. Forty-two cases, fully half of the solo practitioners, can be classified as self-taught, with twenty of them mentioning that they relied upon *Taking the Path of Zen* as

Table 8. Practice Data

Type of Practice	No. Cases	Percentage of Total	Percentage of Subtotal
Some meditation	198	76%	—
Zazen	190	73%	100%
Solo practice	95	36%	50%
Sit with a group	23	9%	12%
Member ZC	32	12%	17%
Other meditation	8	3%	—
No zazen/read only	19	10%	—
No mention/unclear	44	17%	—
Prior ZC experience	49	19%	26%

Table 9. Other Practice Information

Information Provided	No. Cases
Practices kōan	10
Practices breath counting	5
Practices *shikantaza*	3
Sits zazen daily	21
Sits zazen sporadically	17
Has attended sesshin	15
Has attended retreat/orientation	6
Has worked with a teacher (named)	25
Has monastic experience	8

their primary or sole resource. Five mention that they used Kapleau's *The Three Pillars of Zen*. A few others acquired Aitken's orientation tapes from HDS directly or from friends. This suggests a high degree of self-reliance among Western Zen practitioners, at least up to a certain point in their practice. The self-taught, like many other solo practitioners, eventually feel the need for formal instruction and/or guidance from a teacher.

Among the ninety-five Distant Correspondents who practice on their own, approximately one third indicated that they had reached a stage in their practice where they felt the need for a teacher. A few others suggest that the encouragement and support provided by a group, even one without a teacher, would likewise be helpful. One such individual, a thirty-five-year old man who gave up his previous career as an artisan working with stained glass in order to move to the South to care for his ailing father, provides an illustrative example. When he first contacted Aitken in 1978, he had been practicing *zazen* on his own for three years, indicating that for two of those years he had been sitting with the Mu kōan, based on his reading of Kapleau's *The Three Pillars of Zen*. (He did not indicate how he was first introduced to *zazen*, and was therefore not counted among the self-taught.) He eventually began to experience physical and emotional problems arising from *zazen*, which he identified as *makyō*. He tried without success to ignore the experiences, and decided to seek guidance. Since, in his new location, he lived too far from a Zen center to contact a teacher in person, he first wrote to Kapleau for advice. He received an answer, written by an assistant, warning him that undertaking Mu without a teacher is dangerous, and that he should stop immediately. Unsatisfied with that advice, he wrote to Aitken for a second opinion. Aitken responded, "I think it is remarkable that you should be practicing Zen on your own." Commenting that his "symptoms don't sound at all wrong," Aitken encouraged him to resume his practice of Mu. He offered to guide him through "this stale place" in his practice, and recommended that he begin visiting a teacher at least for occasional *sesshin*. Thus began a ten-year correspondence that resulted in a direct student-teacher relationship with Aitken.

Many correspondents comment in a similar vein that they have reached "a point of stagnation," "a dead end," or that they feel "stuck without anyone to go to for guidance." More than one correspondent, mildly alarmed by *makyō* experiences, decided to seek out a teacher for advice. One woman living in Canberra, Australia, who taught herself to meditate, wrote that she was overjoyed to locate a local Zen group, only to become deeply disappointed when she learned that they met without a teacher. Having just heard that Aitken would not visit Australia again for another year, she wrote,

> Now I seem to have hit a brick wall. I struggle & struggle & can't find any way. I feel nauseous, sick in my head & my heart & thoroughly frustrated. Last night during *zazen* I burst into tears and that's when I decided I must write to you although I'm not your student . . .

A high school teacher, trying to guard against just such an eventuality, said that "as a teacher, I know the value of a good teacher to help avoid the pitfalls." He went on to say that, despite good progress in his practice, he hesitated to start Mu without having access to the guidance of a teacher. Other solo practitioners struck a slightly different theme, suggesting that it is now time to "begin a legitimate Zen practice," or "take the next step," or "establish more of a commitment" to the practice of Zen as represented by working with a teacher.

One rather unusual case of solo practice involved a man who longed for the support of a *sangha*, but refrained from attending a local *zazenkai* because he feared that his passing gas would cause a disruption at the *zendo* (meditation hall). He nevertheless faithfully maintained a schedule of twice-daily sitting. Aitken began by saying, "I am moved by your sincerity of purpose and your ardent practice." He then gently admonished the man,

> Please don't be concerned about what effect you might have on others. If you fart, you fart. Treat the zendo like a hospital. Nobody cares what kind of noises you make or smells you produce. It's all very natural. The incense will dominate smells. *Zazen* is best done in a group. You get support this way.

Aitken then included contact information for a nearby Zen group led by one of his senior students.

Distant Correspondents Who Practice with a Group or Zen Center

In *Taking the Path of Zen*, Aitken strongly recommends that people find at least one Zen friend with whom to sit on a regular basis. In his early letters, he occasionally even encouraged his correspondent to consider sitting with a meditation group that practices something other than *zazen*, including eclectic groups in which each individual practices whatever form of meditation that he or she prefers. Several Distant Correspondents wrote to tell him that they took his advice and regularly met with a friend or a group. A man from San Antonio indicated that since he had been unable to locate a Buddhist group of any kind in his area, he usually practiced alone, but sometimes joined a "meditation group" for moral support. Another woman, living in an area of California with Zen groups nearby, chose instead to practice with Quakers, because she found the Buddhist groups disappointing with their "indifference to the politics of living."

In six cases, Distant Correspondents wrote to Aitken for advice about establishing or enhancing a group of their own. A woman writing from

Tucson, Arizona, for example, participated along with her husband in a small Zen group meeting at that time in private homes. She requested information and materials from Aitken, and became a regular correspondent as did her husband. This same group developed into Zen Desert Sangha, as it is now called, the first such group to affiliate with HDS. Another man, writing from Alaska, explicitly requested suggestions for holding *zazenkai* with his own little group, then consisting of only two people, himself included. Inspired by a recent visit with Gary Snyder, he decided to turn to Aitken for practical advice, explaining,

> because you have been the source of my limited contact with formal Zen practice, and because I believe very strongly in the direction that both you and Gary are taking with regard to lay Zen communities here in North America, I would like to establish a more direct tie with you as my teacher.

Aitken responded with a lengthy, handwritten letter, which is very rare in the archive. He suggested that the group could undertake a project as a way of giving themselves definition as a *sangha*, such as prison visitation, hospice work, or whatever seemed appropriate to their place and time. He recommended that they do a study project, reading Zen books that they both like and discussing them. He closed with, "The main thing is *zazen*, of course. Keep the faith!"

In other cases, Aitken responded in a more guarded fashion when Distant Correspondents hoped to found their own group. He warned one beginner that starting a group can be quite difficult without having a strong foundation of one's own in place first. He recommended that instead of founding a group, he work with a teacher and just find one Zen friend to sit with for the time being. A man from Tennessee wrote with great enthusiasm about the rituals his little group had developed for themselves based on their reading of Aitken's books. Aitken's first letter was vaguely encouraging; in it, he suggested that they get in touch with Pat Hawk in Texas, since he was not too very distant from them. The correspondent's next card, obviously written immediately upon receiving Aitken's letter, in a seemingly breathless response, requested "taking refuges, vows, precepts, abhishekas, kesa, names and lineage papers by proxy" and promised that the group would support HDS monthly "as our Dharma home away from home." At this stage, Aitken's tone shifted. He indicated that this approach "probably won't work." He explained that *jukai*, as HDS calls the ritual for taking the precepts, takes time, careful preparation, and close work with a teacher, as symbolized by the sewing of the *rakusu*. There ended the exchange.

In a few cases, Distant Correspondents currently working with other teachers or affiliated with other lineages wrote to Aitken requesting instruction in a manner that breached his sense of student-teacher protocol. Consequently, his responses took on a very formal tone. One young man, a member of a Rochester-affiliated center, became inspired by reading one of Aitken's essays and wrote to describe his current practice and to ask permission to begin the kōan Mu. Aitken responded in an uncharacteristically business-like manner, "Thank you very much for your letter of inquiry dated July 30. You are certainly welcome to write to me, but I will not be able to serve as your teacher, so long as you are affiliated with the Rochester Zen group. It is to Rōshi Kapleau that you should turn for advice." He then provided specific advice about what to tell Kapleau—that he sits for four hours per day, what is happening in his mind when he sits, and what experiences he has had, if any, during *zazen*.

Another young man, this time affiliated with ZCLA, wrote to get Aitken's response to a question and answer exchange he had with Genpo (Dennis Merzel) about the "enormous apocalyptic upheavals and changes we see our planet experiencing." He mentioned to Genpo that Tibetan Buddhism makes prophecies about our times and asked Genpo why Zen has been so silent on the subject. Genpo replied, "'Because it's all a dream' and then he referred me to you, saying that you have a lot to say on the subject." Aitken again responded with great formality,

> The priest Gempō[1] responded directly to the point of your question, and there is no need for comment from me, but since he suggested that you write me, I will try to decorate the lily.
>
> You know, Tibetan yoga is generally taken up with the karmic, temporal side—even its exposition on life after death shows this. Zen people seek what underlies and infuses phenomena, karma, and time, and view the phenomena as a dream, a fantasy, and so on, as the Diamond Sutra says.
>
> Grounded in the dojo of the Buddha, we live in this dream world. I think you are correct in sensing burgeoning destruction . . .

Aitken sent a copy of his letter to Genpo as a professional courtesy, and took the opportunity to send along his personal greetings. On the carbon copy addressed to Genpo, he added a brief note: "Dear Gempo: Thought you should have this reply to your student. I look forward to seeing you soon, and send love to you and Hōbai. Bob."

I noted elsewhere that surprisingly few individuals wrote to Aitken requesting personal counseling, and that those who did were typically current or former members of a Zen center. I would like to provide here some typical examples as well as more unusual cases from this small portion of the study group. The most typical reason for a Distant Correspondence to request personal counseling is grief for the loss of a loved one. A married couple, members of the Chicago Zen Center, wrote to Aitken requesting his help in dealing with their grief related to an abortion they had twelve years earlier. They indicated that their grief was actually heightened by *zazen* and that their sadness deepened in the presence of their two children. Aitken responded in much the same manner he used with other grieving parents. He counseled them that the most important thing was for both of them to say goodbye, the same way they would to any other relative who died. He explained that Yvonne Rand holds a ritual each year for parents like themselves, and provided contact information in case they were interested in that option. He enclosed an essay he had written on abortion and also recommended that they read the relevant section in *The Mind of Clover* if they wished to create their own ritual of farewell.[2] For that ritual, he suggested that they give the child a name—a poetical unisex name if they didn't know the gender—put a picture of the Bodhisattva Jizo or an artistic rendering of a child on their altar, and speak directly to the child. They should explain that the circumstances were such that birth was not possible and "now with all your love you must say goodbye." In his letters to grieving parents, Aitken often stressed that the process of saying goodbye and letting go are critical not only for the parents' well-being, but for the well-being of their surviving children.

Another man, himself a practicing Zen Buddhist at a Zen center in California, wrote to inform Aitken that his brother, one of Aitken's students, had recently died tragically in a car accident. He sent HDS a contribution in his brother's name, and asked Aitken to help his brother "in making the transition." He explained that he and his grieving parents had agreed to donate his brother's organs, and now he wondered if this was an appropriate Buddhist decision. Aitken assured him that they had done the right thing. He mused that while the Tibetans seem certain about the after-death process, "I don't know what happens. Your brother was a bodhisattva in life. Be confident that he would want to continue to serve others in death." He promised that he would dedicate the upcoming *Rohatsu sesshin*[3] for his brother, and signed his letter, "With love, Rōshi."

One final extraordinary example involved a Western woman ordained as a Zen nun who indicated that she had worked closely with an otherwise unidentified Asian Zen teacher for over fifteen years, establishing Zen centers in the United States. She identified herself only with the pseudonym Compassionate Action, and routed her mail through a trusted friend to further protect her identity, and, more to the point, that of her teacher. Her first letter comprises eight single-spaced typed pages describing her situation, as well as that of another woman, an Asian woman she calls "Sue." Her teacher had a violent, abusive temper and he openly admitted that he hated women. Despite his violent outbursts and threatening behaviors, she did not want to leave and lose a "good teacher" of the Dharma. She understood that most people would immediately tell her to leave him, and hoped that Aitken could provide more nuanced guidance. She enclosed copies of several Dharma talks by her teacher, apparently to serve as evidence in his favor. At a time in his career when most responses waited for at least several weeks, Aitken responded with great urgency the day after he received the letter. He said simply, "It is time for you and Sue to go." He had already "discreetly" made arrangements for them to take shelter with one of his Dharma heirs, and had further made arrangements to cover their transportation costs should that prove necessary. Given the contents of the file, it appears that Aitken may have sent along copies of articles describing spousal abuse as further encouragement for her to leave. Subsequent letters from Aitken indicated his growing concern for Compassionate Action's safety. She had not arrived as he had hoped at his Dharma heir's center, and no one had heard from her. Her final letter, written a month later, indicated only that she and Sue had decided to remain with their teacher.

Distant Correspondents with Reading Knowledge Only

Only nineteen people indicated in their letters that they had never attempted to meditate or mentioned that they possessed only reading knowledge of Zen. The only patterns that emerge in reviewing this small segment in the study group are to be found in Aitken's replies. To every individual who made a request for guidance on how to proceed with practice or asked permission to begin meditation, Aitken provided a similar response: Please read, or reread as the case may be, *Taking the Path of Zen*, and begin to practice on your own. Write again if you have more questions. In one early case, dating back to 1981, Aitken recommended that the individual read Kapleau's *The Three Pillars of Zen*. To those few individuals who indicated that they had never meditated and who wrote what amounted to fan mail, that is expressing only appreciation without any hint of an inclination to practice, Aitken simply did not respond.

Minor Patterns

The very first Distant Correspondent identified for this study was a man whose business card identified him as chief instructor and director of a Tae Kwon Do *dojang*, and a seventh-degree black belt. In his letter, he indicated that he was first introduced to meditation through the martial arts, and continued to use it with his own students. Based on my own experience teaching university classes related to Zen, I have found that many Americans assume that there is a deep connection between the martial arts and Zen. Indeed, I expected to find numerous such examples among the study group, given the numbers of my students who have raised the topic in class. It was a mild surprise, therefore, to find that only six individuals mentioned their involvement in martial arts. I can only speculate that Aitken's clearly pacifist stance either deters that segment of the Zen reading audience from writing to him, or convinces them to remain silent on the matter when they do. For his part, Aitken recommended that Zen aspirants keep silent about the martial arts when dealing with other Zen teachers. One college student, for example, wrote to Aitken to ask for help in planning his first trip to Japan to practice in a rural monastery. He likewise mentioned his other aim for the trip, to take up Aikido while in Japan. Aitken offered him some unsolicited grandmotherly advice: "Do not mention Aikido in your letter [to the Rōshi], just emphasize your strong commitment to Zen practice."

A final connection that emerges in a small number of letters relates to the use of *zazen* as a form of therapy. Several medical professionals within the study group indicated to Aitken that they used Zen therapeutically with their own patients. As many as ten other Distant Correspondents mention the mental health benefits that they have experienced with practice, ranging from improved self-confidence, to relaxation and stress reduction, to the reduction of pain during periods of physical illness.

Several prison inmates, for example, indicated that they initially took up *zazen* to control their destructive patterns of anger. Aitken responded positively to all of these comments, accepting therapeutic benefit as one recognized purpose for *zazen*. He commented, for example, to a man recovering from a betrayal by his former lover, "You are handling your pain well. Your practice will see you through the valley of despair. Give energy to your practice and the pain fades and becomes transformed."

In another case, Aitken himself initiated contact with a young woman when he learned she had been diagnosed with cancer. He wrote in order to teach her a therapeutic form of *zazen* to help her cope with the physical pain and mental anguish of her condition. In a beautifully composed, handwritten letter using language that mirrors his instructions in *Taking the Path of Zen*, Aitken guided her through breath counting while lying on her back in her hospital bed. He knew that she would be afraid sometimes, and wrote reassuringly that this was okay. He asked her "to face the bugaboo death and admit you are afraid."

Two individuals wrote to Aitken specifically to ask if *zazen* could heal their mental illness. A man from Texas described himself as having been "purely materialist until about 40." At that time, he began experimenting with automatic writing, which triggered periods of hallucinating. His family eventually had him hospitalized for psychological treatment. Even after six years, he wrote that he had never been the same since. He said, "I feel as if I lost my soul if that is possible. So I am wondering if Zen would help me become normal again?" Aitken replied that Zen meditation might be of some help; at the same time, he strongly advised that the correspondent attempt meditation only under the direction of a good teacher and "with a supporting cast of good mental health professionals nearby." In this case, he specifically recommended working with Maezumi in Los Angeles as someone who could guide him through "basic personal integrative exercises." Aitken explained that Maezumi had experience working with people with emotional difficulties and that there were many good medical professionals associated with ZCLA. In other cases, Aitken invited people who identified themselves as having bipolar disorder or depression to become his students and practice with HDS. He did not, however, recommend that they undertake the rigors of residential practice either at Maui Zendo or Koko An. In their cases, he recommended that they live in the local community and participate in weekly *zazenkai*, meetings, and holiday celebrations.

Conclusions

The present study provides no basis to determine the numbers of Zen sympathizers and solo practitioners in the general population, nor can its results be used to determine the relative numbers of solo practitioners versus sympathizers beyond the study group. Nevertheless, the most important conclusions to be drawn from the data collected for this study related to Zen practice by solo practitioners and self-taught meditators almost certainly reflect patterns that exist beyond the confines of the 261 Distant Correspondents identified from Aitken's files. First, the category of Zen sympathizers, sometimes known as "night-stand Buddhists," includes a substantial number of American Zen practitioners that practice meditation on their own, and would be better called *Zafu* Buddhists. Their commitment to Zen goes beyond sitting in an armchair to read Zen literature and includes sitting *zazen* on their cushions, conducting themselves according to Buddhist ethics, and participating in social justice activities. Like their counterparts who affiliate with a Zen center and practice with a community, they regard *zazen* as the central feature in their practice.

Some of these individuals practice alone by choice, for a variety of reasons. They may have previously encountered negative experiences at a Zen center, they may not yet have found a group to their liking, or they may be otherwise averse to joining groups. The majority, however, practice alone out of necessity; even today, many Americans live beyond the comfortable reach of an established Zen organization. The topics of isolation, aversion to joining groups, as well as commitment to Buddhist ethics and social justice will be taken up in the next chapter.

Many Zen practitioners teach themselves to meditate, at least in the initial stages, by reading books such as *Taking the Path of Zen* or *The Three Pillars of Zen*. In this regard, Zen lends itself to the kind of self-instruction and solo practice one finds in many other alternative religious movements, such as Wicca and other forms of neo-paganism. Americans of the Baby Boomer generation have demonstrated that they are quite comfortable with a do-it-yourself approach to exploring new religious options. It is quite possible that resources available on the internet have already or soon will supersede the modern Zen classics mentioned here as the primary means of self-instruction. A quick search on YouTube suggests that how-to Zen resources are already readily available and widely accessed.

One cannot tell from the number of viewers whether or not the audience for this new visual material is primarily Baby Boomers, or if subsequent generations are attracted to Zen practice.

As many Distant Correspondents found, once an individual's practice is somewhat established, he or she may encounter either unanticipated difficulties or profound religious experiences. Both unpleasant *makyō* experiences and the more pleasurable successes may lead a solo practitioner to conclude that the time has come to consult a teacher. This need for guidance does not necessarily translate into active participation in a Zen *sangha*, but may be confined to a brief interaction with a teacher via mail, email, or telephone. For at least some of these individuals, contacting a teacher, however, may serve as the initial bridge between solo practice and affiliation.

CHAPTER 4

Areas of Special Concern Raised by Distant Correspondents

> It is difficult to follow the Buddha or a religious path of any kind without community. The pressures of our greedy world tend otherwise to drive the sincere individual into isolation—and isolation is death. Even Thoreau had chairs for guests.
> —Robert Aitken, *The Mind of Clover*

Over the course of this research, a series of recurring themes appeared in the letters from the Distant Correspondents that represent concerns within the broader audience of Zen solo practitioners and sympathizers. In order of prevalence, these concerns include: A sense of isolation from a teacher or other Zen practitioners, commitment to social justice and/or Buddhist ethics, the challenges of lay versus monastic forms of practice, resistance to joining a *sangha* or to formally accepting a teacher, questioning the need for a teacher, and feeling the need for appropriate styles and amounts of ritual. In some cases, both the existing literature as well as my discussions with Zen teachers and direct observation of Zen groups supports the fact that these concerns are likewise shared by members of Zen centers and other Western Buddhist *sangha*s. Commitment to engaged Buddhism and preference for lay as opposed to monastic patterns of practice are sometimes identified, for example, as characteristics of American Zen or Western Buddhism in general.[1]

Isolation from a Teacher or *Sangha*

In his portrait of Buddhism in America in the nineteenth and early twentieth century, Thomas Tweed quoted from a letter written by a young American Buddhist convert living in Vermillion, South Dakota to a Buddhist priest in San Francisco: "You cannot know how utterly alone I have felt during the past years . . . knowing of no other person in America attempting to follow the teachings of the Lord Buddha, and how I desire to be of service to his cause." Tweed observes that this young man was perhaps among the most isolated of American converts or sympathizers at that time, since most of the others lived in a few urban areas where they could meet other Buddhists.[2] Approximately ninety years later, in 1988, a woman living in a remote region of Wyoming wrote to Robert Aitken asking his advice regarding her practice. She explained that she had attempted to practice *zazen* on her own for twenty-five years without the benefit of a teacher or a *sangha*. She had recently read *Taking the Path of Zen*, Aitken's most popular book, and found it quite helpful for her practice. She continued:

> In all the time spent pursuing the idea of Zen, which seems to ideally suit my mind type, I have yet to meet face to face another human being who is of the same bent. My family and acquaintances are all Mormons or Baptists or don't seem to give a damn.

It would appear that some things had not much changed in the interim, except perhaps that many more American Buddhists and Buddhist sympathizers experienced a deep sense of isolation in the late twentieth century.

As discussed in the chapter 1, America experienced a rapid growth in the number of Zen centers and meditation groups in the last three decades of the twentieth century. The growth curve of the number of new Buddhist centers illustrated in table 4 closely matches the distribution of the letters from Distant Correspondents shown in table 1, when comparing the data for the same time period. While one could surmise that the growth in Zen centers would reduce the problem of isolation faced by sympathizers and solo practitioners, as many as 40 percent of the Distant Correspondents continued to regard isolation as a serious concern for their practice throughout the 1990s.

While only thirty of the 261 Distant Correspondents explicitly discussed problems arising from a sense of isolation from a Zen teacher or from a community of likeminded practitioners, the issue seems to be lurking just beneath the surface in many more of the letters. Isolation appears to be a factor, for example, in an additional thirty-three cases in which the Distant Correspondent requested assistance in finding a possible teacher or *sangha* within a specific geographical area or requested permission to become Aitken's students and relocate to Hawaii. When one considers additional factors, such as the circumstances faced by Buddhist prison inmates (eighteen cases) and the sometimes self-imposed isolation of former members of Zen centers (twenty-two cases) who wrote to Aitken before they were ready to accept a new teacher, the number of "isolated" individuals grows to 106, nearly 40 percent.

The most common reason that Distant Correspondents identified for their feelings of isolation was their geographical distance from a Zen center or meditation group. Forty-five individuals mention either their physical distance from a teacher or Zen center or request information about finding a teacher or center in their general vicinity. Even with the burgeoning number of Zen centers, many people in North America, Europe, and Oceania still live beyond easy reach of one. Nor is it always practical for individuals to travel relatively short distances to the nearest big city to attend weekly *zazenkai*. Several Distant Correspondents indicate that they are limited in their ability to travel due to physical or emotional disabilities (five cases), their responsibilities for care giving of children or ailing family members (three cases), or for financial reasons (two cases).

Aitken was well aware of the problem of isolation from a teacher or *sangha*, having experienced some of it himself at various times in his life. He remarked in a few early letters to Distant Correspondents that their part of the country was "a wasteland for Zen practice." His early experimentation with the "corresponding membership" category for HDS and *dokusan* by letter was designed to meet the need felt by many solo practitioners and Zen sympathizers.[3] More discussion of Aitken's responses to the problem of isolation will be covered in a later chapter.

Some Distant Correspondents seem to have written simply to make contact with an actual living Buddhist. Many of them were like the woman from Wyoming and had never had the opportunity to meet a practicing Buddhist, let alone a teacher, and needed the encouragement of human contact. In December 1987, a man from Texas wrote in his second letter that although he had been reading about Zen for four years, he never had "any contact with anyone actually practicing it before [receiving] your letter." He found it tremendously encouraging "just knowing someone is out there." Aitken responded warmly with advice about locating a meditation group in his area, and invited him to continue writing. "I have a huge correspondence, but I get to each letter eventually."

In a few cases, correspondents revealed that their apparent proximity to a Zen center based on simple distance in miles was rendered irrelevant by other factors such as the quality of the roads and the weather. A man living in Leavenworth, Washington, reasonably close to Seattle in good weather, explained that his mobility was limited for much of the year because "for 7 months of the year we have 8–10 feet of snow. We get our mail by walking with snow shoes for 2 ½ miles." An individual living in the mountains near Taos, New Mexico described a similar experience of isolation during the winter months, cut off from town by snow and poor road conditions.

Nor is it always practical for individuals living in less remote areas to travel relatively short distances to the nearest big city or town to attend weekly *zazenkai*. Several Distant Correspondents indicated that they were limited in their ability to travel due to their own physical or emotional disabilities. A woman living in New Mexico, for example, indicated that she had practiced Zen for about seventeen years, and in recent years usually sat alone. A friend loaned her one of Aitken's books, and she eventually read *Taking the Path of Zen*. Based on her reading, she began practicing with Mu two years previously, still working without a teacher. She requested Aitken's "guidance for my practice. I know the student usually goes to the *rōshi*, but I have MS." Her question related directly to practice: "Does one concentrate on Mu or on the question, 'Does a dog have the Buddha Nature?'" Aitken responded, "I was moved to learn that you are persevering with *zazen* despite your poor health and chronic pain."

He encouraged her to "remember you are sitting with earnest Zen students everywhere," and assured her, "The relief you feel on experiencing no-self is an unmistakable clue that you are on the right road. Persevere. Breathe MU."

Another case of a man living in rural England seems to combine various forms of isolation including geographic limitation, care giving, and other emotional concerns. He identified himself as a publisher who had practiced Zen for approximately twenty years. He originally traveled regularly to participate in Zen meetings and *sesshin*, but this caused friction in his marriage, so his practice dwindled. His life eventually became more constrained because his wife suffered from bouts of depression and more recently cancer. He felt that he could no longer leave her even for brief periods to pursue his practice. He then found himself struggling with his own depression and alcoholism, and facing a new sense of urgency to practice. "I was desperate for understanding of why we are born? why we die? In the midst of this I was totally isolated, utterly alone, and in need, and still am of spiritual company." Having joined Alcoholics Anonymous, he stopped drinking and was able to practice again, up to thirty minutes daily.

> Just sitting doesn't seem to be helping me get the answers I want. What am I doing wrong? What do I need to do? I have considered founding a group and bringing in a teacher. There is no one here who could fulfill the role of master.

Aitken's reply unfortunately is not preserved in the file, although the man's subsequent note of thanks indicated that he found whatever advice it contained quite helpful.

A few individuals expressed a sense of isolation for reasons that appear unique to their situation; these cases may nonetheless reflect the experiences of other solo practitioners. A woman writing from Texas in 1977 explained her preference for "mail-study" of Zen in the following terms: "I am considered a minority because of race; therefore, it seems important at this time for me to practice quietly-alone causing only personal vibrations. . . . Later, hopefully, I will gain more courage." The membership at most Zen centers, as at other non-ethnic Buddhist meditation centers in the United States, was predominantly white at that time. This was true even at HDS, located in perhaps the most racially and ethnically diverse place in the United States, where whites represent less than 30 percent of the population.[4] As James Coleman notes, this racial demographic is "a matter that has been of considerable concern to Buddhist leaders."[5] This woman's expression of hesitancy may indicate that there is more interest in Zen among minorities than membership numbers indicate. Perhaps some individuals simply do not feel comfortable joining and participating in overwhelmingly white *sanghas* and therefore accept the isolation of practicing alone.

The same woman went on to tell a story from her early life that delighted Aitken. When she was a young woman, she worked with a guitar teacher who assumed she knew more than she did, because he knew that she had previously taken piano. He therefore started her out in a book that proved too hard for her, and "Failure came without question, although I tried very hard. It is my hope that Zen training, practice and learning will be a *slow but sure unfoldment* (smiles)." Aitken responded, "I like your spirit. You understand how little you know and have no preconceptions to get in your way."

A clinical psychologist employed at a university in Arkansas as a student counselor faced a professional dilemma. He wrote to

> seek advice or counsel on my practice, which is two 25-minute periods each day of breath counting. I know it is better to sit with others, but the problem here is that there are no Zen or even meditation groups in town, only contemplative prayer. I hesitate to start a group myself, since it could interfere with my work.

He worried that some students would perhaps want to have contact with him outside of therapy, which could potentially cause problems. For other students, he was concerned that his involvement with Zen could confuse them, "since Zen is so foreign in the Bible belt." While this situation may appear to be unique to this clinical psychologist working at a university in a region without a Zen center, it is suggestive of related types of professional and personal limitations experienced by other Zen solo practitioners and sympathizers. Among the Distant Correspondents, for example, a few Protestant ministers expressed concern that members of their congregation would be put off or even scandalized to learn of their minister's interest in Zen. Several Distant Correspondents, especially prison inmates and people living in the so-called Bible belt, suggested that there was still a stigma attached to practicing a religion other than Christianity. Even today public participation in Zen may entail too much personal cost to be worth the benefits for some individuals.

A few of the Distant Correspondents who identified a sense of isolation as a difficulty in their practice mentioned their unhappiness with the options that existed nearby. A woman wrote from Cologne, Germany that she was determined to improve her English so that she would have options for practice outside of Germany. She had been practicing Zen for twenty years with several well-known teachers, but she still felt a kind of isolation. She wished to meet with Aitken, either in Europe or the United States, to "get clear about that what I call Zen within me and I am at variance with." She explains that her Zen teachers in Germany are all priests and nuns, "and although they are kind father confessors, they do not correspond with Zen within myself and what I encounter in the sutras, Mumonkan and Biyanlu."[6] Thus, while some Distant Correspondents live in cities with existing Zen centers, they did not necessarily find that the local option suited them. American cities supporting multiple Zen Centers remain a rarity, so that few Americans enjoy a choice at all comparable to the choices available for Christians.

While numerous Distant Correspondents made it clear that they could not afford to travel to distant Hawaii (or California, or Sydney, etc.) for *sesshin*, a handful mentioned that they could not even manage a visit to a nearby Zen center. There are other hints of this type of limitation in the archive letters sent by Aitken's students that were not included in this study. Indeed, Aitken himself raised the issue of financial limitations far more often than did his Distant Correspondents. I suspect this is based on his long experience with the genuine financial struggles faced by many of his students.

Financial limitations rarely emerge in scholarly discussions of Zen practitioners in the West, and practitioners are generally assumed to be wealthy. James Coleman's research on what he calls "New Buddhism" in the West indicates that members of Buddhist centers do in fact enjoy above-average income levels.[7] My research with the Distant Correspondents, on the other hand, suggests that one of the factors contributing to their sense of isolation relates to financial constraints. Monetary concerns may hinder a certain segment of the Buddhist solo practitioner and sympathizer population from joining a *sangha*, especially when combined with even minor geographic isolation. While individuals with sufficient disposable income find the travel necessary to maintain a form of Zen practice that includes regular *sesshin* in more or less distant locations within their financial reach, those with more limited income may be priced out of the market. Such limiting factors may skew the pool of possible members toward wealthier individuals thus masking the appeal Zen may have for individuals with lesser means. Aitken himself raised the issue of financing one's practice quite often, warning people that they would need "a good cushion of dollars" if they planned to visit Hawaii for any length of time. In many cases, he had reason to doubt that his correspondents could afford even the modest price of a "corresponding membership" in HDS, much less the plane fare to participate in *sesshin* in another city.

Commitment to Social Justice and Buddhist Ethics

Given Robert Aitken's reputation as an outspoken advocate for social justice issues and his extensive writing on Buddhist ethics and Buddhist approaches to social justice, it is not surprising to find that many of his Distant Correspondents share these concerns. In thirty-six cases (14 percent of the study group), Distant Correspondents made explicit their commitment to these concerns and expressed their agreement with Aitken's suggestions for ethical Buddhist conduct in the world. An additional twelve imply that they share similar sentiments, based on their glowing remarks about the content and importance of *The Mind of Clover* for their own practice; if one includes these less explicit cases the percentage would rise to 18 percent of the study group. I will not, however, include the less explicit cases in the remarks further on.

Regarding social justice concerns, two dates from Aitken's career should be borne in mind. First, in 1978, Aitken cofounded the Buddhist Peace Fellowship, along with his wife Anne Aitken, and his student, now Dharma heir, Nelson Foster. Second, in 1984, Aitken published *The Mind of Clover*, his widely read and highly regarded consideration of the precepts for Zen practitioners within contemporary Western society. The formation of Buddhist Peace Fellowship and the growth of its local chapters throughout the United States and internationally spread Aitken's reputation as a Buddhist teacher committed to socially engaged Buddhism throughout Western Buddhist circles.

Buddhist Peace Fellowship brought together like-minded Buddhists who sought to promote the practice of socially engaged Buddhism, in order to "Bring a Buddhist perspective to contemporary peace, environmental, and social justice movements."[8] Within the first year, Buddhist Peace Fellowship grew to include approximately fifty individuals and was already publishing a newsletter that later evolved into the journal *Turning Wheel*. Today, Buddhist Peace Fellowship has become a network of regional groups and individuals throughout the United States and the world, with chapters in thirty-two states, the District of Columbia, and twelve other countries.

While Aitken's work with Buddhist Peace Fellowship extended his reputation in Buddhist circles, the publication of *The Mind of Clover* made his sentiments known to a considerably more extended audience. After *Taking the Path of Zen*, *The Mind of Clover* is his most widely read and acclaimed book. It established Aitken's reputation as a Buddhist teacher committed to clarifying the precepts as guides for daily living in a modern Western context. Aitken remains today closely associated both with the promotion of socially engaged Buddhism as a social movement writ large, as well as with the application of Buddhist ethics within the confines of everyday life.[9]

The majority of Distant Correspondents who address their commitment to social justice and/or Buddhist ethics do so in the period after the publication of *The Mind of Clover*. It seems likely, therefore, that most of them became acquainted with Aitken's position on the subject from that text, even when they do not directly mention it. Approximately seven individuals, however, raised concerns for social justice or ethics before that publication appeared. The earliest two, writing in 1975 and 1976, make no mention of Aitken's position and may have been unaware of his teachings on the subject. It is of course possible that one, a former peace activist, could have heard about Aitken's stance against the Vietnam War through those circles.

Some of this early group learned about Aitken's regard for social justice and ethics through their connections with Zen centers and other Buddhist groups. In a previously discussed case, a young man from ZCLA wrote because he believed his teacher Genpo encouraged him to consult with Aitken. He requested that Aitken comment on his worries about impending nuclear apocalypse and the environmental devastation of the earth. Another former ZCLA residential member wrote because he heard tapes of Aitken's *teishō* on the first four precepts, sermons that later formed the basis for related sections of *The Mind of Clover*.

> As you know, your perspective in ethical matters is not shared in Los Angeles and in most Western Centers. A discussion of traditional Buddhist values and their integration in the setting of modern American culture is one I have sorely missed; and unknowingly have been waiting for. Your words have softened my recent cynicism and discouragement about Zen practice . . .

This individual's remarks allude to the tensions existing within the Zen community about the proper understanding of the precepts and social engagement for Zen practitioners. Even within HDS, not all of Aitken's students agreed with his emphasis on keeping the precepts nor his interpretation of them during his tenure as head teacher. Since his retirement, the HDS community continues to hold extended discussions about the place of the precepts in Zen practice,[10] and the community now appears to regard commitment to social justice activities as a personal rather than a communal endeavor.[11]

Several Distant Correspondents were themselves deeply involved in social justice activities and encountered Aitken or his reputation through this venue. In one case, dating from 1979, the individual encountered Aitken at an antinuclear demonstration, and this motivated him to write. He specifically mentioned that he was looking for a teacher with whom he felt some affinity in these matters. Similarly, two men who wrote in the early 1980s mentioned their connection with Buddhist Peace Fellowship. The first had seen Aitken speak in England and participated with him in Buddhist Peace Fellowship–sponsored events there. Another man wrote to Aitken after an inspiring visit with Gary Snyder, himself an early member of Buddhist Peace Fellowship, and generally regarded as a founding member.

Eleven of the thirty-six Distant Correspondents in this category identify themselves as activists of some type, including peace activists, antinuclear activists, a war tax resister, and an organizer for Greenpeace International. It was not uncommon for social activists affiliated with other religious traditions, including especially Roman Catholic and Quaker activists, to request permission to spend periods of sabbatical at HDS. One woman, still active today in other aspects of the Christian social justice movement, was affiliated with the Osage Monastery at the time she first wrote to Aitken.[12] In her initial letter, she described her activities in Latin America, specifically her involvement with Catholic Church workers aiding the poor in Peru. In requesting information about coming to HDS for an extended period of practice, she mentioned that she felt drawn to Aitken by his "blending of practice and service." She maintained a long correspondence with Aitken, keeping him informed about her own social justice work, and offering him support and encouragement in his endeavors.

The founding organizer for the Rural Southern Voice for Peace, who identified himself as both Quaker and Buddhist, wrote that he and his family were "looking for a Buddhist center to live in and practice with a community for 3 months as a sabbatical break to prevent burn out." Aitken responded enthusiastically, "You sound like exactly the kind of folks that we would like to have as a part of our community." Aitken and the correspondent likewise maintained a long friendship based on their mutual interest in social justice and its basis in religious practice.

One man writing from a federal penitentiary in Texas explained that he had previously written to Aitken from a Connecticut prison, when he was serving a one-year sentence for an act of civil disobedience at the Pentagon.[13] He began by thanking Aitken for the advice that he provided earlier and for sending *Taking the Path of Zen*, which allowed him to progress in his practice while in prison, including undertaking the Mu kōan. When his first prison term was reduced to six months served, he moved to Iowa. In the year he was out, he helped to establish a Zen community in Des Moines "for non-violent resistance to social injustice and service to the poor." Initially, he said, the group practiced *zazen* together regularly, but the practice then became sporadic. He attributed this failure to his own laziness. Now, incarcerated for a much more serious offense, this time civil disobedience at a nuclear weapons plant, he faced a sentence of twenty to thirty years. He observed that back in prison his practice had once again become more consistent, but he believed he wasn't yet ready for kōan work and had returned to breath counting.

Aitken's response to this man's letter reflects his deep sense of respect for those who took much bolder steps to express their commitment to peace and justice than he himself ever took. He began, "You have our profound respect and support," speaking apparently for himself and Anne. He advised that it is normal for the regular pattern of practice established in prison to "go to pot" when one gets out, "so don't call yourself names." Regarding the request for advice about his current practice, Aitken recommended, "Follow your own nose in your practice. If it seems right that you should stay with breath counting, then by all means do so. If you get to 10 easily and feel bored, go back to Mu." As was his custom, Aitken enclosed a book for the inmate, appropriately a copy of the just-published *The Mind of Clover*.

Five individuals in the subgroup made specific reference to their interest in Buddhist Peace Fellowship. One man writing from Madison, Wisconsin, for example, indicated that he was disappointed with the Zen groups he had visited to date, because he preferred "more social consciousness in my teacher." He requested information about establishing a local Buddhist Peace Fellowship chapter in his own community, hoping that it would bring together a community of like-minded Buddhists. An inmate serving time in Pennsylvania on drug-related forgery charges said that he converted to Buddhism three years earlier in prison. He indicated that he "wanted to write to Diamond Sangha because I was so impressed by two of your essays and your involvement with Buddhist Peace Fellowship."

Several individuals wrote to Aitken for help in deciding a moral dilemma. A member of Buddhist Peace Fellowship from England had recently heard about his teacher Maezumi Rōshi's drinking problem. He had arranged to take *jukai* with Maezumi before he knew about the alcoholism, and felt conflicted about his decision. "I read in *Taking the Path of Zen* where it says that faith in the *rōshi* is essential. Faith does not mean expecting perfection. In light of Maezumi's foibles, should I receive *jukai* from him?" Aitken deeply respected Maezumi despite his drinking problems and maintained his friendship with him until his death. He did, however, recognize Maezumi's weakness. His response, not surprisingly, reflected his own mixed feelings. "Regarding *Jukai* with Maezumi Rōshi, this is a tough one, and something ultimately that must be your decision. If it were Baker Rōshi (too many unresolved questions) or Eidō Rōshi (clearly a wrong 'un), the path would be clearer."

Other Distant Correspondents asked Aitken for advice in interpreting Right Livelihood, Right Action, and Right Effort for contemporary Western life. A real estate lawyer from the Pacific Northwest asked questions about integrating Zen into his life and profession. He contemplated other career choices, including ordination as an *unsui* and the academic study of philosophy. Can the latter, he wondered, "go along with practice?" His final question is quite blunt: "Is it possible to be a real estate lawyer and practice Zen?" Aitken did not attempt to answer the question himself. Instead he deferred to "a good friend," a real estate attorney in San Francisco who had written pieces on Right Livelihood for *Blind Donkey*, an HDS publication.

A former student of Maurine Stuart expressed his concerns about the relationship of Right Action and the concept of emptiness. He said that he was troubled about the question of Right Action as it relates to the story of Iwasaki Yaeko found in Kapleau's *The Three Pillars of Zen*.[14] Iwasaki was a young Japanese woman who practiced *zazen* for the last five years of her short life, under the direction of Harada Sogaku Rōshi. At age twenty-five, she attained an enlightenment experience while on her deathbed, just days before passing away. The Distant Correspondent asked, "What is the relation of the fact that there is no-one to save to Right Action? Ought one transcend the delusion of having a noble Purpose in life?" Aitken responded that while Iwasaki experienced the void very clearly, as did the Buddha, the Buddha got up after a week and taught for thirty-nine years, but Iwasaki had no time to do so. The same individual related that he recently read *In His Steps*,[15] a nineteenth-century work of Christian devotionalism, and suggested to Aitken that the question "What would Jesus do?" would function well as a Western kōan. Aitken rejected the idea, saying that the question is not a kōan, but rather a guide to compassionate action.

One Distant Correspondent from New Zealand explained that he, like other New Zealanders, needed to amass enough wealth during his working years to support himself in later life. He was contemplating investing in the stock market, but saw a potential problem (in his words an "anomaly"). What would be appropriate action? He conceded that the question was still academic, since he had not yet made any investments. Aitken responded at some length.

> Everything is so intertwined that the over-scrupulous investor is likely to feel paralyzed. I tend to pay very little attention to money, except to be sure that I am not involved with tobacco, liquor, arms and industries that are destructive to the Earth.

He mentioned the existence of American directories listing green businesses and investment funds that limit their activities to beneficial industries and suggested that the correspondent look for a New Zealand equivalent. He also provided the names of two Buddhist friends from California that were actively involved in the stock market and had given the issue a lot of thought.

A final example involving a war tax resister illustrates many aspects of Aitken's epistolary interactions with fellow activists. The woman, an active member of a California Zen center, wrote for Aitken's advice regarding Right Effort. She related that for the first time in many years she paid all of her taxes, without excluding any portion as a protest against federal military spending as had been her practice for several years. She described her recent experience caring for her ill mother over an extended period of time. She found the experience "direct and focused," feeling "no gaps between what I needed to do and what I wanted to do." As a result, she no longer felt compelled to withhold tax dollars, but she harbored lingering doubts about her motives. She wondered, "How can I know when I am making right effort?"

Aitken began by remarking, "We are on the same wavelength." He explained that for many years he and Anne likewise paid only the portion of their federal income taxes that the Fellowship of Reconciliation estimated would be used for non-military spending. "But it doesn't work like that." And then, he said, they got caught,

> and the ensuing trauma was too much for Anne, so we decided not to pursue the practice. We felt we had made our point. Actually, I think our point didn't make a dent. I now feel it is best to devote one's energy somewhere particular in peace and justice and ecological fields where one can make some difference.
> Doubts are healthy. Hitler had no doubts—Gandhi was full of them. As to my doubts, I wonder what I will be when I grow up.

Aitken typically related to fellow activists with just this style of warmth and humor, treating them as friends, even when they clearly related to him as the "expert" and "teacher."

Challenges of Lay and Monastic Forms of Practice

The topic of lay and monastic practice was discussed at some length in chapter 2, and this section will not repeat that material. In at least twenty-one cases, Distant Correspondents and Aitken discussed the tensions between lay versus monastic practice, as well as the challenges inherent in those options as they apply to contemporary practitioners in the West. Several expressed their longing to take up a monastic life, in a few of the cases despite being "happily married." In one such case, a married man wrote on behalf of himself and his wife, although his signature alone was attached to the letter. He identified his monastic urge as the basic practice-related problem that he would like Aitken to address. He asked, "Is there any reason why a married couple without children (I'm sterilized) can't train in Buddhism at a more or less monastic level of commitment without becoming effectively unmarried; and do you know where we can do it?" He and his wife had already sold their home in order to finance a three-month Buddhist retreat, so they currently retained the financial resources sufficient only for purposes of relocation, and not an extended residency at a Zen center. Unfortunately, Aitken's reply is not included in the file; there is only a small notation "ans" in Aitken's hand, indicating he did write.

Of the seven correspondents who described feeling the monastic urge, only one was a woman. Writing in 2002, she explained that she had waited thirty years to be ordained so that she could raise her children. She wrote to Aitken in deep despair because when she finally approached the Zen monastery with which she had been affiliated throughout that time, the teachers recommended that she remain a lay person and continue to serve the community by practicing law. In her case, the urge for monastic practice did not fade with time. For others, it seems to have appealed in one phase in their life. One man described his religious history, which began when he became intensely religious when he married a Catholic woman and converted. He admitted that he became devout "to the point that my wife used to joke that if it weren't for her and the children I would probably run off to the nearest monastery. She may have been right at the time." He eventually left the Church, disillusioned by internal conflicts over Church teaching. He found that he could "not accept the Church's authority on things such as birth control, and became disenchanted with the notion of a personal God." By the time he discovered Zen, his interest in monastic options had waned.

Another correspondent had participated in residential practice at SFZC for several years, and then wrote to Aitken in 1982, "looking for a new way to practice and a new teacher." While he did not explicitly say that he had become disenchanted with the monastic option, he asked pointedly whether or not "it is possible to achieve enlightenment within practice, but not necessarily within the context of a residential community? Can one realize true self while living completely as a lay person— employed and with a family?" It seems likely that as he grew older, the desire for wife and children became more appealing. He eventually accepted Aitken as his new teacher and practiced as a distant member of HDS, coming for *sesshin* annually and maintaining his relationship in the interim with letters.

The concerns of the unaffiliated Distant Correspondents regarding lay versus monastic practice reflect similar tensions and conflicts found within the membership of many non-ethnic Western Buddhist communities. The issue is not unique, however, to the Western world, although that seems to be the basic assumption in much contemporary Zen literature. The world of Japanese Buddhism has experienced a great deal of turmoil regarding monastic celibacy throughout its history, but especially in the modern period.

An American living outside of Tokyo in the early 1990s wrote to ask Aitken for advice in finding a compatible place to practice Zen in Japan. Their ongoing correspondence discussed the possibility that the individual would establish a relationship with Sanbōkyōdan, the lineage with which Aitken and HDS were then still affiliated. The correspondent expressed confusion when he learned that the Sanbōkyōdan *rōshi* was not an ordained monk. Aitken explained that this was the norm within Sanbōkyōdan, and indicated that he would understand if the man preferred to find an ordained teacher. What Aitken did not mention is that whichever Japanese Zen teacher the man eventually chose to work with, ordained or not, the teacher would almost certainly not be a celibate monastic. Over 90 percent of all Buddhist clergy in Japan, including high-ranking *rōshi*, are married men. This fact is well understood by experts in the field of Japanese religion, hence we rarely mention it. Indeed, it remains a sort of "open secret" in the world of Japanese Buddhism.

It is generally understood in Western Buddhist circles that throughout Asia, Buddhist meditation is a monastic practice, while in the West, most forms of non-ethnic Buddhist practice are undertaken by laypeople. Books related to Western Buddhism rarely discuss the complicated case of Japanese Buddhism. Readers without a background in Japanese Buddhism are thus left to erroneously assume that the same pattern of monastic practice found in China and Korea holds true in Japanese Zen. Such a monastic pattern was in fact the norm in Japan during the premodern periods, when famous Zen teachers such as Dōgen or Hakuin lived and worked. Adding to the confusion, many Western Buddhists seem to understand that the modern Sanbōkyōdan lineage of Harada and Yasutani differs from other Japanese Zen lineages because it promotes lay practice and its teachers are themselves not ordained. What is not widely understood is that today ordained Japanese Zen priests are likewise usually married men.

The three major denominations of Japanese Zen, Sōtō, Rinzai, and Ōbaku, along with most other denominations of Japanese Buddhism,[16] gradually took on the new pattern of married clergy in the modern period, after the Meiji Restoration in 1868.[17] Today, ordained Japanese Zen priests live as celibate monastics only while residing at a training monastery, typically a period limited to a few years at the beginning of their career while they complete their seminary training. The vast majority of Zen priests leave the monastery and return home to marry and to serve as local parish priests. Indeed, most of them will actually inherit a temple from their father, who typically served as their first Zen teacher. The large Zen training monasteries in Japan continue to follow traditional patterns of monastic meditation, where the priests live as celibate practitioners while they are in residence. On the other hand, most Zen temples found in city neighborhoods, as well as towns and villages throughout the country, operate like small, local churches, where the priest and his wife serve a local parish of lay practitioners. Local Zen priests provide funeral and memorial services and offer special services and festivals on the various Buddhist religious holidays. In this regard, Zen priests function in much the same manner as priests from all other Japanese Buddhist denominations. *Zazen* is neither the focus nor the primary practice at the local Zen temples, for the laypeople or their priest.

The majority of Japanese Zen teachers who come to the West, whether they are ordained (as is typical of most Sōtō and Rinzai teachers) or not (as is typical of teachers from the Sanbōkyōdan lineage of Yasutani and Harada), are likewise married men. Some of them come to serve the ethnic Japanese Buddhist community, and like their colleagues in Japan, primarily provide funeral and memorial services for their parishioners. They may offer weekly meditation sessions, but as likely as not, their Japanese American parishioners will not number among the participants. *Zazenkai* held at Japanese ethnic temples are typically attended by white Americans who only rarely officially join the parish. The two types of attendees thus form a pattern similar to the "parallel communities" identified by Paul Numrich at ethnic Theravada temples.[18]

Well-known Japanese teachers such as Maezumi Rōshi at ZCLA or Eidō Shimano at Dai Bosatsu in New York who oversaw Zen centers with a monastic option were themselves both ordained priests and married men. Residential members of the Zen centers may well understand this, but Distant Correspondents certainly do not appear to. Nor did I find evidence that Aitken ever explained these matters to his sometimes confused correspondents. He typically addressed only the immediate issue of practice, and left the details of Japanese Buddhist history to academics.

What Aitken did make clear in his letters is that HDS did not offer a monastic option, despite having a residential program. An American woman living in Nagoya wrote to Aitken while planning her relocation to the United States. Her new location was yet to be determined, based upon what she learned about Zen practice options in various cities. She identified herself as a beginner at *zazen* that had visited several monasteries in Japan. One Japanese teacher recommended that she "throw everything out and start again." As a former Maui resident, she wondered if relocating to Hawaii "to sit *zazen* and do it" would make the most sense. Aitken replied, "We would welcome you as a student at either [the Honolulu or Maui] center." He went on to provide his standard advice for individuals looking to relocate at HDS. If she preferred the residential option, she should contact the head residents at the two centers, whose addresses and phone numbers he provided. He explained that HDS preferred people to live in Honolulu for a while before they applied for residency at Koko An. He recommended that she settle down somewhere in the local community and establish a home and a career while taking up the practice of *zazen*. "We are not a monastery, and none of us are ordained, so if you settle down here to practice, then you should settle as a lay person." In many cases, he added the recommendation that an individual should contact Maezumi Rōshi at ZCLA if she or he preferred a more monastic environment.

A prison inmate from the Midwest had been practicing *shikantaza* on his own for six years, after reading a book about Sōtō Zen. He continued to read widely in Zen literature and commented on several of Aitken's writings. He wrote specifically to thank Aitken for composing *The Dragon Who Never Sleeps*, a short collection of *gathas*, or Buddhist verses, designed to encourage people in their practice. He asked if Aitken could explain more "about the lay path of your lineage." Aitken replied that "Lay Zen Buddhism is a matter of daily *zazen*, attending *sangha* meetings as frequently as possible and *sesshin* the same, and the application of one's understanding in daily life."

Resistance to Joining a Zen Community

A small but significant number of Distant Correspondents (sixteen cases) indicated that they felt some resistance either to joining a community or committing themselves to a teacher. Since Zen teachers and scholars alike wonder why people with viable options choose to practice alone rather than affiliate with a group, this category deserves close attention. I have done my best to categorize the reasons these individuals expressed in their letters. The most common issue mentioned (seven cases) relates to doubts regarding particular groups or teachers that the individual had already encountered. Others (five cases) indicated a deep sense of independence from or fear of submitting to authority. Finally, some individuals (five cases) expressed doubt regarding all organized religion or religious communities, or suspicion regarding all religious teachers. Although the doubts related to specific groups and teachers are more numerous, I will begin with the other more universal expressions of doubt and resistance to affiliation.

A man with fifteen years of experience in practicing Zen, which included six years working with Katagiri Rōshi[19] and serving as his *anja*, in this case a personal assistant to the teacher, before his death in 1990, provides a long account of his spiritual journey. He left the business world at age thirty-nine in order to travel throughout Asia and the Middle East and to undertake volunteer work. He eventually returned home to care for his ailing father. Despite what appears to an outside observer to be a deep level of commitment to Buddhist practice, the individual admitted that he had never been able to "let go and commit to a lineage or teacher." Limited now in his ability to travel and practice with a teacher, he conceded, "I need to feel as if I am discussing practice/path issues with an authentic teacher. I wish I knew you—or you knew me—well enough to accomplish this, but I hope to make do with writing."

A young American writing from Japan expressed his deeply conflicted feelings about finding a teacher and joining a *sangha*. Despite his strong desire to practice, he admitted he had "an unnamable fear of taking up formal Zen practice. There is something however about submitting to an authority, even though I want to, that perturbs me at a deep level. Perhaps it is a strong independent Americanness." Aitken reassured him that his instincts were healthy ones, and that at HDS he would be free to take his time deciding if he was comfortable enough to enter into a student-teacher relationship with Aitken.

In 1977, a man who recently relocated to Hawaii contacted Aitken to explore the possibility of working with him and affiliating with HDS. He explained that he had been practicing for approximately one year, working with a teacher in San Francisco for six months of that period. He indicated that he had been trying to work on his own in Hawaii, using books as his guides, because he "always hated groups." Now, he was reconsidering his options because he needed a teacher to help him through a period of stagnation in his practice. Aitken replied that it would be good to affiliate with a *sangha*. He suggested that he investigate Koko An and the other groups then available on Oahu. "Organizations are not bad, per se. . . . The *sangha* is an expression of the Buddha Dharma, that everyone and everything are elements of the same organism. Besides that, I think you would enjoy knowing other Zen people." Aitken felt the need to remind several Distant Correspondents, as he did here, that the *sangha*, with all its faults, is nevertheless one of the Three Treasures.

In the mid-1980s, Aitken received several letters from individuals who expressed both universal and specific concerns about trusting Zen teachers and communities as a result of the publicized scandals at several Zen centers. A Polish couple that corresponded with Aitken several times in 1986 and 1987 expressed their aversion to organized religions of all kinds in one early letter. They described the terrible experiences of a Polish friend who recently returned to Poland from the United States after residency at an unnamed American Zen center. "Our optimism that Zen is something better may not be justifiable. Although all these facts make me doubtful about organized religion (all the great Japanese sects and their wealth and power) I still believe in Shakyamuni's original experience."

In 1986, a nurse who worked in intensive care and conveyed that his work made him "feel the impermanence of life rather acutely" began by asking some general questions about teachers who drink or abuse their female students. He then shifted abruptly to the particular, without any indication of the source of his doubts regarding the teacher he mentioned. "Would it damage a student to study with Eidō? I don't know if I'll practice alone or join a group very warily. I am afraid of receiving a harsh answer, but I need to ask." Aitken responded, "You are quite right to be cautious. Accepting a teacher involves transference, and if this relationship is not handled appropriately from both sides and allowed to mature, then there is real trouble." Aitken here avoided directly answering the question as asked. Instead, he recommended a different teacher in the man's general vicinity.

One of the more interesting cases, dating to 1984, in which a Distant Correspondent expressed concerns about joining a specific community and working with their teacher raised the specter of cults and their potential danger for the unwary, a concern then prevalent in the United States. The correspondent was a university professor in the Midwest who began to practice initially based on reading *Taking the Path of Zen*. He had recently attempted to affiliate with a nearby Zen group affiliated with the Kwan Um Zen School, headquartered in Providence, Rhode Island, but the experience "raised questions and concerns." As a part of his affiliation process, he wrote to Seung Sahn, the group's founder and teacher. In his reply, Seung Sahn told him to stop breath counting and instead to say "clear mind, clear mind, clear mind" when inhaling and "don't know" when exhaling.

He also told me to consider why I want enlightenment and find the answers to the following: 1. Why is the sky blue? 2. Why do I eat every day? 3. When does sugar become sweet? I suppose these are sort of "kōans." Also, I was encouraged to bow 108 times morning and evening and recite mantras such as "Kwan Seom Bosal."

I have decided not to attend the upcoming retreat, because I believe it involves a shift in consciousness which is brought about by lack of sleep, food and crowded living space. Now, please, I understand that there are usually these conditions at *sesshin* but something about the whole approach troubles me greatly. I'll finally come to the point of this letter now.

When religious organizations seem to be this "well oiled" and have blanket panaceas for anyone's ills they smell to me like cults. I don't want to be a part of that. So I'm confused.

He went on to explain that he was firmly established in his present location and didn't want to relocate in order to be near an alternative Zen center. He concluded, "Can you recommend a less 'cultish' approach? I cannot now and I do not want to make such a radical change in my life style."

Aitken took some care in his response. He began by observing that part of the problem arose from the fact that the correspondent was trying to bridge the gap between the teaching styles of two teachers, in this case himself and Seung Sahn. "We are good friends, but we have different views. You will have to choose. I think there is a teaching for every person, a person for every style. Please don't try to cramp yourself to a particular style, but choose one that is most comfortable." Aitken explained that he himself recommended different styles of practice for different students, depending on their purposes. He concluded, "There is definitely a cultish flavor in any insistence that 'ours is the only way,' and if you don't give up everything for our way, then something is wrong with you. I am sure that Seung Sahn agrees with me on this point." Without denying the validity of the correspondent's feelings, Aitken nevertheless defended a fellow Zen teacher from the implied charge of being a "cult leader."

One final example comes from another university professor, this time a physicist. He described the only local Zen teacher as a "hard-core Soto" type, who belittled his desire for *kenshō* as contrary to the Bodhisattva ideal. He asks,

> Is it wrong to want kensho? My question to you is, is it so wrong for me to focus at this stage on achieving some kind of opening? What should my (beginners) attitude towards my practice be after I have the more basic things down?
>
> I would like to know if you have any advice on how to find a compatible teacher. How should I balance my own unenlightened gut feelings with submission to the guidance of someone with so much more experience? How can I know, as an unenlightened person, if this lack of emphasis on kensho is just a different perspective, or is it just covering a lack of realization.

Aiken responded,

> The notion that one must not seek realization developed in the late 19th century in a Sōtō setting. It seems to run contrary to natural human aspiration, (which brought you to your field of physics in the first place). When Dogen Zenji and other worthies say that everything is all right as it is, they are talking about peak experience. It is up to us to practice bringing that rightness actually into being, a lifetime task.
>
> You express bodhicitta (aspiration for bodhi) very clearly. That is your incentive, and you can use it. Of course you do not practice holding the notion of *kenshō* foremost in your mind, but rather (under the guidance of a teacher) focus on the *upaya* which can lead you in that direction.

Writing from retirement in 2002, Aitken recommended that the man consider working with his Dharma heir Nelson Foster.

Is a Teacher Necessary?

A mere one in twenty of the Distant Correspondents (fifteen cases) overtly ask the question, Is a teacher necessary for the practice of Zen? Bearing in mind that one third of the correspondents are actively looking for a teacher and over 40 percent are explicitly seeking the advice of a Zen teacher in their letter, it would appear that the overwhelming consensus answered this question in the affirmative. The few Distant Correspondents who did raise the question present a wide spectrum of opinion on the subject, from grave concern that they could be harmed without a teacher's guidance (four cases) to a firm denial that a teacher is necessary at all (two cases). The majority posed the question in a less emotionally charged manner. Some appear to be asking permission to practice alone, and others seem to enquire whether or not they have progressed far enough to require a teacher.

In writing and publishing *Taking the Path of Zen*, Aitken clearly acknowledged the possibility that would-be Zen practitioners can begin to practice *zazen* on their own, even to the extent of undertaking the Mu kōan. Nevertheless, he affirmed in various ways that all serious Zen practitioners eventually require the guidance of a teacher at some stage of their practice. In the preface to *Taking the Path of Zen*, for example, Aitken explains that he intends his book to serve as an introduction for the first few weeks of Zen training (p. xi). Later, in the chapter related to establishing a relationship with a Zen teacher, he becomes explicit that working with a teacher is necessary, saying that a person who says that they do not need a teacher is not ready to begin *zazen* (p. 89).

In responding to the fifteen cases considered here, he repeatedly reaffirmed that necessity and strongly urged the majority of this group (nine cases) to find a teacher. For precisely this reason, the two cases in which he allowed for the possibility of continued solo practice warrant special attention to see how they differ.

Four correspondents indicated that they had grave concerns about the safety or advisability of pursuing their practice without guidance. A man who first learned to meditate from his karate teacher explained that the same teacher later warned him to "beware or you will go in the wrong direction." Aitken provided a few tips for continuing with his breath counting, but confirmed that, "Ultimately, you should be working with a teacher." He then provided a specific recommendation for a teacher in his general vicinity.

A woman who had previous experience sitting at a few Zen centers when she lived in California had moved back East. She explained that she never actually worked with a teacher in California, and raised some mild concerns about her continued ability to progress without guidance. She asked, "Do I need contact with a Rōshi? Do I need the sustained focused environment of a Zen Center?" Aitken responded, "There is so much room for self-deception in the human psyche, and Zen training is so subtle and rigorous, that at a certain point after introduction to the practice, a teacher is certainly necessary." Sensing her wariness about her current practice, he reminded her that she is fundamentally all right.

One correspondent appeared deeply distressed by the possibility that he could cause himself harm by practicing without a teacher. He had been practicing on his own for an unspecified period of time in Texas, where there were no qualified teachers at the time. He recently read an article by Rōshi Taisen Deshimaru[20] that clearly frightened him, and he suspended his practice while waiting for a response from Aitken. In this case, Aitken responded in completely reassuring terms, "So long as you are in good mental health and are careful about following correct instructions, sitting alone can be quite productive." In other parts of this study, we have seen that in cases involving mental illness, Aitken warned against practicing without the guidance of both an experienced Zen teacher and skilled mental health professionals.

In one other case, Aitken approved of a Christian minister continuing in his solo practice using the kōan Mu. The man sought reassurance that his approach to the kōan was appropriate. He indicated that he "doesn't try to make a synthesis of Zen and Christianity," although he sometimes "struggles with the contradiction." He tried to work on Mu as a Zen Buddhist would. Aitken reassured him,

> I think the reason most masters say that you should not work on kōans by yourself is that (1) you may fall into a kind of false confidence after a small experience, which would be difficult to throw off once you met a true teacher. I would judge by the tone of your letter that such a thing would be unlikely in your case. (2) If you have an experience, you will have no way to get it checked.
> ... I have experimented with doing *dokusan* (personal interviews) by mail, and somehow it doesn't work.

While Aitken ultimately recommended that both of these men work with a teacher, he suggested that the issue is not immediately urgent in their particular cases. It was preferable that they continue to practice, rather than overreact. Not surprisingly, Aitken took a completely different tone with other Distant Correspondents who rejected outright the notion that they would need a teacher.

In 1982, a Distant Correspondent began writing to Aitken subsequent to his decision to sever ties with his former teacher and community after three years as an active member. Based on internal evidence, the man was most likely a student of Walter Nowick at Moonspring Hermitage in Maine. Nowick resigned as teacher that same year, and several students left the community at that time. The correspondent spelled out his numerous concerns related to Zen practice and working with a teacher within a *sangha*. In the first letter, he asked, "whether or not one is able to vigorously continue to practice alone?" He requested that Aitken identify any critical points and specific dangers he should look out for during solo practice. He asked pointedly, "Why is a teacher needed at all?" His additional questions provide the only hint as to the problems he encountered with his former teacher. "How much direct and open instruction and guidance should a student expect? What are the criteria for judging harmony/disharmony between student and teacher?"

Aitken responded with a long and detailed letter, providing one of his most extended arguments for the necessity of working with a Zen teacher, in this case despite negative experiences from the past. He indicated that while the correspondent should certainly continue to sit alone, he should remember that when he does so he sits with everyone and everything in the cosmos. He emphasized the importance of finding a teacher he could trust, even if they worked at a distance, so that he could attend *sesshin* at least once a year. Aitken spelled out two reasons for this: "First the mind is devious and you need the teacher to hold up the mirror. Second, the exchange in *sanzen* [an alternative term for *dokusan*] is the Tao of the Buddha in sharpest focus."

Continuing on the theme of *sanzen*, Aitken made use of the term *suki*, derived from Aikido.[21] In *sanzen*, Aitken explained, the teacher does not so much listen to the content of the student's words, but rather looks for the move that indicates his or her point of vulnerability. The *teishō* (Zen talk) serves a similar function. Zen study rests on three pillars: *zazen*, *sanzen*, and *teishō*.[22] In response to questions about student/teacher relations, Aitken maintained that "harmony/disharmony can be judged using ordinary Western standards of good communication and social health."

Aitken provided a slightly different sort of rationale for working with a teacher when dealing with a former student of Baker Rōshi. In this case, the man was already searching for a new Zen group, and exploring options for visiting Hawaii. He asked what kind of practice they do at HDS, and for any thoughts Aitken had "about how necessary it is to have a teacher. If everything is illusion, why bother?" Aitken replied,

> There is no way anyone can study Zen without a teacher. You can learn to sit quietly and to reach a pleasant place in the inner world, but from my point of view, that is not true practice. As to

the world being delusion, so why bother, the world is not delusion. The world is ephemeral. We are deluded when we think otherwise.... Only through *zazen* can the truths of the Dharma be realized.

In typical fashion, Aitken's tone here is firm, but not harsh. He only became harsh when responding to apparently self-taught individuals who reject the notion that they could ever need a teacher. In one such case, the Distant Correspondent attacked both Aitken's teaching style and his published writings in numerous letters, all the while quoting extensively from translations of classical Zen texts. Internal evidence in the correspondent's letters suggests that he read at least some of the classical texts in the original Chinese. The individual apparently resisted all of Aitken's suggestions that he begin practicing with a teacher. In his final letter, Aitken warned, "Zen practice is not for the 'autodidact,'" and marked all subsequent letters from this correspondent "no ans."

Questions Regarding Zen Ritual

Ritual poses something of a problem within the non-ethnic world of Western Zen Buddhism. Many Westerners, including many solo practitioners and sympathizers, understand Zen as a non-ritualistic tradition. Some of the early Western enthusiasts of Zen, including the Beat poets, celebrated the antinomian qualities of Zen, including its apparent rejection of "empty ritual." Western enthusiasts were aided in their creation of the popular Western image of Zen by early twentieth-century Japanese Buddhist apologists, such as D. T. Suzuki, who likewise downplayed the role of ritual in Zen practice. Even now, popular literature about Zen suggests that while ritual concerns the exterior trappings of religion, authentic Zen focuses inward, toward true nature and awakening. For individuals harboring such assumptions, entering a traditional Zen monastery in Asia, or even a typical *zendo* in the West, would produce a rude awakening of another sort.

As is obvious to most scholars of East Asian religions, Zen in Japan, along with Chan from which it derives, is a highly ritualized religious tradition, despite the existence of antinomian and anti-ritual passages in certain classical Chan and Zen texts.[23] This becomes readily apparent from all but the most casual of visits to a Zen training monastery in Japan, as well as from a review of recent scholarship related to Zen. Many Western Zen practitioners and sympathizers, being well read, are well aware of these facts. I have nonetheless observed a kind of tension within Zen communities related to ritual. Some active members find the rituals they have observed and/or participated in distasteful. They would prefer that Zen practice become "more Westernized," by which they imply less ritualized. To some, the ritual represents a vestige of the Japanese cultural trappings, which could readily be discarded without damaging the heart of Zen practice.

The discussion that follows here focuses primarily on the issues of ritual raised by Distant Correspondents themselves. It does not include any analysis of the place of ritual within Aitken's HDS nor other Zen centers in America. Jeff Wilson has already provided a very rich discussion of ritual within contemporary Zen communities in *Mourning the Unborn Dead*. His research suggests that non-ethnic American Zen communities, once resistant to both the inclusion of ritual and the understanding of *zazen* as a ritualized practice, are becoming more open to the use of ritual in the twenty-first century, a period not covered by the Aitken archive.[24]

In *Taking the Path of Zen*, Aitken directly addressed the place of ritual within Zen practice.

> The rituals and ceremonies of Zen practice may be understood in a number of ways. For present purposes, let me offer only two primary explanations. First ritual helps us to deepen our religious spirit and to extend its vigor to our lives. Second, ritual is an opening for the experience of forgetting the self as the words or the action become one with you, and there is nothing else. (p. 29)

Later, in describing the sort of space a Zen practitioner could fashion at home that would be conducive to daily meditation practice, Aitken explained that incense, devotional images, and flowers serve as aids in one's practice that "help put us in touch with the wellspring of universal spirit" (p. 35). One Distant Correspondents picked up on these passages, remarking that he found that ritual and devotion do serve to make Zen more than just "pop therapy" or self-help. While he regarded himself as "guilty of these faults," he expressed the intention to make Zen "the religion in my life," and therefore requested suggestions for books that have Zen rituals and devotional prayers to use in his practice.

Only a small percentage of Distant Correspondents (eighteen cases) brought up the topic of Zen ritual within their letters. In most cases (thirteen cases), like the individual discussed earlier, these correspondents took a positive attitude toward ritual. They requested assistance in incorporating more ritual into their daily practice, asked for instruction in a specific ritual, such as the ritual for miscarriages and abortions (*mizuko kuyo*), and requested permission to participate in a ritual, such as taking the precepts (*jukai*) or a reaffirmation of their marriage vows. In a very few cases (three cases), correspondents voiced negative attitudes toward ritual. Positive attitudes thus outnumber negative attitudes by a margin of four to one.

The clearest pattern that emerges in analyzing the requests for ritual instruction or participation in a specific ritual is once again the issue of isolation. Nine of the thirteen correspondents who made overt requests for ritual guidance likewise mentioned isolation from a *sangha* or teacher as a problem they faced in their practice, and all of these individuals were included in the earlier section on isolation. Unable to participate in any communal practice at a Zen center, several of these individuals expressed an interest in participating vicariously by following the daily HDS ritual schedule as closely as possible. One man requested information not only about taking vows (*jukai*) at HDS and what sutras they chant and when, but likewise requested details related to the dietary restrictions they observe, the work schedule and requirements that they keep, as well as what they were reading and discussing as a *sangha*. Another man requested "liturgical formulae and a calendar of observances" as well as instructions for observing a "long-distance *sesshin*"!

Two correspondents requested information about ritual not only to enhance their own practice, but also as a means to facilitate establishing small Zen groups in their isolated locations. In a case discussed earlier, a man living in Alaska wrote, "What would be helpful now would be some specific direction in conducting *zazenkai* for our little group. I feel the need for a little more structure and ritual in my practice, and that might be a start." In response, Aitken offered to send him a copy of the daily sutras chanted at HDS, along with "some new sutra dedications." A young man in Florida made a similar request for advice, although he was self-taught and lacked any experience at practicing Zen within a *sangha*. In his case, Aitken provided more detailed recommendations, such as setting a cooking timer for periods of *zazen*, and suggested that he lead his group in chanting the Four Great Vows at the beginning of their meditation meetings. In both cases, Aitken recommended that the fledgling groups undertake "a study project, reading Zen books . . . and discussing them as a regular part of your ritual."

At least three of these individuals requested permission to participate in *jukai*, the ritual for receiving the precepts, *in absentia*. Aitken sometimes allowed his Distant Correspondents, especially those limited from traveling by disability or incarceration, to receive *jukai* via mail. Preparation for *jukai* via letter was not at all unusual for HDS members living outside of Hawaii. Aitken routinely sent the requisite forms and instructions by mail for students preparing to receive *jukai* at their next visit for *sesshin*. On these forms, individuals answered questions regarding an appropriate choice of Zen name, to be created and granted by the *rōshi*, as well as instructions for them to compose a statement expressing their understanding of the precepts. Other instructions described in detail the process for making a *rakusu*, a small garment symbolizing Zen monastic robes.

Many Distant Correspondents took to heart Aitken's positive attitude toward ritual expressed in his writings. Several of the isolated correspondents described for Aitken the rituals that they created for themselves. One young man still in high school, for example, described to Aitken his own private ritual for taking *jukai* in front of his small home altar. Others enumerated the sutras and vows that they chanted, either alone or with others, and a few detailed the reading projects that they engaged in as a part of their practice.

In three cases, Distant Correspondents requested information about conducting rituals for "the death of an unborn child," known in Japanese as *mizuko kuyo*. While none of the correspondents explicitly mentioned it, Aitken included a short discussion on abortion in *The Mind of Clover* (pp. 21–22) as well as providing his own version of the *mizuko kuyo* ritual used at HDS in the appendix (pp. 175–176). In two of the cases, men wrote to Aitken on behalf of themselves and their partners; in the third case, a woman made the request on behalf of "a group of women who want to begin a ritual circle for women who are choosing or have chosen abortion."

One of the men, living in Europe, indicated that he was writing for information "about rituals for couples coping with abortion." He explained, "My partner and I made this choice at the beginning of the year, and have wanted since then to honor our difficult decision and the life that we stopped joining us as a child." He made no reference to either one of them practicing Zen, and Aitken made no such assumption in his response. Aitken's letter indicated that he enclosed a copy of *The Mind of*

Clover, referencing the ritual in the appendix. He also spelled out some suggestions they could use to personalize the ritual. He suggested that they might wish to substitute a hymn or a reading for the sutra. He recommended that they find a picture of Jizo in a book on Japanese Buddhism or Buddhist art, and have it open while they do the ritual. Finally, he explained how to create a Dharma name for the unborn child, and indicated they could use any name they chose. In this case, perhaps because the couple lived outside the United States, Aitken did not recommend that they contact Yvonne Rand, a Sōtō Zen teacher known for conducting *mizuko kuyo* services.[25]

All three individuals who expressed negative feelings toward ritual in their letters had previous experience practicing with a Zen *sangha*, two of them as longtime members. None of them made more than passing reference to ritual, and none suggested that they decided to leave their previous affiliation due to their distaste for the rituals they experienced. In each case, the comments seemed to be only a small piece of a much larger pattern of negative experiences. Indeed, they expressed feelings similar to those I have heard from current HDS members as well as some Zen teachers: the chanting conducted in foreign languages is incomprehensible and meaningless; the foreign flavor of Asian rituals is unappealing to Westerners and/or inappropriate in a Western context.

In the first case, a current member of SFZC was actively seeking a new teacher and community during the period of upheaval in 1982; he eventually affiliated with HDS and became Aitken's student. He asked, "Is the discipline of Buddhism possible without uncomprehensible [*sic*] chants, black robes, incense and ceremony?" Aitken did not directly address this question, responding instead to practical issues related to attending *sesshin* at HDS and the process of affiliating with a new *sangha* should he make that choice.

The second case involved a former member of Kyudo Nakagawa Rōshi's New York community. The correspondent explained that he initially became interested in Zen while studying East Asian culture at Columbia University as an undergraduate and therefore came to the study of Zen in its East Asian context. He had experience practicing with several other Zen teachers before he joined Kyudo's *sangha*. He mentioned that at first he greatly appreciated the simplicity he encountered there, "the lack of ritual that is off-putting for a Westerner, even one familiar with Japanese Buddhism." Again, Aitken responded to the more urgent issues, discussed later, and ignored the matter of ritual.

The third case involved a university professor, discussed previously in this chapter, who had recently experimented with joining a nearby Zen center affiliated with the Kwan Um Zen School. He mentioned that he was encouraged "to bow 108 times morning and evening and recite mantras" as a part of his laundry list of elements that led him to find the group "cultish." Although he provided no other comment, I was reminded of a member of a Zen *sangha* on the mainland who once remarked to me after a service that "Americans don't like to bow." Indeed, in Tworkov's short biographical sketch of Aitken, he admitted that he was initially appalled by the practice of bowing during his first experience of *sesshin* in Japan.[26]

Since discomfort with ritual was not the primary focus of these three correspondents, Aitken's replies make no mention of it. Aitken encountered resistance to ritual from a few of his students at HDS, and he responded not only in his published writings mentioned previously, in a few instances his responses are preserved in other letters in the archive. In a 1994 letter Aitken wrote to one of his distant students, Aitken defended the use of ritual within the Zen context and life as a whole.

> Don't knock ritual. This letter is a ritual. Saying hello and goodbye is ritual. With ritual our ancestors come alive and our future children stir. Without ritual there can be no love. Life is dry and stale. Lubricate your life with ritual.

Aitken thus regarded ritual in very positive terms as a necessary component in religious practice as well as other forms of human social interaction.

Aitken sometimes anticipated that ritual would prove problematic for particular individuals and raised the point himself. In one response addressed to a self-identified Quaker, for example, Aitken mentioned that Zen rituals sometimes cause discomfort for participants, especially for Quakers whose services are relatively devoid of ritual elements. Aitken explained that HDS services necessarily entail much more ceremony than the correspondent might be accustomed to. He therefore recommended that he prepare for the possibility by reading up on Zen practice, including *Taking the Path of Zen*.

It would appear from this small sampling of Distant Correspondents that the negative tensions related to ritual arise primarily among individuals who already have experience participating in communal services. Solo practitioners obviously have the freedom to establish for themselves the style and amount of ritual that they prefer. On the other hand, it is apparent that some solo practitioners recognize a deep need for ritual in order to make Zen Buddhism their religion. Some of them appear to crave the very devotional behaviors that cause others discomfort.

The areas of concern identified in this chapter, isolation from a *sangha*, the understanding of the precepts for contemporary Western practitioners, the challenges posed by both lay practice and monastic practice, the role of the teacher, and the proper form and balance of Buddhist ritual, are not exclusively Zen concerns. Nor are these concerns limited to solo practitioners and sympathizers. Most of them are likely shared in common by other Buddhists living in Western cultures, regardless of their denominational preference. Many individuals actively affiliated with a Buddhist community likewise share similar concerns.

Concerns related to isolation stand out as perhaps the most critical problem identified by the Distant Correspondents as a limiting factor for their ongoing practice. Their concerns in this regard provide a significant counterpoint to many previous studies of Buddhism in America. By stressing the rapid growth of interest in the tradition in the late twentieth century, existing studies create the impression that most if not all Americans enjoy access to a Buddhist community and teacher. The Distant Correspondents testify that this is not the case. In addition, the present study highlights related problems such as financial constraint and family obligations that compound geographical distance in limiting access for many sympathizers and solo practitioners to ordinary affiliation with a Buddhist community—issues that have previously received little attention.

It is possible that the steadily growing access to the internet has ameliorated the sense of isolation expressed by many of the Distant Correspondents in their now-old-fashioned paper letters. In the last decade, more and more people feel comfortable with participating in "virtual" interactions with like-minded people. Some individuals seem now to regard membership in a virtual community as an adequate substitute for participation in face-to-face interactions. It would be fascinating to see what concerns are raised in email exchanges with a Buddhist teacher, and if isolation has faded.

Resistance to joining a community emerged as a relatively minor theme in terms of percentages in this study. I would argue that this is most likely a function of the self-selected nature of the study group. Precisely because these individuals have elected to write to a teacher, many of them with the stated intention of identifying a *sangha* with which to practice, they represent a less resistant segment of the broader sympathizer and solo practitioner community. Nevertheless, they express feelings that are likely shared by many Buddhist sympathizers and solo practitioners that prefer to remain anonymous in their belief or practice.

The following chapter will continue the process of identifying special concerns raised by the Distant Correspondents, but from a different angle. The focus shifts to an examination of identifiable subgroups within the study group, such as prison inmates and former members of Zen centers, and an exploration of the problems and issues that they face in their practice.

CHAPTER 5

Special Constituencies within the Distant Correspondents

> We can gain a glimmer of understanding by recognizing that in Zen all statements by masters are presentation. They are not explanations or interpretations. If you ask an eight-year-old child to show you a fire engine, and he has none, then perhaps he will say, "I don't have one." But if you ask his four-year-old brother to show you a fire engine, you are likely to get an ear-splitting, vocal siren and the roar of the motor, right there in the living room.
> —Robert Aitken, "The Zen Buddhist Path of Self-realization"

In the course of my research, I identified several subcategories of correspondents for closer investigation. Listed here in order of occurrence, they include: the "Walking Wounded," which refers to former members of other Zen centers (twenty-two cases), "Seekers and Dabblers" (twenty cases and eight cases, respectively), Long-term Correspondents (eighteen cases), and Prison Inmates (eighteen cases). I believe that these subcategories reflect significant segments of the broader community of American Buddhist sympathizers and solo practitioners. The stories and concerns expressed by these special constituencies are therefore significant for understanding portions of the larger community of Zen sympathizers and solo practitioners who are largely beyond the scope of more traditional scholarly studies.

The "Walking Wounded"

Twenty-two correspondents can be identified as either former members of a Zen center, former students of a Zen teacher, or current members actively seeking a new affiliation and/or a new teacher. While this category of correspondents represents a relatively small percentage of the study group as a whole, their letters are among the most compelling. Moreover, they represent a portion of the American Zen community that is rarely discussed in scholarly literature. While much attention is paid to the misconduct of teachers and the related scandals, very little has been written about the students who were injured by them. Most of the walking wounded in the study group expressed the desire to continue to practice Zen, and their letters to Aitken appear to serve as a means to promote self-healing as well as an exploration of re-affiliation with a new *sangha* and a new teacher.

The "walking wounded," as one correspondent dubbed himself, stand out as distinct from other parts of the study group in several discernable ways. First and foremost, they represent the most experienced portion of the Distant Correspondents in terms of active meditation practice with a teacher and as members of a practicing community. Fifteen of the walking wounded reported their years of practice: the spectrum ranged from two years to over thirty years of active Zen practice, while the median years of practice was seven. The walking wounded also included a higher proportion of women than the overall study group, with a ratio of two males to one female. This proportion is closer to Zen center membership data than to the three-to-one ratio of the study group as a whole.

Of the sixteen individuals who directly identified their former affiliation or teacher, five were associated with SFZC, three with ZCLA, two each worked with Kyudo Nakagawa and Eidō Shimano, and one individual each worked with Jiyu Kennett, Walter Nowick, and Rochester Zen Center. One individual had worked with a Tibetan Buddhist teacher, Chogyam Trungpa. Based on internal evidence, it seems likely that two other individuals from the group also worked with Nowick at Moonspring Hermitage, although they do not explicitly name him or the group. Two individuals explained that their former teacher died, representing a very different experience of loss, but nevertheless posing a serious challenge to their continued practice.

One correspondent whose teacher died indicated that he had worked with Maurine Stuart until her death. Having subsequently practiced alone for three years, he felt ready to accept a new teacher. In 1993, he wrote to Aitken to request permission to come to Hawaii to work with him. Aitken wrote to welcome him, although it is unclear from the file whether or not the correspondent made the transition. The second correspondent, a prison inmate serving time in Ohio, explained that his former teacher, identified only as a woman from California, had recommended that he seek help from Aitken before she died. The timing of the teacher's death relative to the letters is somewhat ambiguous. The two letters preserved in the file are dated September 22, 1996 and October 8, 1996, shortly before Jiyu Kennett Rōshi died in November of the same year. It seems likely that she was the inmate's previous teacher, and he acted on her recommendation before she died.

Each of the individuals in the walking wounded category has a story to tell of pain, disappointment, betrayal, or loss, and yet nearly all of them display an obvious reticence to explicitly address their experiences in writing. A few correspondents requested to meet with Aitken in person, and mentioned that they would be willing to discuss their concerns face to face. Aitken expressed appreciation to these individuals for their discretion, and his replies were invariably couched in similarly guarded terms, despite knowing detailed information about many of the circumstances. In six cases, the correspondent made either no mention of the problems experienced or was so vague that no determination was possible. In other letters, correspondents provided sufficient information to allow for categorization of their comments, however tentative. The categories include, in order of frequency: No longer trust the teacher (seven cases), feelings of disillusionment (seven cases), verbal betrayal by the teacher (two cases), lack of guidance due to conditions caused by scandal (two cases), escalating dis-ease with the style of practice (three cases), verbal (and possibly physical) abuse (one case), and sexual abuse (one case). Some individuals fall under more than one category.

Seven correspondents indicated that they needed to sever ties with a teacher or a community because they no longer trusted the teacher(s). The most expressive individual among these was a former member of ZCLA, who had been active for two and a half years before he quit. He wrote to Aitken in 1985, a few years after Maezumi's drinking problem became public knowledge. He opened with the observation that "American Zen is in crisis. If Glassman Sensei and Gempo Sensei [two of Maezumi's Dharma heirs] are examples of what happens when one sits, why sit?" He also expressed reservations about Maezumi, whom he still respected: "I would not want to become like him." A second "long-time Maezumi student" wrote that he felt uneasy returning to practice with Maezumi, because as a recovering alcoholic himself, he had misgivings about placing his full trust in the teacher.

Seven individuals appear to have suffered no direct abuse from a teacher, but express deep sentiments of disillusionment as a result of scandals affecting their *sangha*. A former ZCLA member, writing in 1983, expressed his dismay at the scandals rocking both ZCLA and SFZC that year. He wrote with some regret about his "recent cynicism and discouragement about Zen practice." Another former ZCLA member observed, "I have not lost faith in the sitting process or in Buddhism, but I have lost faith in Zen as practiced by the Japanese. People pass kōan study but are still so deluded by greed and worry, that something is wrong with the practice."

Two correspondents wrote to Aitken after suffering negative experiences working with Kyudo Nakagawa in New York City that left them feeling betrayed by their teacher. Aitken reacted to these letters with surprise and special concern, because he had personally met and liked Kyudo in Japan, and had actually recommended him to some of his former students. One correspondent, a therapist, indicated in 1984 that he had just read Aitken's "book on ethics" (*The Mind of Clover*) "and it has spoken to me so directly that I felt compelled to write." He explained that he had revealed some private matters to Kyudo in *dokusan*, and later realized that the *rōshi* had repeated them to other students. He left the *sangha*, feeling betrayed. He indicated that while he was not yet ready to look for a new teacher, he felt that "teacherless Zen may be a problem." He also explained that due to severe back pain, he could "only do *zazen* in yoga 'corpse' position," and he was seeking clarification on how to proceed practicing on his own. Specifically, he asked whether or not he should he continue to meditate with Mu?

Aitken responded that the correspondent should continue with his practice to the extent he was able. He indicated that he felt certain that the student's back trouble was directly related to his feelings of betrayal, although some meditators do encounter problems related to the postures they use. He explained his own rather relaxed policies regarding postures for meditation at HDS.[1] He mentioned that he had heard horror stories about nerve damage caused by overly strict Zen center policies "and am more than convinced that my rather anarchist style is the best way for lay practice."

The second former student of Kyudo provided no explanation of what had befallen her, indicating that she had other outlets for coping with the trauma and that "I have survived, bruised, but intact." She explained that a mutual friend had recommended Aitken to her as a possible teacher, and that she was requesting permission to attend *sesshin* with HDS. "What I seek from you is a little nudge back onto the path of Zen, as you call it in your lovely book, and away from the cynical nihilism that threatens always as a result of such a battle as I have survived. (Not to speak of the impotent rage.)" Unfortunately, in this case Aitken's responses are not preserved in the archive.

The single correspondent who acknowledged experiencing verbal abuse from her teacher was discussed at length in chapter 2. An ordained Buddhist nun who had been active in helping her teacher to found Zen centers, she would perhaps be a familiar name to members of the Buddhist community. For this reason, she wrote to Aitken anonymously, using the alias Compassionate Action. She likewise employed other means to preserve her identity as well as that of her teacher; she took the precaution of sending her letters to an intermediary, who then posted them to Aitken. In this way, the postmark and return address provided no geographical clues that would have allowed Aitken to identify her.

In her first letter, comprised of eight single-spaced typed pages, Compassionate Action described her situation at great length. She portrayed her teacher as having two distinct personalities. On the one hand, in private he behaved as a violent man, with an abusive temper. He openly expressed his feelings of hatred toward women, and showered abuse on the women with whom he worked closely. In his public persona, he presented himself as a "good teacher of the Dharma," and Compassionate Action admitted that she was loath to lose access to his teachings. She and another female assistant had become increasingly the brunt of the teacher's anger and verbal abuse, and her letter suggests her growing fear of the potential threat of physical violence. She wrote to Aitken for guidance as she struggled to decide whether or not to leave her abusive teacher, and in her final letter stated that she and the other woman were determined to remain with him.

The Walking Wounded includes only one definite case of sexual abuse. Because the correspondent did not directly reveal this information in her letters, her case is discussed in a different section further on. The woman was one of two former members of HDS who were sexually abused by Eidō Shimano in the early 1960s. Information about her case emerged from reading other parts of the archive, and I identified her case by piecing the story together.

The Walking Wounded wrote to Aitken at different stages of transition. Approximately eight had not yet made their exit from the practicing community, although they indicated in some way that they planned to leave. Thirteen individuals had already made the break, and identified themselves as former members or former students. A few of these, in the immediate aftermath of departure, wrote to Aitken without any clear plan for how they would proceed with their practice. Some acknowledged that they are not yet ready to seek out a new teacher, although they recognized that they would someday reach that stage. Still others having already practiced alone for some years were actively seeking a new Zen teacher, and wrote to Aitken for permission to work with him. Even in the latter category, some displayed a certain reticence at the prospect, perhaps in the same manner that an abused spouse would shy away from future intimacy.

Several of the members of the walking wounded decided to reach out to Aitken because they were aware of his reputation as a Zen teacher who stressed the imperative for ethical conduct among Zen practitioners and especially within the student-teacher relationship. In his third book, *The Mind of Clover*, published in 1984, at a time when several Zen centers were already engulfed in scandal, Aitken addressed the issue directly.

> For the teacher of religious practice, the opportunity to exploit students increases with his or her charisma and power of expression. Students become more and more open and trusting. The fall of such a teacher is thus a catastrophe that can bring social and psychological breakdown in the *sangha*. (pp. 12–13)

More than half of the walking wounded made mention of Aitken's writings as a source of comfort, inspiration to persevere in their practice, or the basis for writing to him as a potential new teacher. Based on their reading of his published work and his reputation, wounded individuals often commented that they regarded him as a trustworthy teacher before seeking his advice regarding ways to continue in their practice; as one man put it, "I trust your basic sanity."

As discussed elsewhere, Aitken's clear stand on matters of ethical conduct and his contemporary Western interpretation of the precepts was among the characteristics that attracted a significant number of other Distant Correspondents to write to him as well. Three of the walking wounded specifically mentioned that Aitken's handling of ethical issues in *The Mind of Clover* was critical for them in their handling of their feelings of betrayal or disillusionment. Three others made reference to hearing Aitken speak about the precepts in 1983, just before *The Mind of Clover* was published. Aitken based the book on sermons and lectures he had previously given, so that one may assume that all six were responding to similar statements, whether spoken or written.

Three former members of SFZC mentioned that they had heard Aitken give a *teishō* (Zen talk) on the precepts at SFZC in 1983, during the initial period of upheaval when the Baker scandal was becoming public knowledge. One of them encouraged Aitken "to continue to criticize bad teachers and sick training situations." He wrote to Aitken because he felt the need to discuss his meditation experiences with a teacher he could still respect, since he believed that his previous "instruction seems permeated with Baker's sickness." Aitken agreed to correspond with him in the interim, but strongly encouraged him to find a new *sangha* and consider working with a new teacher.

Another former SFZC member commented that he liked Aitken's "assessment of our general level of practice" when he gave his *teishō* on the precepts. He indicated that he departed SFZC after "Baker's demise" and had moved on to Dai Bosatsu, Eidō Rōshi's monastery in New York. Now, some five years later, he was contemplating a move to Hawaii to try working with Aitken. He concluded, "I think you a trustworthy teacher although, frankly, you appear a bit straitlaced. Are you?" Aitken replied, "I would be very glad to work with you. I think you are wise to accumulate a good dollar cushion."

Another correspondent, a former member of ZCLA, likewise wrote to Aitken in 1983, after hearing a tape of his *teishō* on the first four precepts in the same year. He wrote,

> In the last few months distressing news has come out about Zen teachers in Los Angeles and San Francisco. As you know, your perspective in ethical matters is not shared in Los Angeles and in most Western Centers. A discussion of traditional Buddhist values and their integration in the setting of modern American culture is one I have sorely missed; and unknowingly have been waiting for. Your words have softened my recent cynicism and discouragement about Zen practice . . .

Aitken responded first with an update of conditions at ZCLA, including the news that Maezumi had decided "to spend 30 days at Scripps Hospital" for treatment for his alcoholism.[2] He invited the correspondent to regard himself as "indeed a part of Diamond Sangha."

Many Distant Correspondents, caught up in their own situation, mistakenly assumed that Aitken had written or spoken specifically about their own former teacher. Indeed, in a few other cases discussed previously, loyal students wrote to vehemently defend their teacher from Aitken's apparent attacks. In fact, Aitken saw for himself very early on within his own community the harm that an unethical teacher could cause. In most cases when he wrote or spoke out about the issue, he did so with that personal experience in mind. One of the women harmed by Eidō's sexual abuse eventually wrote to Aitken for assistance with her continuing solo practice, and she is included within this category.

In her first letter, written in 1977, the correspondent explained that she recently read *Taking the Path of Zen*, and that it was "like meeting an old friend." In the same letter, she expressed her anger, not only at Eidō, but also at Aitken and herself for "participating in a conspiracy of silence." Indicating that the nearest *sangha* was too far away to represent a practical possibility, she asked whether or not someone at HDS would be available to help her via mail with her questions about practice. The tone of Aitken's first response is distinctly different from his later, more open, letter. Initially, he expressed his hesitation to write about her experience with Eidō, although he expressed his desire to meet with her in person. In that context, he indicated he would be willing to give her all the time she needed to talk about what had happened. At this point in time, Aitken was willing to write only that Eidō had "not really thrived," as she might think, and that "no one gets off scot-free."

Aitken typically responded to his wounded correspondents with a compassionate tone. In several cases, he made special arrangements to meet with them in person to discuss matters too sensitive to commit to paper, or offered to correspond with them until they were prepared to find a new *sangha* and to work with a new teacher. At least six of them eventually became members of HDS and accepted Aitken as their teacher. One such correspondent wrote, "Thank you for your time and patience. You seem to have become the American patron saint of 'Lost Causes,' a Zen St. Jude, indeed."

In almost every case, Aitken wrote encouraging words that they continue in their practice as best they could, and that they remain open to the possibility of finding a trustworthy teacher in the future. To one man, Aitken wrote that he gets many letters from the "walking wounded" and that he tells them two things:

> The first is to continue, if possible, with *zazen*. I say, "if possible," because some people are so negative that they can't sit under any circumstances. It is best to sit with others, of course. The second is to gather with other wounded in a group with a skilled facilitator and work through feelings together. So far as I know, nobody has followed this second part of my advice.

On at least one occasion, Aitken took his own advice and made use of a facilitator within his own community when he felt that they needed assistance in healing wounds caused by internal friction.

In one or two cases, Aitken's compassion took the form of stern and admonishing words. To the former ZCLA member, for example, who wrote bemoaning the state of American Zen in general and criticized several American teachers by name, Aitken responded,

> I do not think that we can blame the religion for the way people use it. I do not believe that we can blame Muslim terrorists upon Islam. We cannot blame the Crusades on Christianity. We cannot blame corrupt Rōshis on Zen. . . . I think that you and I should accept this teaching in our hearts and practice it as earnestly as we can, set the best example possible, and correct others when it is possible to do so in an inclusive and loving way.

Seekers and Dabblers

For the purposes of this study, I use the term "seeker" for any Distant Correspondent who mentioned previous experience practicing another alternative religion (that is, excluding a mainstream form of Christianity or Judaism), indicated that they continued to pursue at least one other alternative religious practice simultaneously with their practice of Zen, and those who self-identified as a seeker on a spiritual quest. Twenty individuals fell into this category. I use the term "dabblers" for those few correspondents who explicitly stated that they did not practice Zen in a serious or consistent manner. Eight individuals fell into this category.

The twenty seekers mentioned experience practicing or studying a wide variety of alternative religious beliefs and practices, predominantly originating from Asian traditions. Only one of these individuals mentioned multiple, but exclusively Buddhist forms of practice. The traditions that received more than one mention include: the teachings of Krishnamurti (five), Taoism (three), Hatha Yoga (three), Tantra (two), and Vipassana or Insight Meditation (two). Also mentioned were the Book of Miracles, Spiritual Alchemy, Baha'i, Tai Chi, Raja Yoga, Tibetan Buddhism, telepathy, and spiritual healing.

Based on the general content of these letters, I estimate that fourteen of the seekers had little or no understanding of Zen teachings or practice. A few examples will illustrate this point. One correspondent, who described himself as "a seeker who has tried many religions," began to practice *zazen* based on his reading of *Taking the Path of Zen*. He requested "liturgical formulae" for his daily rituals as well as Aitken's guidance in conducting a "long-distance *sesshin*." A "sometimes art teacher" described his spiritual interests as including, "self study, along with Taoism, Tibetan Buddhism, Tantra, Kundalini Yoga and the Ocean." He wrote to Aitken for information to aid him in his search for "a spiritual community that is Taoist-Buddhist." Aitken responded to his "interesting letter" and included brochures for both Maui and Koko An Zendos.

In several cases, Aitken felt compelled to explain to a seeker that Zen represents a distinctive path, different from Yoga, or Taoism, or the teachings of Krishnamurti. He encouraged several seekers to select one path, whichever seemed the most comfortable or appropriate for their needs, and to pursue it. In several letters, he repeated his belief that there is no single true path, but rather a path for every person. Implicit, if sometimes unwritten, was his common refrain that "the important thing is to begin your meditation."[3] To an English professor, who appeared more interested in engaging in literary exchanges than Zen practice, for example, Aitken admonished, "The way is *zazen* but it must be applied."

One seeker acknowledged that while he had only read about Zen, including Aitken's books and Kapleau's, what he had "glimpsed in them" made him "feel that Zen is a proper path to follow. While I am not a deeply religious man, I know that there is more to this life than making money and collecting possessions, and I know that there is 'something', God, karma, Cosmic energy, Tao?, or whatever, and I want to find it." Ironically, the only request he made of Aitken was that he send him Kapleau's mailing address. The HDS secretary replied that Aitken was on sabbatical, but provided Kapleau's address, along with information about Aitken's publications, a rather pointed recommendation that he read *Taking the Path of Zen*, and information for an HDS affiliate group in the man's immediate vicinity.

The number of individuals who admitted to being "dabblers" in Zen represents a quite modest percentage of the study group, only 3 percent. I include them here as much for contrast to the norm (since the vast majority of the Distant Correspondents seek to make clear to Aitken their serious commitment to Zen practice) as for the inherent interest in this segment of the Zen audience. These are the individuals that I would classify as "sympathizers" rather than solo practitioners. One woman referred to herself as an "amateur" at *zazen*, another man said that he had merely "dabbled" with Zen meditation, yet another admitted to using Zen as little more than a form of "pop therapy." In five of these cases, the dabblers explicitly requested Aitken's assistance in becoming more serious and committing themselves to a more formal and consistent form of practice.

One dabbler, who described his letter as a form of "Zen center shopping," tells an amusing story of his youthful enthusiasm for Zen. Twenty years previously, circa 1964, he approached Alan Watts after listening to him lecture at a university. He told Watts that he had "read lots of his stuff as well as the works of [D. T.] Suzuki, and I thought it was the most logical thing to take up the practice of Zen in earnest. Watts replied, 'I'd think about it some more if I were you." The correspondent concluded his letter with the observation that perhaps two decades of "thinking about it" was enough, and he was ready to begin.

In two cases, Aitken responded to dabblers with unsolicited and relatively concrete recommendations for deepening their practice, and the correspondents wrote back to express their surprise. In one case, the correspondent initially wrote to express his gratitude for *Encouraging Words*, which, he commented, "has been like regaining a language I'd neglected." He described it as "an ideal book—informal, personal . . . it has rejuvenated not practice, but seeking." Aitken sent him detailed information about a small Zen group that met in his area, where one of his Dharma heirs led *sesshin* on a regular basis. The correspondent admitted that this information came to him as a kind of "challenge," because he had always "shied off groups."

In the other case, the correspondent conveyed in his first letter that he possessed only a reading knowledge of Zen, and that came mostly from the works of Krishnamurti and Alan Watts. Aitken responded rather routinely by sending HDS brochures, application forms, and the year's *sesshin* schedule along with a brief letter. The correspondent replied to express his shock at this implicit invitation to practice, when he had never gotten beyond the "hobby stage."

Long-term Correspondents

The vast majority of Distant Correspondents, 210 cases or 80 percent of the study group, wrote to Aitken only a few times (one to three letters), and slightly more than half, 141 cases or 54 percent, wrote him only one letter. The subgroup of eighteen long-term correspondents wrote to him over a period of one to several years, and I came to measure their contacts with Aitken in terms of the number of file folders they filled, rather than counting individual letters. The range of years stretches from approximately one year to twenty years, with the median being ten years of correspondence. Most long-term correspondents filled only a single file folder (twelve cases), some with as few as ten letters. On the other end of the spectrum, the twenty-year correspondent filled eight file folders, and the eighteen-year correspondent filled eleven file folders. In several cases, correspondence may have continued well beyond the time period included in the archive, perhaps down to the time of Aitken's death, since he maintained a steady pattern of answering correspondence to the end of his life, in later years conducted largely via email.

Under close inspection, a clear pattern of isolation emerges among the long-term correspondents, although the cause of isolation was not always geographical. Twelve of the correspondents experienced significant geographical isolation from a Zen center or smaller meditation group. Seven of the eighteen individuals lived in remote regions of the United States, without a Zen center for hundreds of miles. In two of these cases, the correspondents actually described being nearly cut off from civilization during lengthy winter months, when the only means to reach the nearest town was walking several miles with snowshoes. Five correspondents lived outside the United States, with little access to a Zen teacher in their home country.

Nine long-term correspondents experienced isolation due to other factors. Three were prison inmates, who had no access to any Buddhist prison ministry and enjoyed at best only limited access to a prison meditation group. They are discussed in the following section. Two correspondents described physical or emotional disabilities that severely limited their access to the outside world. Two others were classified as "walking wounded" and preferred to remain solo practitioners working via correspondence with a distant teacher. One correspondent served as the primary caregiver for his aging father and was therefore unable to travel to distant Zen centers. Another long-term correspondent began to write to Aitken while he was still a minor, and had no independent means to travel to a Zen center.

In cases in which isolation was not imposed by factors beyond the individual's control, such as incarceration or physical disability, Aitken made an effort to identify a Zen community that the person could contact and recommended a teacher or teachers with whom to practice, even if the relationship would necessarily remain long distance. Six of the individuals eventually attended *sesshin* in Hawaii or at another HDS affiliated center and became Aitken's students. In four other cases, Aitken successfully identified another community or teacher, although these individuals maintained their correspondence with Aitken for at least a limited time afterwards.

While Aitken provided all of the long-term correspondents various kinds of encouragement in their practice over the years, in only two cases did he undertake directing kōan practice, including written versions of *dokusan*, via long-distance mail. In the first case, which began in 1975, Aitken encouraged a correspondent living in a very remote area in the Pacific Northwest to consider undertaking the kōan Mu. Aitken provided the necessary guidance at the beginning, and the correspondent appears to have made steady progress. Portions of the file have apparently been removed, presumably because the individual passed at least one kōan. The file contains clear evidence that the individual passed the Mu kōan and moved on to other kōan cases. Approximately one year into this twenty-year correspondence, in late 1976, Aitken wrote, "Mail and the written word just don't do it. Not your fault or mine. Your experience will keep. I suggest that you continue with Mu—this is my kōan too, after I have completed kōan study. Only Mu." They reserved their work on other kōans when they could work face to face during *sesshin*. After this early experiment with *dokusan* by mail, Aitken did not attempt this level of teaching by mail again with a Distant Correspondent for over a decade.[4] Aitken's concerns regarding long-distance teaching are discussed in chapter 7.

In 1988, Aitken received a poignant letter from a man living with partial paralysis in his arms and legs, residing in rural England. He began his correspondence with Aitken by thanking him for the inspiration provided by his writings, including HDS newsletters and journals. He wrote, "I am deeply grateful to you and your books and writings for you have provided the only real teaching in Zen that [my wife and I] have ever had." He indicated that despite his isolation from a teacher and a *sangha*, he practiced meditation regularly and that he regarded his physical disability as "good training ground" for *zazen*. Clearly moved by the first letter, Aitken responded that the couple should certainly regard themselves as "distant members" of Diamond Sangha. The couple later requested and received *jukai* via mail, and Aitken offered to direct the man's kōan practice via written correspondence. In this case, materials do not appear to have been removed from the file, suggesting that the individual did not make significant progress before his disability precluded further correspondence.

Prison Inmates

Robert Aitken and HDS have a long history of prison ministry, one that deserves more attention than can be given within the confines of the present study. I hope to provide more thorough coverage in a future project; for the present purposes, I include a few details about the HDS prison ministry to establish the context for Aitken's correspondence with prison inmates who fit the classification as Distant Correspondents. Sometime during the 1970s, during the Maui Zendo years, Aitken and some of his students began visiting with inmates and teaching *zazen* at various prisons within the Hawaii correctional system. They facilitated weekly *zazenkai* (meditation meetings) for inmates and provided "spiritual counseling" and encouragement. The program became so successful, in fact, that at some time in 1990 or early 1991, Tom Van Culin, then head chaplain for Hawaii Department of Public Safety, requested that HDS coordinate a meditation program for the entire state prison system.[5]

The subcategory of prison inmates who corresponded with Aitken is far larger than the cases discussed here. Indeed, many letters from Hawaii inmates had to be excluded from the present study, precisely because the individuals already had established a student-teacher (or at least a "ministerial") relationship with Aitken before they wrote their first letter to him, and thus did not fit the criteria as Distant Correspondents. Among the eighteen inmates included in the study group, Hawaii inmates account for five of the eighteen cases, and they represent most of the more extensive correspondence within the category of prison inmates. This is not surprising, since the local prisoners had the opportunity to meet with Aitken and his senior students, and to establish more lasting relationships. In most of these five cases, the men wrote to request permission for an initial meeting with Aitken and to secure his support for joining the *zazenkai* meetings. Subsequent letters served to supplement personal meetings.

Aitken described his Hawaii-based prison ministry in a 1982 letter to an inmate serving a life sentence in Australia. Aitken did so in order to contrast the purposes and practice of most participants at the Maui Correctional Center with the correspondent's more serious intentions, which included a request for "assistance in making progress toward *satori.*" Aitken related that the Maui inmates were all transient, awaiting trial, or serving a sentence of less than one year. "Thus, their motives are different from yours. So far not a single one of them has come to the Maui Zendo upon his release. I have an idea that your purposes are much more serious." Indeed, Aitken was eventually proven correct. Ten years later, after his release from prison in 1992, the individual went to live at the Sydney Zendo, an HDS affiliate. His final letter to Aitken after release described the apparent discomfort of the resident teacher when they first met. The file ends on that discordant note.

Wherever they were serving time and no matter the sentence, prisoners made similar requests. The two most common requests, coming up in one third of the cases, were for reading materials and for letters of support addressed to the prison chaplain or other prison administrators. Inmates typically have only limited access to books, and depending on the correctional facility, may only be permitted to receive books donated by a recognized religious organization. When they requested that Aitken send them a specific title, typically one of his own, they often included clear instructions for the proper procedure to follow. Several inmates later wrote to inform Aitken that they had shared the books he sent to them with other inmates interested in Buddhism, or that they donated them to the prison library. In a few cases, inmates also requested a list of book recommendations. Archive materials make it clear that Aitken routinely sent books to inmates, whether they requested them or not. While the files for the study group included only six requests for books, the files contain evidence that Aitken sent or ordered books at least eleven times for these eighteen prison inmates.

Many of the prisoners mentioned that they had encountered difficulties with prison chaplains and administrators regarding their practice of

Buddhism. Many commented that the chaplain was heavily biased against non-Christian religions, and only recognized requests that supported the practice of Christianity. A prisoner serving on Oahu, for example, wrote that "the chaplain is biased towards his version of Christianity and regards other beliefs as cults." Prisoners therefore needed to request letters from an outside source that could authoritatively support their demands for a variety of privileges. The prisoners in the study specifically requested Aitken's assistance in securing the following: access to a vegetarian diet, permission to use a cushion for meditation, permission to own a Buddhist altar, or permission to meet with other Buddhist prisoners for meditation and religious services. As with book requests, it was not uncommon for the request to include detailed instructions about the use of letterhead, religious titles, and the like. In most cases, Aitken sent along a copy of his letter for the inmate to see, and copies were likewise included in the archive files.

Three inmates acknowledged to Aitken that they had initially learned to meditate as a means to control their anger or despair. An inmate on death row in Florida wrote, "I never took the time to look into Buddhism until about 9-10 months ago, when I realized that if left unchecked any longer my anger was going to destroy me . . ." A prisoner from Texas related that he was first drawn to Zen by the movie *Sharky's Machine* and purchased *Taking the Path of Zen* so that he could learn how to meditate. He began sitting *zazen* while in prison, and had been doing so for four years at the time that he first wrote to Aitken in 1992. He explained that he "needed help with anxieties about dying, and feeling life is futile with death on the horizon." He started to use "What's the use?" as his kōan, until he had a religious experience while meditating. He described it as "the feeling of the world as BIG beyond words." He continued to practice, because he "want[ed] that feeling back." He inquired whether or not it is "the goal of Zen to 'hold on' to those feelings?" and expressed his disappointment that, unlike people in Zen literature, who never seem to "relapse" from their experience of enlightenment, he had.

Aitken responded to the inmate's description of his religious experience by confirming that it was "genuine and deep." He encouraged the man to consider taking up Mu as his new kōan, and to join a *sangha* upon his release. He sent along contact information for Pat Hawk, with whom the inmate did eventually connect. As for his concerns about backsliding, Aitken confided,

> The initial experience of realization is just a peep into reality. It exposes the open gate. You must take yourself in hand and walk through it. . . .You are right in asking why there is no discussion of backsliding in Zen. I guess the intention was to accentuate the positive.

Approximately a year after these exchanges, the inmate wrote to report that he had been released, was going to school, and still meditating every day.

Between 1997 and 1999, three inmates, all at the same Texas prison, wrote for Aitken's support in gaining permission to set up a Buddhist meditation group. They requested his advice regarding strategy in approaching the administration, practical procedures once it was established, and advice about including or excluding other inmates based on their motivations. Aitken explained to one of them that he was retired and undergoing chemotherapy at the time; he offered in various letters to continue answering their questions as he was able. After one long delay, he apologized

> I am very remiss in not answering you [sic] good letter of so long ago. I am like the Chinese poet who closes his brushwood gate and sits in his garden sipping wine and watching the passing of the seasons. Except that I sip ginger ale and there isn't that much change of season here in Hawaii. Mail comes in and the stack of unanswered correspondence gets bigger and bigger.

Aitken then went on to carefully answer each of the five or six questions regarding Buddhist teaching and practice that the man had listed in his letter. When asked by another of these men if reading is truly necessary for the Path, he sent along a bibliography of his writings, and generously offered to order and have sent any of them that the inmate requested.

Among the many interesting stories that emerge from the letters from prisoners, one in particular stands out, although the inmate and Aitken exchanged only one letter each. In May of 1991, Frankie Parker, a death row inmate convicted for murder in Arkansas, wrote to Aitken. "After reading about Zen Buddhism I think that that's for me. Zen I understand is the best form of meditation." He then requested a copy of *Taking the Path of Zen*, which had been recommended to him. He also asked Aitken to guide him in his practice of Zen Buddhism. "If you can't help me could you possibly direct me to someone who could?" Aitken sent him the book, and included a few brief suggestions in his letter, based on his prior experience working with inmates. "Sit on your bunk, and wrap a couple of books in a blanket to use as a cushion. Or just sit on the edge of the bunk with your feet on the floor. Write me again when you have questions."

Frankie Parker continued to study Zen and practice meditation, primarily on his own, and no further letters were exchanged between him and Aitken. Nevertheless, the archive file contains other materials that tell more about Frankie Parker's story. There are newspaper clippings, including one from the *New York Times*, dated May 29, 1996, that describe Frankie's conversion to Buddhism in prison. He was ordained as a Zen Buddhist monk by Kobutsu Malone just a few days before his death. The file also includes an announcement of his execution on August 8, 1996, sent to members of the Buddhist community who had participated in an unsuccessful movement to save his life.[6] Elsewhere in the archive is Aitken's letter, addressed to then Arkansas governor Mike Huckabee, in which Aitken described Frankie Parker's conversion to Zen and the transformation he underwent as a result of his practice. Aitken requested that the governor stay the execution and commute Frankie's death sentence to life in prison.

The recent history of Zen in America has been punctuated by several public scandals that either ended or seriously altered the careers of the teachers involved and damaged their communities. Most accounts of the scandals have, not surprisingly, focused on the teachers most directly involved in the misconduct and the impact their actions had on their (former) Zen centers. In most cases, the affected Zen centers experienced a drop in membership as students withdrew from active engagement with their former community. In a few cases, the community completely dissolved as a result of the crisis. These public aspects can be readily observed in the literature. Largely lost from view is the perspective of the students who previously practiced with these same teachers or were members of the relevant practicing communities.

Many Zen students who worked directly with teachers implicated in scandals also suffered considerable harm as a result of their teacher's misconduct. Some were the immediate victims of the teacher's abuse of power, while many others experienced serious disillusionment in response to events. While some of these disaffected members eventually turned to other teachers and joined a new *sangha*, others have found it difficult or impossible to resume practice under the direction of a new teacher. The letters composed by the walking wounded help to document the stories of these individuals.

In a similar fashion, the letters written by inmates provide an initial glimpse into the practice of Zen inside prison walls. Much more can be done in this area of research in the future. The Aitken archive contains several types of materials related to his prison ministry, including letters exchanged with inmates that did not fit the definition of Distant Correspondent. There is also correspondence with prison officials and with Aitken's students who contributed to the prison ministry project. In addition, many other Zen groups are engaged in prison ministry, and some may be willing to share information about their experiences working with Buddhist prisoners.

The correspondents identified in this chapter as dabblers exemplify my understanding of the category of Buddhist sympathizer as distinct from solo practitioner. These individuals were influenced by their reading on Zen and other forms of Buddhism, and they felt drawn to the tradition. By their own accounts, however, they had not undertaken any serious attempts to practice meditation. The seekers represent a different type of religious individual, one who may participate in a variety of alternative religions or spiritual practices either simultaneously or consecutively. Some of these individuals appear to be more interested in constructing a spiritual path for themselves, by selecting teachings and practices from multiple sources, than in settling into an established religious path like Zen. Others may become engaged with Zen for a time and then move on to a new option, much as they have moved on from earlier religious experiments that they mention in their letters. While scholars may have reasons to exclude these seekers and dabblers from the category of Buddhist adherent, they nevertheless represent an important form of influence on the American religious or spiritual landscape.

PART II

The Rōshi Responds

CHAPTER 6

Robert Aitken's Zen Ministry by Mail

> The good teacher is necessary for two reasons. She or he will encourage you and offer you guidance. She or he will also deny you the complacency of a plateau and urge you on to the peak of your potential and even beyond. Too often I meet people who have the confidence that comes with a spontaneous spiritual experience outside any discipline or practice. When I check them and tell them, "Not enough," they tend to become angry and to argue. Sometimes they disappear, which is too bad. So faith in the teacher is important. If she is worth her salt, she *knows*, and you must swallow hard and accept the fact that you probably don't have it yet.
> —Robert Aitken, *Original Dwelling Place: Zen Buddhist Essays*

In a very deep sense, Robert Aitken was a man of letters. All of his adult life he immersed himself in great literature, the Zen classics and other forms of Buddhist writings. He was an unrepentant bibliophile. Books were his favorite gifts to give and to receive. He likewise felt comfortable expressing himself in writing. In some ways, it would seem that he was more comfortable writing than speaking. He was sometimes awkward socially, but even his most informal writing seems graceful. Michael Kieran recalls that Aitken always wrote out his *teishō* (Zen talks) before delivering them, and he read them off in a manner reminiscent of the formal performance of a *teishō* in a Japanese Zen monastery. In traditional Japanese Zen contexts, the *rōshi* would compose his *teishō* in classical Chinese and then read the text aloud in the Dharma hall, rendered into classical Japanese, as a formal presentation of the Dharma. Although Aitken used colloquial English for his talks, he maintained the formal element of reading from his script.

Aitken came from a generation that wrote letters to family and friends as the standard means to maintain relationships. His patterns of letter writing were well established during a time when speaking long distance on the telephone was prohibitively expensive for most everyday purposes, and instantaneous communication via the internet was, of course, far away in an unforeseen future. Communication through the written word was Aitken's element. He continued to enjoy written correspondence throughout his life, long after most of us found it more convenient to use the telephone. It must have been a natural extension of his love for letters to create his ministry by mail.

Robert Aitken received designation as a Zen teacher with the authority to independently instruct students from Yamada Kōun Rōshi in 1974. In the thirty-six years after that, Aitken endeavored not only to guide the students who came to work with him directly at HDS and affiliated centers, but to simultaneously spread the Dharma to as wide an audience as possible in the West through his published writings and public appearances. I argue that his correspondence with individuals who wrote to him for advice, those that I have dubbed Distant Correspondents in this study, represents a third, distinctive element in his teaching ministry. Aitken's teaching extends to three concentric circles of Zen students and sympathizers: members of HDS, Distant Correspondents, and the broad audience for Zen literature.

The innermost circle of Aitken's teaching audience naturally comprises Zen students who directly practiced *zazen* under Aitken's guidance. This group includes both the active members of HDS who formally claimed Aitken as their teacher, as well as the hundreds of individuals who participated in one or more *sesshin* under his guidance either at HDS or an affiliated Zen center. This group of Zen students listened to his Zen talks and encountered him privately in *dokusan*. The more active members worked closely with him as part of the HDS community, building and maintaining Koko An, Maui Zendo, and/or the current site at Palolo Zen Center. Whether the student-teacher relationship was deep and long-lasting or merely the duration of a single *sesshin*, these practitioners shared with Aitken the focus on *zazen* as the central feature of their practice of Zen. As Aitken commented to one correspondent in the context of discussing the establishment of a local Zen group, "The main thing is *zazen*, of course."

The broadest circle of Aitken's ministry encompasses the entire reading audience for his numerous books and articles, regardless of their personal commitment to Zen practice or belief. This circle includes individuals who have never progressed beyond curiosity about Zen as well as individuals who attempt to practice on their own, with only books for guidance. Aitken regarded reading and study as critical to the development of Western Buddhist practice, and he encouraged Zen practitioners and sympathizers to read widely. As early as 1974, Aitken concluded his article "The Zen Buddhist Path of Self-realization" with a short list of recommended Zen titles and the admonition, "In the process it is good to read. Americans and Europeans lack the background of Zen Buddhism that an Asian, even a modern Asian, has to some degree."[1] He himself continued to write and publish in his retirement. As with many of his students, Aitken was first drawn to Zen through reading Zen literature. He therefore understood the printed word as a powerful teaching device.

The Distant Correspondents represent an intermediate circle, not yet students, but less anonymous than other readers, since they themselves put pen to paper to write to the *rōshi* and to share with him pieces of their lives and their practice. Throughout his teaching and writing career, Aitken treated his work with Distant Correspondents, these strangers who wrote to him from afar, as a critical part of his Zen ministry. The correspondence files preserved in the Robert Baker Aitken Papers attest to this, whether they are taken as a whole or analyzed by individual example. Aitken maintained the files that supported this particular part of his work throughout his career (as he continued to do in retirement) because of his willingness to enter into correspondence with anyone who expressed a sincere interest in Zen.

Indeed, Aitken's willingness to correspond with Distant Correspondents appears to be a manifestation of the same imperative to teach and to write that arose from the responsibility he felt as a *rōshi*. His letters and his work habits provide clear evidence that he felt this imperative to respond to Distant Correspondents. It was not uncommon, for example, for him to transition from the introductory niceties of a letter to the main topic with a comment about getting down to "your urgent questions." Until his retirement, Aitken balanced the considerable demands of his HDS students, travel to distant Zen centers, writing obligations, and public appearances with the demands he placed on himself to keep up with his correspondence.

When Aitken retired at the end of 1996, he stopped accepting new students. This is clear not only from discussions with HDS members, but from the archive itself. One finds numerous examples in the later letters such as the following comment Aitken sent to a prospective student in January 1996:

> I am glad that your practice is going so well, and that you are noticing good changes in yourself. . . . I am retiring at the end of the year. Nelson Foster will take my place. So no new students for me. The closest Dharma heir [of mine] to you is Pat Hawk . . .

Although Aitken allowed for a transitional period when he continued to work with a limited number of students, he routinely referred new students to one or the other of his Dharma heirs. Evidence from the archive letters suggests that he began to increasingly refer prospective students to his heirs in the year or two before his actual retirement. His teaching responsibilities for the innermost circle thus restricted, Aitken reserved his energies for other aspects of teaching.

In retirement, Aitken shifted his focus to writing as his primary vehicle for teaching. Nevertheless, he continued to employ a secretary not only to assist with what he referred to as his "writing program" for publication, but also to help him maintain his correspondence. In 1999, when Aitken was living in retirement in Kaimu and still recovering from cancer treatments, he responded to a letter from an inmate on death row, "Though this letter is delayed, and I have a writing program to maintain, I'll be your friend and will respond to your questions when I can." In September 2008, his secretary informed me that the Distant Correspondents remained a high priority for him, and that he still tried to spend a portion of each day responding to their letters. It is my understanding that he maintained this practice until just before he died, whenever his health permitted him to work.

I spoke with Aitken only once about this project, shortly after completing the archival research while I was still drafting an initial version of the manuscript. The occasion was a social call after his ninety-first birthday and not intended as a working visit. We chatted about family, his current writing project, and his health. The latter was not his favorite topic. Eventually he asked the inevitable question, "What are you working on now? Will there be another book soon?" I replied, "Rōshi, you'll think it's just dried spittle," a Zen expression for something worthless. He listened to my description of the project and how compelling I had found his Distant Correspondents. He beamed and clapped his hands. "They still write to me, you know. I get a new letter every week. And I still answer them." Aitken understood the value of archives and archival research for scholarly purposes, which was why he donated his papers. He agreed that the Distant Correspondents constitute an important part of the story of Zen in the West. Why else would he devote so much of his time writing to them? For practical purposes, he suggested that I consider making it a "crossover" project that would appeal to the practicing Zen community. He recommended a publisher and gave me his address. His primary concern was that I protect the identities of the correspondents while still letting their voices be heard. "All the quotations can come from Mr. Anony Mouse and his relatives."

"Corresponding Membership"

From the beginning of his teaching career, Aitken understood that many would-be practitioners of Zen had no access to a Zen teacher. He therefore offered "counseling by mail," an invitation that appeared along with his mailing address in the article "The Zen Buddhist Path of Self-realization." At about the same time, he created the category of "Corresponding Membership" for HDS as an alternative for individuals who could not personally visit HDS but who wished to receive HDS publications and to consult with a Zen teacher.

In a letter composed in June 1977, Aitken described "Corresponding membership" to a woman requesting "private instruction by mail" in the following manner:

> Corresponding membership, which includes the bulletin with my talks every other month and personal letter writing, is $20/year. For an additional $15, you get tapes periodically, about once a month—also *teisho*. . . . The measure of commitment expected is nil. The measure of commitment that you will need to get anywhere is something more than that. Positive possibilities of mail study are that I will answer your letters. Negative possibilities are that we can't strike the sparks at a distance that we can nose to nose in the interview room.

Aitken routinely waved the membership fee for "personal letter writing" for individuals whom he judged could not afford the expense. In most of these cases, he offered to continue writing to them as a "Zen friend." On a few occasions, he took a further step and asked the HDS staff to provide complementary subscriptions to their newsletter and periodical publications.

Many of the Distant Correspondents who opted for corresponding membership enquired about the proper form of address they should use for Aitken, what topics were appropriate to discuss, and how regularly they should write. A typical example of Aitken's responses to this kind of question was addressed to a young woman recently returned to the United States from an extended period living and traveling in Asia, in June 1979. Aitken answered, "Please write as you wish. There is no particular form, and your salutation [Dear Rōshi] is correct. It is not at all necessary to confine your letter to *zazen* matters, in fact I am always interested in the other life matters." Aitken's concern to hear about other life matters arose from his genuine interest in other people as well as his conviction that the practice of Zen extends beyond the time spent on one's cushions.

Aitken eventually decided to abolish the corresponding membership category sometime around 1982. He explained the reasoning in a letter to a high school teacher who enquired whether or not the offer for "counseling by mail" that he saw in *What Is Meditation?* was still available seven years after the publication date. Aitken replied, "We discontinued the Corresponding Membership category because I wrote people whether or not they were members. Please write as often as you wish. I'll respond eventually." As his promise suggests, the decision to discontinue the membership category had no negative impact on his maintaining an extensive correspondence program.

Standard Procedures for Correspondence

The following observations related to the standard procedures Aitken followed for his correspondence with Distant Correspondents are based largely on evidence found in the archive files. In the course of preparing the archive for transfer to the university, I had extensive discussions with three of his secretaries, and also learned some details about more current procedures from their comments. I never attempted to discuss the details of his correspondence program with Aitken. By the time I was conducting this research, he was already ninety-one years old and showing the normal signs of aging.

It appears from the files that Aitken personally handled the early HDS correspondence, relying on his wife Anne Aitken for assistance. Eventually the organization grew large enough to require the services of a secretary, whose duties included, among other things, typing up the letters for Distant Correspondents that Aitken would dictate. In most cases, HDS secretaries were Zen practitioners, and many of them participated in the HDS residential program during their years of service. Handwritten notes on several letters suggest that Anne Aitken continued to routinely sort and prioritize Aitken's mail for many years.

When Aitken traveled, his secretary sometimes composed routine replies, especially to answer straightforward questions, such as enquiries about *sesshin* schedules, HDS residential options, or contact information for Zen centers elsewhere. In cases requiring the Rōshi's attention, the secretary would write to indicate the reason for the delay, and to convey the promise that Aitken would respond when he returned. Several letters bear notations such as "refer to rōshi." In some of the very early correspondence, before Aitken had designation as a full Dharma heir, there are likewise notes to "refer to rōshi." In these early letters, Aitken seems to have made the notation himself, intending to discuss the matter with Yamada.

When the services of a secretary were not available, especially on his travels, Aitken either typed or wrote his letters by hand. He sometimes made disparaging remarks about his poor typing ability or the illegibility of his handwriting. (Well earned, on both counts.) In a few cases, he indicated that the confidential nature of a particular letter made dictation inappropriate. For example, in a letter addressed to a prospective Koko An member who had not yet had a chance to meet Aitken personally, since he was then living at Maui Zendo, Aitken remarked that a discussion of her goals for practice is "too personal to dictate, so I am typing (badly)." Many of the longer, more involved letters discussed in this study bear telltale signs that Aitken typed them himself.

Aitken would instruct a correspondent to mark his or her envelop "confidential" whenever the exchange would include materials related to kōan work that would normally be conducted face to face in the *dokusan* room. Like most other Zen traditions, HDS regards such exchanges as private. The secretary would then know to leave the letter for Aitken's eyes only. This happened only rarely with Distant Correspondents, but was somewhat more common with other students. Envelopes were not retained when the library staff processed the correspondence files, but before that time I recall seeing several marked as confidential. In some cases the letter was still tucked inside.

Most of the letters in the archive composed by Aitken are carbon copies of typed letters. From very early on, it was HDS practice to conserve paper and reduce expenses by recycling paper. For this reason, the archive letters do not have the appearance of typical business files, and are written on the back of all manner of used paper.

In numerous cases, Aitken's response is not preserved in the files, although the contents of the file nevertheless indicates in some way that he wrote one or more letters. My records indicate that in forty-five out of the 261 cases (17 percent), the archive files contain no copy of Aitken's response to the Distant Correspondent; in twenty-eight of these cases there is clear evidence in the file that a response was actually sent. In many cases, subsequent letters from the Distant Correspondent make mention of Aitken's answer(s). Most often, Aitken wrote a brief annotation for himself, such as "Ans," "Ans. no carbon," or "card sent" on the original letter from the correspondent, often with the date it was posted. In a very few cases, the missive carries an emphatic "NO ANS." In all, the archives suggest that Aitken left at most seventeen Distant Correspondents (7 percent) unanswered.

Aitken made other notations for himself, sometimes writing brief comments in the margins, such as "done" or "sent." In many cases, he marked passages from the Distant Correspondent's letter with red ink, underlining key words, or jotting stars or numbers in the margins. These markings appear to be aids for later composing his answers during dictation sessions. They provide further evidence of the care that he took in reading and contemplating his responses. In some cases, it appears that Anne made notations to expedite the process.

Beginning sometime in late 1987 or early 1988, Aitken began appending personal notes for some correspondents at the end of "General Letters" that he produced for his regular correspondents at fairly regular intervals. The timing for this new practice coincides with the rapid increase in HDS membership, including the members of affiliated Zen centers, as well as an exponential increase in letters from Distant Correspondents. The General Letters were apparently originally designed to provide distant HDS members with updates of events in Honolulu. Aitken did not always send General Letters to Distant Correspondents, many of whom still received longer personal responses. It does appear to have been a time-saving device, and he often also used a mass mailing of the General Letter to catch up with his considerable personal correspondence with friends and family.

In the early years, Aitken appears to have been able to handle the relatively light level of correspondence quite readily; his answers are typically dated within a few days to one week of the original. By the late 1980s, however, when the correspondence peaked in volume and Aitken was often traveling or busy with publishing deadlines, it generally took him much longer to answer. By this time, even with secretarial help and Anne's input, he composed most replies approximately one month after receipt of the original letter, and in some cases longer. Selected letters, apparently flagged as urgent, still received his more immediate attention. It was only in retirement, especially when he became ill with cancer and underwent treatments in the late 1990s, that his pattern for replying became erratic. Starting in the late 1980s, it is not unusual to find that Aitken began his letters with an apology for the delay.

In most cases, Aitken's letters are relatively short and to the point. The average response is generally one to one and a half typed pages of text. He only rarely took an impersonal tone such as one finds in traditional business correspondence, characterized by phrases such as "In response to your letter of . . ." Rather, he is business-like in the sense that after a few introductory remarks, he sets about replying to specific questions and enquiries in an efficient manner. In this regard, Aitken seems to prefer a very practical approach to his written encounters with Distant Correspondents. He nevertheless routinely includes information that correspondents did not specifically request, perhaps understanding that they do not always know what kind of information would be useful.

Aitken typically sought to make a personal connection with the Distant Correspondent in his opening paragraph, making comments such as "I was moved" or "I was impressed" and referring to specific details from their letter. And he regularly showed his deep respect for the correspondent by calling their questions urgent or commenting on the seriousness of their situation or the sincerity of their endeavor to practice Zen in difficult circumstances. He wrote "encouraging words" as often as possible, generally taking a gentle, compassionate tone. The rare occasions when he adopted a truly harsh tone, instances in which he assumed a stereotypical "master's voice" of authority popularly associated with Zen teachers, stand out as the exceptions.

I cannot say how unusual Aitken's correspondence patterns are in relation to other Zen teachers. To my knowledge, no other teacher has opened their files for examination by scholars or the public. My best guess is that few Zen teachers commit such an extensive amount of time and effort to correspondence, whether conventional, via email, or more recently on social media, especially with strangers. First-generation Japanese and other Asian-born teachers would likely not have had the language facility to make an extensive mail ministry possible even if they had the inclination. American Dharma heirs could potentially undertake this form of ministry if they so choose. Given the demands on many teachers, it seems unlikely that it is common practice. Michael Kieran, head teacher at HDS, for example, indicates that he doesn't have the time or the inclination to respond to such enquiries for instruction by mail. This is not to say that HDS does not field requests for information, but that responsibility falls to the office staff, as it does at most of the larger Zen centers.

Aitken's willingness to conduct his ministry by mail probably derives from a variety of factors and influences. First, his generation of Americans routinely conducted their long-distance relationships by mail. It was simply the most convenient method of communication before telephone costs declined and internet became readily available. Second, as discussed earlier, by predisposition, Aitken preferred to express himself through writing. In addition, Aitken could readily empathize with his correspondents' feelings of isolation and desire to learn more about Zen from a qualified teacher. He knew from his own experience that a need existed and he actively welcomed the possibility to fill the need. He wished to take advantage of any opening to spread and promote the Dharma.

In reading his letters as a corpus, it becomes clear that Aitken had a rather limited agenda that governed his responses to the Distant Correspondents. He undertook specific goals in his Zen ministry by mail, goals that are quite distinct from those undergirding his public sermons and his published writings. In his responses to Distant Correspondents, he offered very little direct teaching of Buddhist concepts, and only occasionally addressed the basic procedures for meditation. He had already covered these topics in his published writings, and routinely directed the correspondents to existing resources, including his own writings when appropriate. When writing to the Distant Correspondents, he sought first and foremost to encourage them to undertake *zazen*, to persevere in it, and to regard it as the central feature in their practice of Zen. Toward that end, he strongly recommended that they provide themselves with the necessary supporting structures, the communal practice of Zen meditation, seeking out and accepting the guidance of a qualified Zen teacher, as well as self-education through reading relevant Buddhist literature. These patterns of Aitken's responses are taken up in detail in the next chapter.

CHAPTER 7

These Words Are Your Words

Patterns in Aitken's Responses to His Distant Correspondents

> If you listen as a member of an audience, you may tend to listen passively, as though I were simply expressing an opinion, not necessarily for you. This is not the act of pure listening. It is important to listen as though I were speaking to you alone. It is the same with reading. These words are your words.
> —Robert Aitken, *Taking the Path of Zen*

With these words from the preface to *Taking the Path of Zen*, Robert Aitken invited his readers to understand the book as personal instruction composed just for them. When he wrote letters to Distant Correspondents, Aitken frequently repeated the advice set out in his published works, especially *Taking the Path*, even to the extent of cutting and pasting portions of text on the computer in later years. To the reader of the archive, Aitken's repetition of set answers takes on the appearance of a steady refrain. To his correspondents, however, the words may well have sounded far more personal—compassionate instruction from an admired Zen teacher.

The primary patterns that emerge from an analysis of Aitken's responses include: an encouragement to find a Zen group with whom to practice *zazen*, recommendations for reputable teachers and Zen centers with whom to consider affiliating for guidance and more intensive practice, and suggestions for reading Buddhist literature to enhance one's practice. In addition, Aitken raised a few special concerns of his own in the context of certain letters, including practical constraints that could hinder a correspondent's practice such as financial limitations, marital and family responsibilities, and problems that could arise from long-distance guidance.

Encouragement to Affiliate with a Zen Group

Throughout the archive, Aitken consistently encouraged his Distant Correspondents to find a group, affiliate with a Zen center, and accept the guidance of a trustworthy Zen teacher. He echoes the same message found in *Taking the Path of Zen*, often making use of precisely the same suggestions for locating a group and similar wording to explain the advantages of communal practice within a *sangha*. His constant refrain entails the following points: It is best to practice with others. As he wrote to one correspondent, "Besides, the real point of the practice is that the other is no other than myself. This is hard to realize if your practice is exclusively alone." He advised many correspondents that they could form their own tiny *sangha* with one Zen friend and reap the benefits of mutual support and greater motivation to maintain the practice.

Aitken's advice developed somewhat through time, as conditions changed in the broader society. In the early years, when Zen groups were few and far between, Aitken sometimes suggested that meditating with another kind of meditation group could also be beneficial. In a 1978 letter to a man living in the Philippines, for example, he distinguished the types of yoga meditation styles that could form "a good basis for later Zen practice" from those that would be "confusing" and best avoided. Such suggestions disappear from his letters after about 1985, when many more options for practice with a Zen group existed.

Whenever possible, Aitken conveyed specific suggestions, complete with names, addresses, and telephone numbers for contacting Zen centers or groups in the individual's general vicinity. In the earliest period, when few such centers existed, he often recommended that Distant Correspondents subscribe to the publications and newsletters of distant centers, including HDS, ZCLA, and SFZC, while simultaneously scoping out the possibility that a local meditation group already existed. He recommended contacting an academic Department of Religion or Department of Philosophy at a nearby university or college, since professors who teach about Buddhism often have information regarding local meditation groups, many of which meet on or near college campuses.[1] As one moves through time, Aitken eventually began to recommend HDS-affiliated groups as well as his own Dharma heirs. Aitken appears to have recommended only those teachers that he personally knew and trusted.

In 1977, in a letter written to a recent transplant to Hawaii who indicated he was contemplating affiliating with HDS, despite his distaste for groups, Aitken writes,

> It is good to affiliate. I suggest you investigate Koko An and other groups on Oahu. Organizations are not bad, per se. . . . The *sangha* is an expression of the Buddha Dharma, that everyone and everything are elements of the same organism. Besides that, I think you would enjoy knowing other Zen people.

To another man who enquired about the process of locating and selecting a teacher and group, Aitken responded with one of his standard rationales for communal practice. "Mutually conspiring to practice is very helpful logistically, and it also is a confirmation of the inner fact, 'the other is no other than myself.'"

Aitken regarded solo practice as difficult at best, although he recognized that for some individuals it remains the only viable option, at least for periods of time. For these individuals, Aitken sought to minimize their sense of isolation with encouraging words that they should bear in mind, even when they sit alone, that they sit *zazen* with all living beings. As he said to a man living in rural Oklahoma, "When you sit, remember you are sitting with everyone here at Diamond Sangha, and everyone in the whole world. There is no such thing as isolated practice." To a woman limited by a physical disability, he remarked, "remember you are sitting with earnest Zen students everywhere . . ."

Aitken's advice for individuals living and practicing in isolation eventually became standardized, as is exemplified by the following exchange from 1995. The Distant Correspondent, a solo practitioner for ten years from Alabama, asked, "1. How can I sustain my practice in this situation? 2. Can I modify my practice in a way to increase its efficacy?" Aitken responds,

1. Sit down with the consciousness that you are sitting with everyone and everything everywhere.
2. Attend *sesshin*s with good teachers when you can. The nearest to you is Pat Hawk in Amarillo . . . [provides telephone

number.] Call him and get a schedule. Don't write, it will take
   too long.
3. Read some each day. Widen your reading of Zen books by
   browsing in a good bookstore or library and choosing those
   that interest you.

Although the student asked only two questions, Aitken added the third point about reading, a regular item on his recommendation agenda.

Distant Membership

In the aforementioned letter, we find one version of Aitken's advice about how to establish and sustain a new form of Zen affiliation, the pattern of practice that I call Distant Membership. Aitken sometimes encouraged isolated correspondents to regard themselves as "distant members of Diamond Sangha." The label Distant Member likewise suits the pattern of long-distance affiliation Aitken recommended for solo practitioners with the freedom and financial means to travel. The pattern came to invariably include the following suggestions: 1) The Distant Member should continue to practice *zazen* as regularly as he or she could manage, preferably at least once a day. 2) The individual should seek out communal support somewhere in their immediate geographical vicinity and attend group meditation sessions, ideally once or twice a week. Aitken routinely commented that in some cases this would entail finding a single "Zen friend" with whom to sit with once a week. 3) The Distant Member would need to establish a teacher-student relationship with a qualified teacher whom they could trust. 4) Finally, a Distant Member would need to travel to attend *sesshin* with their teacher at least once a year.

At the same time that Aitken encouraged individuals to affiliate with a group and find a teacher, he recognized the need for exercising a certain care in committing oneself to another's authority. His early experience with the harm caused to fellow HDS members by the unscrupulous behavior of Eidō Shimano in the early 1960s informed his advice to Zen students throughout his career. He therefore consistently provided support and affirmation for any expression of caution that correspondents expressed in their letters. To a man who asked whether working with Eidō could damage a student, presumably himself, Aitken affirms his concern: "You are quite right to be cautious. Accepting a teacher involves transference, and if this relationship is not handled appropriately from both sides and allowed to mature, then there is real trouble." In many other instances, when Aitken sensed doubt, however implicit, in a correspondent's words, he supported their need to feel completely comfortable with a group and its teacher before committing themselves.

Aitken encouraged prospective students to take their time and consider all their options before making a commitment. His concern ranged beyond the possibilities of harm arising from an unethical teacher, to his basic conviction that teacher and student must be suited to one another. He wrote to several correspondents seeking a teacher that he believed that there was a teacher for every student and a student for every teacher. For correspondents dabbling in several forms of Buddhist and/or other religious practice, he made similar comments: "There are many kinds of religious paths, and each more or less fits particular kinds of people. To get down to cases, there are *shikantaza* people and there are kōan people. No invidious comparisons to be made." He encouraged such individuals to make an informed choice and then get down to the critical step of beginning their practice.

In some cases, correspondents shared with Aitken their fears related to accepting any religious affiliation. A woman from Colorado had been reading about Zen for six months, including *Taking the Path of Zen*. She had not yet taken any steps to contact a Zen community because her "experience of religion is that it seeks to remake people in its own image, but Zen seems different." She asked Aitken for advice in how she should proceed. He replied,

> The fundamental human fear is of dying. The religious path exposes that fear, and gives it an important twist. ALL true teaching, including Zen, encourages dying to the self. This does not mean getting rid of the self, for that cannot be done except by suicide. Rather, the expression points to the experience of forgetting the self completely in the act of uniting with someone.
>
> In this profound experience of uniting with one thing, one unites with all things. . . .
>
> All this takes practice, and practice begins, continues, and ends with meditation. Zazen is one such path of meditation.

He invited her to reread *Taking the Path of Zen*, to experiment with *zazen*, to consider finding a community, and to keep in touch.

Aitken made no exception in encouraging appropriate caution to individuals contemplating making a premature commitment to himself and HDS. When an engineer with the financial means and the freedom to spend six months practicing Zen contacted Aitken to establish a connection sight unseen with HDS, Aitken suggested that he first visit at least two Zen centers, HDS and ZCLA, in order to gain some perspective in making a decision. In another case, a man that had recently registered for his first *sesshin* at HDS requested to receive *jukai* without even the benefit of an initial interview with Aitken. Aitken wrote back to strongly recommend that he get acquainted with HDS first and that he be certain "this is the lineage you want to make your home." In yet another case in which a young man expresses fear about taking up formal practice with Aitken, a teacher he admired, Aitken responded,

> I think it is healthy to be leery of authority. It is misused, even in Zen Buddhism, perhaps especially in Zen. Come with diffidence and give yourself time to feel comfortable. In our dōjō, people can attend all meetings except *sesshin* without any commitment at all. (At *sesshin*, everyone comes to *sanzen*, which we call *dokusan*, so some commitment is necessary.) But I'm not a guru and you can pull out anytime.

In numerous cases, Aitken encouraged his correspondents to trust their instincts. If they felt uncomfortable in any way, they should take their own feelings seriously and leave their options open.

Aitken's Recommendations for Special Cases

Whenever a Distant Correspondent described an experience that Aitken deemed genuine or significant, he confirmed that it represented a "milestone" in their practice and offered words of encouragement so that they would persevere. In addition, if they did not say as much themselves, he usually indicated that they had reached a critical stage in their practice at which they needed the guidance of a Zen teacher. Aitken made clear in his published materials and in his letters that anyone seeking to practice *zazen* with any degree of seriousness would eventually require a qualified teacher to guide their efforts.

In certain cases, Aitken's advice to immediately seek out face-to-face instruction with a qualified Zen teacher took on special urgency. In one such example, Aitken enumerates his arguments for working with a teacher in great detail.

(1) Please don't suppose that your pilgrimage is a common one. It most certainly is not. It is rare to have such talent, and it is important to follow through with what you have.
(2) Without a teacher, it is natural to treat an experience such as yours as something be-all and end-all, and to scorn organized religion. . . .
(3) The *Sangha*, with its failings and fellow students with their failings nonetheless form the Third Jewel of the Dharma. Without them you are isolated, just laughing at the Buddha and abusing the Ancestral Teachers. . . .
(4) The teacher is frustrated waiting for someone with your realization and potential to show up. Put yourself in his hands. He will challenge you to attain your own best potential. He will not let you stay on the plateau you reached initially.
(5) How about *zazen*? You don't mention it. There is no fulfillment without it. Maybe the reason you are doubtful about kōan study is because you haven't tried it on cushions.

Despite being couched in the third person, one nevertheless senses that this represented a rare bid on Aitken's part, indeed the only one I found in the archive, to convince a particular Distant Correspondent to consider working with him. In other cases, Aitken retained a more neutral tone when encouraging the correspondent to seek out a teacher. In his second letter to this correspondent, Aitken confirmed the impression that he hoped to gain a student, "I feel that I have found a friend when I thought there might be a possibility I had found a student. Much better." The two men carried on a five-year correspondence that fills four thick folders.

In at least three cases, Aitken not only recommended that a correspondent who had an experience he deemed genuine seek out a teacher, but he took the liberty of asking "checking questions" in his initial letter of response. Checking questions are queries designed to further test a student's understanding of his or her kōan when the teacher senses a glimmer of realization. Zen teachers usually make use of checking questions in the context of *dokusan*, when meeting face to face with a student. Early on in his mail ministry, Aitken concluded that written correspondence was usually ineffective for this type of student-teacher exchange. Nevertheless, in rare cases, he departed from his own standard procedure.

In a case already discussed, a Catholic priest wrote to Aitken for confirmation of religious experiences he had while meditating with the kōan Mu. Aitken responded that his experience sounded authentic and suggested that they meet for *sesshin*, presumably so that he could check the experience face to face in *dokusan*. Apparently unwilling to await a reply, Aitken immediately offered to attempt checking questions via mail in case *sesshin* should prove impossible. "The first question is, 'What is the height of Mu?' Please be sure to continue to mark your envelopes 'Confidential.'" Subsequent letters indicate that their schedules were incompatible, and they seem to have never met in *sesshin*. There is no evidence in the file whether or not the correspondent replied to the checking questions. It is possible that he did, and that the material was later removed from the file.

In only one case that I found did Aitken appear to withdraw from a teacher-student relationship with one of his Distant Correspondents. In 1992, a solo practitioner from San Diego wrote to Aitken to request guidance via mail and permission to become his student. Although she admitted that she sometimes attended the local Zen Center of San Diego, she had not yet found a teacher. In addition, she indicated that she was willing to visit Hawaii annually for *sesshin*. San Diego Zen Center was at the time served by Charlotte Joko Beck, a teacher that Aitken knew well; in his first letter, he recommended that she be in touch with Beck and he provided her telephone number. He offered to call Beck himself to introduce the correspondent's situation so it wouldn't be a cold call. The correspondent wrote again to explain that she was going through a divorce and could not afford to join the local Zen center "at least for a few months." Aitken replied,

> Though I have agreed to be your teacher—let's face reality. You may have to work with somebody else for a while—given your situation. Joko Beck at ZCSD will be a good teacher for you and won't mind if you have already made contact with me. We are good friends. Please be patient with your practice. Start where you are. Let there be only "one" at that point in the sequence—then only "two"—and so on. Your eye is on each point—rather than upon the sequence.

It would thus appear that Aitken felt the need to put some limits on his ministry by mail. A solo practitioner without any apparent physical impediment, with a viable option within easy reach, and clearly lacking the resources to make good on her promise to visit HDS for *sesshin* could be gently cut loose.

Specific Recommendations of Other Teachers and Zen Centers

In reviewing the 216 cases in which Aitken's response is preserved, I have identified seventy cases in which he made specific recommendations of either a particular Zen teacher or a Zen center in the Western world (see table 10). In nearly every case, Aitken included contact information of some kind, usually both mailing address and phone number. In certain cases, he included additional instructions to the individual about how to go about making contact. Some teachers, for example, respond more readily to phone enquiries, while others prefer a particular type of written self-introduction from prospective students.

In all but five cases, Aitken recommended a teacher affiliated either with the Sanbōkyōdan lineage or one of its offshoots, including, of course, his own Dharma heirs in the Diamond Sangha lineage. Indeed, even in those five outlying cases, Aitken recommended only two other

Table 10. Recommendations for Specific Teachers

Name or Teacher/Center	No. Referrals	Time Period
Maezumi Taizan	10	1977–1982
Seung Sahn	3	1977
Bernard Tetsugen Glassman	4	1981–1987
Ring of Bone	13	Begin 1984
Joan Rieck	4	1984–1987
Robert Jinsen Kennedy	1	1985
Willigis Jager	3	1985–1889
Nelson Foster	3	Begin 1985
John Tarrant	5	1988–1995
Marian Morgan	3	Begin 1990
Pat Hawk	9	Begin 1990
Jack Duffy	3	Begin 1990

teachers. In 1977, Aitken recommended Seung Sahn, a Zen teacher from Korea who founded his own Kwan Um School of Zen, to three individuals living in the Northeast. He also twice recommended Yvonne Rand to couples looking for assistance with *mizuko kuyo*, the ritual for unborn children. This latter type of referral is actually quite distinct from all the others, and is therefore excluded from the analysis.

Factors that seem to have influenced Aitken's choice of referrals include primarily geographic proximity, preference for his own Dharma heirs, as well as special interests expressed by the Distant Correspondent. For example, Aitken routinely recommended a teacher with Christian credentials for Distant Correspondents who mentioned a Christian affiliation. Since several such teachers were on his recommended list, including Joan Rieck, Willigis Jager, Pat Hawk, and Robert Jinsen Kennedy, geographic proximity likewise played a critical role in Aitken's choice. As previously mentioned, he favored Maezumi Rōshi for people who mentioned mental health issues.

Aitken very rarely made negative comments about other Zen teachers, except in a few instances when he confirmed serious doubts raised by the correspondent him or herself. He much preferred to use implication, saying that there were no (other) teachers that he regarded as trustworthy in a correspondent's region. For example, in 1987 a woman wrote to him asking for a referral for a Zen teacher and *sangha* on the East Coast. After eight years of solo practice, she wanted "to dedicate myself more fully to Zen practice, attend *sesshin* and *jukai*, and be accepted by a teacher." Aitken provided her with the name and address for Bernard Tetsugen Glassman's community in Yonkers, and further made the observation that "other 'would-be teachers' [in the area] aren't very competent." In 1993, a member of ZCLA wrote to ask if there was an HDS branch in his area, explaining that as a recovering alcoholic, he felt uneasy resuming his practice with Maezumi. Aitken responded, "I appreciate your discretion, and share your concerns. I am unable to recommend a teacher in your area. . . . Your situation is like that of many others scattered across the country. There just aren't that many good teachers." Aitken sent him a Diamond Sangha brochure that included the names and contact information for four of his Dharma heirs, penciling in the name of a newly designated fifth heir.

In two instances, Aitken learned of problems related to a teacher he had previously recommended, Kyodo Nakagawa, as previously described in chapter 5. In his response to the second of these individuals, Aitken described his surprise at hearing these stories and his chagrin that he had more than once recommended Kyodo to former students who moved away from Hawaii. He indicated that he had already written letters of warning to his former students. A review of the archive files confirmed that he did so. In a letter to two former students, he admitted that his recommendation of Kyodo was based on a casual meeting as well as on positive hearsay from Zen students. Now that he had received contrary evidence, he wrote to warn them, and requested that they be discrete about his comments.

Recommendations for Reading

In 1995, a solo practitioner from the state of Washington wrote to Aitken to ask his opinion about the role of reading and philosophy for Zen practitioners. The correspondent noted that in the two years since his baby daughter died from SIDS, he had been reading Buddhist philosophy and practicing *zazen* more avidly. He noted that "a lot of Zen teachers downgrade reading and philosophy, and yet most of the great Zen masters were well versed in the Sutras and Shastras and even the teachings outside Buddhism." He went on to observe that when he spoke with most of his fellow Zen students, "they have no acquaintance with the basics of Buddhist philosophy. What is your view on this? Where does Buddhist philosophy come in? Why did the masters bother to write the Sutras?" Aitken responded, "Of course you should read. I'd rather have speculation than ignorance and there's not that much risk of speculation. Contemporary teachers who say 'Don't read' have their own agenda."

Throughout his teaching career, Aitken made urging Zen students to read a critical part of his agenda. He explicitly recommended reading in most of his early publications, and often included a listing of specific suggestions. He likewise consistently raised the topic throughout his letters to Distant Correspondents. Specifically, Aitken recommends reading in thirty-eight letters, sometimes making a general statement about the benefits of reading and other times mentioning a specific work or works that would benefit the correspondent. This amounts to one in five of the cases for which his letters are preserved. The recommendation to read can thus be regarded as one of the standard patterns in Aitken's letters.

Many Westerners assume that reading and other forms of intellectual enquiry are in some sense antithetical to Zen, and one finds this attitude reflected in a handful of letters from Distant Correspondents as well. In 1977, for example, one correspondent commented that he was "now studying (books), although I know it is useless" for Zen practice. Aitken replied, "It is not useless to study. Westerners in particular need to know the background tapestry of Zen practice."

In fifteen cases, Aitken recommended a specific text for a beginning practitioner to use as an introductory guide for the early stage of their practice. The recommendation invariably included parallel suggestions for finding a Zen group or teacher. Before he published his own introductory guide for meditation, Aitken routinely recommended Kapleau's *The Three Pillars of Zen* in his letters to novice practitioners, with a few editorial remarks. After 1982, he switched to recommending *Taking the Path of Zen* and later still sometimes added *The Mind of Clover* as a companion text for beginners. Aitken included a bibliography of recommended books at the end of *Taking the Path*, and he sometimes suggested that more advanced practitioners look there for inspiration in their reading selections. In later years, he made similar suggestions based on the bibliographies for his later publications. On a few occasions, he offered to send a photocopy of a bibliography to individuals without ready access to a library.

Aitken recommended extensive reading as a form of support for more advanced practitioners who found themselves isolated from a *sangha*. To one of the walking wounded who wrote that he could not yet bear to seek out a new group, Aitken recommended extensive reading, since "Zen is a Gnostic process, after all." This comment was sandwiched between Aitken's reminder that when he sits, he does so "with everyone and everything" and encouragement to find a new teacher that "he can trust, even if it is at a distance and attending *sesshin* only once a year."

Aitken sent copies of his published writings as gifts of encouragement for several Distant Correspondents, especially for individuals living and practicing in isolation. When Aitken corresponded with prison inmates as well as people with severe physical disabilities, he routinely sent or offered to send copies of his books as well as copies of other materials, such as newsletters and essays. In a few cases, he sent along sections of not-yet-published materials as a special gift for physically handicapped individuals who were already familiar with his available work. Even in retirement, living on a fixed income in Kaimu, he continued the practice of sending books, sometimes ordering copies of his own books to be shipped by Amazon directly to the correspondent. He may have continued to do so after he returned to Oahu in 2004, but the archive currently extends to January 2002 and thus does not cover the last nine years of his life.

When Distant Correspondents wrote to Aitken for advice about establishing a Zen group of their own, he invariably recommended that they undertake reading projects as a part of their communal practice. Reading can thus serve to enhance and inform not only an individual's solo practice of Zen, but likewise to enrich communal practice. Aitken intended the circulation of HDS publications, newsletters, and tapes of Zen talks (*teishō*) to serve a similar purpose.

Special Concerns Raised by Aitken

Robert Aitken understood that his students and his Distant Correspondents carry out their practice within the confines determined by their daily life. This is the nature of lay practice in the Western context that Aitken himself championed. Aitken made it clear in his letters that he appreciated that his correspondents, like his students, did not have unlimited resources, whether it be money, or vacation time from work, or the freedom to leave behind even temporarily responsibilities for children, aging parents, and so forth. In his letters, he often raised these concerns before the correspondent mentioned them, anticipating the realities of lay practice.

Aitken was generous with Distant Correspondents whom he thought lacked financial means. He routinely offered to write to people for free if they could not afford the nominal cost of corresponding membership, and he made gifts of his books to prison inmates and individuals with physical handicaps who typically live on limited incomes. Although current research suggests that most members of Zen centers enjoy higher than average income, Aitken never assumed that a correspondent had ample means unless the letter provided clear evidence to that effect.

For individuals expressing an interest in coming to Hawaii for an extended period of practice, Aitken typically warned them about the financial challenges they would face here, and recommended that they arrive with "a cushion of money." This pattern remained consistent from the very earliest letters through the entire time period covered by the archive. In 1988, for example, a former resident of SFZC wrote in order "to explore possibilities of moving to Hawaii to practice." Aitken responded, "I would be very glad to work with you. I think you are wise to accumulate a good dollar cushion . . ." Aitken's language is nearly identical in letters dating from 1968 and 1977: The practice of Zen will require substantial financial resources, a "cushion of dollars." In 1980, when an American couple wrote from Japan, hoping to relocate in Hawaii to practice with Aitken at HDS, he explained the realities of the situation in straightforward terms. "Maui is rural and beautiful, but with few jobs and few houses. Honolulu is economically easier." Aitken's awareness of the economic realities expressed in the letter apparently contributed to his decision to close Maui Zendo and concentrate his work on Oahu, where more individuals would be able to manage the expense of Zen practice.

In several cases, Aitken made a concerted effort to ameliorate the harsh financial conditions Distant Correspondents would face if they did decide to come to Hawaii. In at least two cases, he arranged for home stays with longtime HDS members. In other cases, he identified potential roommates for sharing an apartment. One Distant Correspondent identified himself as a house painter, a profession he hoped would be readily transferable to Hawaii. Aitken was initially skeptical, and urged caution. He then did some research, and when he determined that there was in fact demand for a painter's skills on both Oahu and Maui, he wrote back in encouraging terms.

In much the same way that Aitken expressed concern for financial constraints, he routinely raised issues related to marital and family responsibilities in his letters to Distant Correspondents. Aitken faced serious difficulties of his own in this regard as a younger man, especially when he left his first wife and young son to travel to Japan in 1950. The separation almost certainly contributed to the breakdown of his first marriage, and after the divorce Aitken felt very keenly his separation from his son Tom when he was living alone in California. That separation motivated his return to Hawaii in 1958. Based on personal experience, Aitken encouraged married men to secure the emotional support of their wives for the practice of *zazen* in order to reduce the likelihood of feelings of abandonment and resentment. He would ask quite directly, "How does your wife feel about your practice?" or "Does [your practice] cause friction at home?" In cases involving a correspondent caring for an ill spouse or an aging parent, Aitken would gently explore the possibilities for travel to *sesshin*, always careful to express his awareness that circumstances might preclude the option at least for a time.

In conversations with me about the possibility of retaining second- and third-generation Zen practitioners, Aitken voiced his concern that the children of active members may naturally feel resentful of their parent's involvement in the practice. For the children, he observed, parental involvement in Zen practice necessarily entails a kind of loss both during the daily period of withdrawal for meditation and the more extensive demands of attending *sesshin*.[2] While Aitken did not explicitly raise these particular concerns in any of his letters to Distant Correspondents, he did indicate his awareness that coming for *sesshin* "may be difficult with careers and children." He encouraged parents to come "if you can do so without disrupting your life."

Another area of concern raised by Aitken in his letters to Distant Correspondents involves the limits he himself recognized in the enterprise of offering advice by mail. Aitken mentioned this type of concern in at least seven letters. His early experimentation led him to conclude that mail correspondence was not an effective alternative for the kind of teacher-student exchanges typically conducted face to face in *dokusan*. As early as 1977 he wrote to a correspondent, "I have experimented with doing *dokusan* (personal interviews) by mail, and somehow it doesn't work." He also sometimes expressed a recommendation in tentative terms, since without the benefit of personal contact to back up his impression of a situation, he could not offer the suggestion with full confidence. When writing to a woman experiencing serious physical manifestations during *zazen*, for example, he suggested that she experiment using a focus, such as breath counting. He then explained that he was "not making this as a firm suggestion, because we are not working face to face." In another case, he closed his letter to an active member of an unaffiliated Zen center seeking "a new way to practice and a new teacher" with an apology. "All this is counseling at long distance. I am not able to look at your face and eyes, so I may be in error. If so, please forgive me. I do hope you can find ease of mind and body."

Aitken responded to issues related to drug use with only a handful of correspondents who admitted to having used drugs in their past. He spelled out his attitude toward alcohol and drugs at some length in *The Mind of Clover*. In the chapter on the Fifth Grave Precept, which he renders "Not Giving or Taking Drugs,"[3] he explained that habitual use damages the body, which is "none other than the dojo of the Buddha" and that even occasional use clouds the mind and interferes with meditation (p. 58). He thus preferred himself to abstain from both alcohol and drugs. Nevertheless, he was not judgmental about others. It is clear from the archive letters that Aitken needed to discuss these matters with his students and those who came to practice with HDS, because drug use was so common in the population that was attracted to Zen and other alternative religions, especially in the 1970s. In a letter addressed to a man applying for residency at Maui Zendo in 1970, Aitken made clear his drug policy for residents, "No drugs, alcohol or tobacco." He went on to explain something of his attitude,

> If there were no drug problem, there would be no Maui Zendo, as drugs have opened the doors for religious possibilities for literally all of our young members, so I don't knock drugs, but simply accept them as part of the scene from which our people come.

Drug use created an opening for Zen practice, and Aitken was prepared to take advantage of it.

When dealing with correspondents who had already worked with a teacher or were accustomed to meditating in a different style from his own, Aitken typically expressed concern about the transition and sometimes offered advice. For correspondents who had practiced yoga, Vipassana, or Tibetan Buddhism, he generally reminded them that the paths were different and they would need to choose. He would encourage them to make their decision and get on with it. When students had practiced with another Zen teacher, Aitken could readily ease the transition, since his own style (derived from Sanbōkyōdan) incorporated a variety of possible practice styles depending on the student's proclivities. Nevertheless, he would warn them to anticipate a gap to be crossed in transition. In several letters Aitken indicated that he and Maezumi found it easy to share students because of their common background with Sanbōkyōdan and the similarity in their teaching styles.

A final concern sometimes raised by Aitken was that he be able to match a style of practice to suit the purpose of the Distant Correspondent. In a letter dating from 1982, he explained the process he was then using in initial interviews with prospective students when they met in person. Aitken's letter was addressed to a new member of HDS whom he had not yet met, because she was living on Oahu while he was residing at Maui Zendo. In her letter, she asked him to explain the four options for Zen practice mentioned in *The Three Pillars of Zen*.[4] Aitken answered that these options came from Yasutani and Yamada, his teachers from Sanbōkyōdan, and that he previously used to outline the same four options in his orientation sessions. "However, in the last few years, I have not used them, but have merely asked the student why he or she wants to do *zazen*. Then I simply decide on the basis of the student's own wording what she or he wants and needs by way of practice."

In at least seven letters to Distant Correspondents, Aitken made statements or asked questions that echo this process. In a relatively early letter from 1975, for example, Aitken responded to a new corresponding member, "Your sitting should be keyed to your purpose and to your situation. Your letter expresses quite vividly the wish for realization. I would think that breath-counting might be the best way." In 2001, he identified the same purpose as expressed in another Distant Correspondent's letter, this time using different language. "You express bodhicitta (aspiration for bodhi) very clearly." In this case, since Aitken was already long retired from teaching, he recommended that the person contact Nelson Foster.

In other cases, Aitken apparently assessed the purpose of the correspondent to be something other than realization, and his recommendations varied accordingly. In 1983, a Distant Correspondent from Australia wrote to ask Aitken's advice about his suitability as a Zen student, and whether or not Aitken would recommend attending a *sesshin* at Sydney Zen Center. Aitken responded,

> Practice should be in keeping with purpose. I think your purpose is to become more at ease with yourself, which differs from most people who attend the Sydney Zen Center. They are seeking spiritual knowledge—grappling with existential questions. I hope you won't mind the difference.

In a rather unusual case from 1982, a Distant Correspondent wrote to Aitken that meditation made her feel happier and more self-confident, and that she was "trying to hear God's voice in my meditations." Aitken responded that meditation is a means to "get in touch with yourself" and to gain self-confidence, but "not the superficial kind they teach in real estate class." In keeping with her theistic purpose, he suggested, "To hear God and distinguish his voice from your own, is a matter of learning to focus and become completely silent in your meditation."

A Few Words about Silence

It is always difficult to make an argument based on silence, but a few words on the topic are appropriate when discussing the teaching patterns of a Buddhist teacher. Silence has a venerable place in the Buddhist tradition, which maintains that the historical Buddha refrained from answering certain questions that would not be conducive to good practice. Aitken likewise remained silent in reference to some questions that his Distant Correspondents asked. In this instance, I refer primarily to Aitken answering some, but not all of the questions addressed to him by the same Distant Correspondent, rather than his apparent lack of response when the file preserves no letter of response at all.

In the vast majority of cases in which a Distant Correspondent asked questions and Aitken's reply is preserved in the file, he carefully answered each question or request. Letters typically bear markings, presumably made by Aitken himself or by Anne, to facilitate his effort to identify all questions to be answered. In some cases, he even numbered the questions in the margins of the original. Requests for particular materials or information were generally each marked "done" or "sent" in the margin. This general pattern of careful response makes the rare examples of silence all the more obvious. While it is not possible to determine why Aitken maintained silence in these cases, one can at least seek patterns in the types of questions he passed over.

In at least two cases, Aitken ignored requests related to practice that may have appeared inappropriate to him. In 1982, an individual writing to set up a time to visit Hawaii for an initial interview and *sesshin* with Aitken simultaneously requested that Aitken assign him a kōan in the meantime. Aitken provided all the necessary information to set up a visit, as well as additional, unsolicited information for possible visits to ZCLA to meet Maezumi Rōshi as an alternative *sangha*. Aitken does not mention the request for a kōan at all. In 1988, a man without ready access to a Zen center requested assistance in maintaining a solo practice. He asked for information about "liturgical formula and calendar of observances" so that he could incorporate them into his practice. Finally, he requested guidance for sitting a long-distance *sesshin*. Aitken responded with a warm, informative letter that provided suggestions and invited further questions. A marginal note indicates that he sent along a copy of the HDS sutra book and calendar of events. Aitken made no mention, however, of the requested guidance for the proposed "long-distance *sesshin*."

In two cases, Aitken remained silent when the Distant Correspondent appeared to cross the line in terms of asking inappropriately personal questions. In 1984, a woman requested assistance "in distinguishing a path" for herself. She related her attraction to and experiences with Jack Kornfield's Insight Meditation and the teachings of Krishnamurti, and her ongoing interest and skepticism for Zen. She asked, "How have you reconciled *zazen* with Krishnamurti's observation that any 'practice tends to reinforce the sense of "me" rather than diminish it'? Why did you leave

Happy Valley School and what do you now think of Krishnamurti's perceptions?" Aitken answered her at some length. He pointed out that Zen, Vipassana, and the way of Krishnamurti are three very different paths. He interpreted her condition of despair in selecting a path as symptomatic of a true religious quest, a Dark Night of the Soul. He let her know that it was very important that she find a teacher, and encouraged her "to go to Barre, MA for a retreat with Jack or Joseph, or come to Hawaii." He said that he didn't want to discourage her from listening to Krishnamurti, but his teachings wouldn't make her any the wiser. He thus answered all her questions except the one about himself and his reason for leaving Happy Valley School.

In one intriguing case, a well-known retired filmmaker wrote to enquire about becoming Aitken's student. He provided extensive information about his daily practice patterns, his background in Buddhism, and his experiences at ZCLA. He asked whether or not he should practice celibacy as a means of overcoming his sexual fantasies from the past that continued to torment him. "Will meditating longer help?" He also asked for advice about what he should do with his free time, indicating that he was "having trouble finding zest and joy in living." Aitken replied with a short but cordial letter. He indicated that he was "moved by the honesty and sincerity of your letter" and glad that the correspondent had started his practice at ZCLA because the transition would be smooth. "If you decide to move, I would be very glad to work with you." He suggested that they meet and offered possible dates. He did not undertake answering any of the more personal questions put forward by the correspondent.

In addition to "ignoring" certain questions, Aitken also appears to have decided not to respond to some letters and other types of communications he received from Distant Correspondents. There are several examples of letters, poems, sketches, and other items on which Aitken wrote "No Ans." In several of these cases, this appears to be an intentional "response of silence," sandwiched as they are between other exchanges in the file. In a few cases, the option of silence brings to mind the bell that Zen teachers use in *dokusan* to signal the end of the interview when the student's answer warrants no response.

Encouraging Words

After reading Aitken's correspondence with hundreds of his students as well as the Distant Correspondents, it appears to me that his basic purpose, expressed somewhat differently in all of his letters, is simply to encourage his correspondents in their practice. In most of his letters, encouragement takes the form of practical advice and information. Occasionally, encouragement is expressed through stern words of warning, when Aitken perceived danger signs of "autodidaction." For those who wrote to him from places of isolation or personal anguish, Aitken responded with direct expressions of his concern.

Aitken frequently used the expression "dark night of the soul" to validate the seriousness of a correspondent's struggles, and to place them in a new light as a clear sign that the individual is indeed on a valid religious path. In much the same way that he validates pleasant experiences achieved through meditation as milestones, he reinterprets certain forms of religious despair as positive markers on the spiritual path. To a man living thousands of miles from a teacher or *sangha* who expressed his feelings of desperation, he exclaimed, "Your goals are altogether exemplary." For the woman with MS who could not take herself to a teacher, he advised, "The relief you feel on experiencing no-self is an unmistakable clue that you are on the right road. Persevere."

In several letters, Aitken acknowledged the encouragement he felt in return on reading a Distant Correspondent's letter. When a woman, then serving as dean of students at a large law school, wrote, "just to thank you for all the help you've given me along the Buddhist path," Aitken replied, "Thank you very much for your encouraging letter—yes, *rōshi*s need encouragement!" In a similar vein, he wrote, "If you were encouraged by my writing, I am encouraged by yours" to another woman who wrote to thank him for speaking out against sexual exploitation in the *sangha*. Aitken recommended practicing with a group as a means of support and encouragement, and he likewise envisioned similar forms of support through written exchange and saw himself as an active recipient as well.

Aitken's words to Distant Correspondents are largely consistent with his published teachings, and often run in parallel with them. As a Zen teacher, he employed the published word to make the Dharma available to as wide an audience as possible, and then supplemented that work with invitations to participate in personal correspondence. He used his letters to both students and strangers alike to encourage them in their practice. Like the vast majority of his Distant Correspondents, Aitken regarded *zazen* as the heart of Zen practice. He understood the guidance of a qualified teacher to be crucial for the serious practice of Zen meditation, and therefore made it his primary responsibility as a Zen teacher to help the Distant Correspondents locate communal practice within a *sangha* under the direction of a qualified and trustworthy teacher. For those outside the easy reach of a Zen center, he constructed a new option for practice that I have called Distant Membership.

Conclusion

> I have heard some people say that since Zen says we must be grounded in the place where there is no right and wrong, it follows that Zen has no ethical application. But if there were no application of our experience of the unity and the individuality of all beings, then Zen would be only a stale exercise in seclusion, the way of death.
> —Robert Aitken, *Taking the Path of Zen*

Scholars who study New Religious Movements often argue that one of the primary benefits derived from studying these movements is that we can see played out in front of us processes of community formation, doctrinal, scriptural, and ritual development, and so forth, that occurred historically in the major religious traditions of the world during time periods now largely lost from sight. In much the same way, studying the development of Buddhism in the West in the twentieth century gives scholars an opportunity to watch patterns of introduction, assimilation, acculturation, misunderstanding, change, and the like that occurred as the tradition moved into China, Tibet, Korea, and Japan in the distant past. Differences exist in each case, of course, but many of the patterns are nonetheless familiar.

The words of famous Zen teachers through the ages have been duly recorded and are available for study. The responses from their audiences, on the other hand, are largely lost from reach. We cannot know how the messages were received or acted upon by monastic and lay disciples who may have been illiterate and were generally themselves too ordinary to be the subject of any preserved text. The Aitken archive has the great virtue of allowing us to hear in their own words how modern Western sympathizers and solo practitioners appropriate the Buddhist tradition and make it their own. I have never encountered sources quite like this in my study of Japanese Buddhism, certainly not collected in one place. With the exception of diaries, it is nearly impossible to find writings by ordinary people who were attracted to new forms of Buddhism in early Edo period Japan, much less texts that discuss what the tradition meant to them or how they practiced it.

The correspondence between Robert Aitken and his Distant Correspondents provides an unusual window to view the broad spectrum of American Buddhism and Zen practitioners that cannot be seen by visiting Zen centers, interviewing teachers and members, or reading contemporary Zen literature. Scholars cannot readily observe Zen sympathizers, or gain any insight into the impact Buddhist teachings have on their beliefs and patterns of living. Nor can they document how solo practitioners, those without any affiliation with a Zen center, practice meditation in the privacy of their homes. Zen sympathizers and solo practitioners have therefore remained largely invisible from view, out of the reach of participant observation and self-reporting survey devices.

The time period discussed in this study, however recent and familiar, is nevertheless gone by. For the most part, Robert Aitken served as a teacher for Zen students of the Baby Boomer generation, many of whom shared his commitment to meditation as the heart of Buddhist practice and his social activist ideals. Boomers remember writing with typewriters and carbon paper, even if we hardly ever use them anymore. We remember writing letters by hand and relying on conventional mail, which didn't need an adjective back then. It was just the mail. Today, people communicate via email or Facebook, not paper letters. They get their information about the nearest Buddhist temple online, not from phone books at the library or by calling the Religion Department at their local university. Anyone interested in attending a *sesshin* at HDS or most other Zen centers can apply online.

In at least one sense, the three decades discussed in this research project represent a distinctive period in the history of Buddhism in the West. Technology has made the methods of communication that Aitken and his correspondents relied upon obsolete. But that does not mean that the experiences of the Buddhist sympathizers and solo practitioners are likewise things of the past. Many of the concerns raised by the correspondents still resonate with Western practitioners of Buddhism. In the future, however, we will need new methods to study the unaffiliated. A colleague recently told me about his sister-in-law, an ordained Sōtō priest, who is working on Second Life in order to reach out to Buddhist practitioners that congregate there. Zen teachers continue to reach out to the sympathizers and solo practitioners that they know are out there. Scholars will need to follow their lead and conduct research in virtual worlds such as Second Life and on social media sites to find out about current generations of unaffiliated Buddhists in America.

The present study employed letters from the Robert Baker Aitken Papers, an unusually rich resource for the study of contemporary American Zen, to bring these portions of the American Zen scene into focus. Some of the findings merely confirm what scholars have already surmised, presented here with the benefit of concrete evidence (available for cross-checking by other scholars) to support the suppositions. Other findings provide additional support for conclusions previously reached through field studies and participant observation. Beyond confirming what we already know, however, the correspondence also extends our knowledge of American Zen.

The Distant Correspondents' letters confirm that most Americans who become Zen Buddhist "first recruited themselves to Zen" through reading Zen literature.[1] Nearly all of the Distant Correspondents had acquired at least a rudimentary understanding of the Zen teachings before they contacted Aitken, although it is impossible to determine from the letters how many already actually regarded themselves as Buddhist when they wrote. Beyond confirming the known, however, the letters also inform us that many of these "self-recruited" individuals do more than familiarize themselves with Buddhist doctrine and the Zen perspective on the teachings. Many of them likewise use Zen literature to teach themselves to meditate and begin to practice on their own. Others elect to participate in formal meditation instruction, such as provided at orientation weekends or short retreats at a nearby Zen center or at a class held at a local community center. Whether self-taught or not, many "sympathizers" thereafter practice primarily alone in the privacy of their home. They become, in effect, solo practitioners of Zen.

Some solo practitioners may maintain their pattern of personal practice for extended periods of time before feeling the need to contact a teacher or make an effort to affiliate with a Zen center. Indeed, we can only suppose that many solo practitioners never make any such effort. Solo practitioners of Zen thus participate in a pattern of religiosity that has been widely observed by scholars in Europe, Japan and, to a lesser extent, the United States, "believing without belonging."[2] In the case of

Zen solo practitioners, this would perhaps be more accurately labeled "practicing without belonging." While some of these individuals may self-identify on national surveys of religious affiliation as Buddhist, others may not.[3]

The present study suggests that solo practitioners of Zen share many attitudes and concerns with affiliated members of American Zen centers. Both members and solo practitioners, for example, typically regard meditation as the central feature of Zen practice. Like nonresidential members, solo practitioners must balance their religious practice with everyday concerns, such as work and family responsibilities. In many cases, they struggle with similar ethical considerations of how to live a Buddhist life in contemporary society, and they contemplate how to understand the Buddhist precepts as lay practitioners of a traditionally monastic tradition. The study also suggests that for a significant minority of the solo practitioners, their understanding of Zen teachings informs their direct involvement in social justice activities. Early studies of Zen centers in the United States found similar patterns. Tipton reported that approximately 20 percent of SFZC members had actively participated in a social justice service organization and that as many as 50 to 60 percent had participated in political protest against the Vietnam War.[4]

Unlike members of Zen centers, however, solo practitioners typically experience feelings of isolation from a practice community and a teacher. While studies that illustrate the rapid growth of Zen centers across the United States may suggest that this problem would have declined steadily during the decades under consideration here, the findings do not bear this out. Even late in the 1990s, Distant Correspondents continued to express their concerns about isolation from a *sangha*. What the study illuminates is that the experience of isolation entails many factors other than simple geographical distance from a Zen center. Financial restraints, family responsibilities, health concerns, and highly individual factors such as ethnicity and profession may serve as limiting factors, effectively cutting off solo practitioners from affiliating with a Zen center, thus exacerbating feelings of isolation.

As the demographic profile of the study group indicated, the age of the Distant Correspondents closely mirrored that of affiliated Zen students throughout the study period. In the 1970s, the typical correspondent was in his or her twenties, and less likely to be limited by family obligations and career considerations. Moving through the decades, the typical correspondent would be older and more likely to encounter precisely the encumbrances associated with the householder stage of life. For these reasons as well, the need for alternative options for practice remained steady instead of decreasing.

Studies of Zen centers and their membership have suggested that Zen practitioners represent an elite portion of American society, at once better educated and wealthier than the average American.[5] While the data collected from the letters of the Distant Correspondents sheds little light on the educational level of Zen sympathizers and solo practitioners, it does suggest that for many of them, financial constraints play a significant role in determining their patterns of practice. The study suggests that monetary concerns may hinder a segment of the Buddhist solo practitioner and sympathizer population from joining a *sangha*, especially when combined with issues of geographic isolation or family responsibilities. Individuals with sufficient disposable income may find regular participation in *sesshin* at a distant Zen center within their financial means, while others with more limited income may be unable to afford the luxury. Similarly, childcare or elder care services that would enable a solo practitioner to attend weekly *zazenkai* meetings at a nearby location may pose an insurmountable obstacle for some individuals. One question beyond the scope of this study to answer is whether or not the rise of internet access may alleviate the feelings of isolation experienced by solo practitioners, since the internet allows for like-minded individuals to create online communities of support.

The experience of the Distant Correspondents demonstrates that some solo practitioners, especially those that meditate regularly, eventually reach a stage at which they feel the need for more expert advice in order to continue their practice. They may enter a "stale period" in their practice and require encouragement to push through the stage, they may encounter *makyō* experiences that frighten or disturb them, or they may experience pleasant or powerful breakthrough experiences that motivate them to seek confirmation from a teacher. Any of these factors that render solo practice problematic may motivate an individual to take a first step toward affiliation.

"Distant Membership" as a New Form of Zen Affiliation

Aitken and his Distant Correspondents mutually participated in creating a new form of Zen affiliation for Americans, "Distant Membership." This pattern of Zen affiliation falls somewhere between full and active membership in a local Zen *sangha* on the one hand and going it alone as a solo practitioner on the other. Aitken initiated the process with published invitations to contact him as a teacher of Zen meditation, qualified to direct a student's practice. Based on his own experience, Aitken understood that many people were drawn to the Zen tradition based upon their reading of Zen, and he recognized that many of them would not know how to begin to establish a practice or contact a teacher.

Moreover, based upon his years of Zen training, living in Hawaii and visiting Zen teachers in Japan, Aitken understood firsthand the many problems and challenges that solo practitioners would face: periods of isolation from a *sangha* and teacher, the financial drain on resources to support extended visits with a distant teacher, and the challenges of balancing family responsibilities with religious endeavors.

For their part, many of the Distant Correspondents used writing to Aitken as a bridge between solo practice and affiliation with a Zen center. Their letters represent a form of reaching out to a trusted Zen teacher, requesting assistance in some manner. In many cases, the correspondent already acknowledged the need to find a teacher and a community to support his or her practice, and directly requested Aitken's help in securing that connection. In other cases, the correspondent apparently preferred to maintain a pattern of solo practice, but wanted the benefit of occasional advice and encouragement from a trusted expert. Whatever the case, they then encountered Aitken's strong recommendation to affiliate, if at all possible, even if only as a Distant Member.

Through a process of trial and error, Aitken created a mail ministry that developed through time from "corresponding membership" to "distant membership." Early on, Aitken offered individuals living outside of Hawaii the option to receive the HDS newsletter and the opportunity to consult him via mail, a category he dubbed "corresponding membership." Aitken provided corresponding members personal words of encouragement to persevere in their practice, practical advice about sitting *zazen*, and, whenever possible, detailed information about teachers and Zen centers that were more geographically convenient for possible affiliation. Aitken's early experiments with conducting *dokusan* exchanges via traditional mail with corresponding members convinced him that there were serious limitations to long-distance teaching. He therefore began to develop a new pattern of "distant membership."

In his responses to Distant Correspondents, Aitken began to encourage the following pattern of practice: First, to practice *zazen* as regularly as they could manage, preferably at least once a day. Instructions for this were laid out in *Taking the Path of Zen*, and in orientation tapes originally prepared for HDS members. Second, he advised correspondents to seek out communal support in their immediate geographical vicinity by locating a small meditation group. If all else failed, Aitken encouraged his distant members to sit with a single "Zen friend" once a week. Third, he encouraged correspondents to establish a teacher-student relationship with a qualified teacher that the individual regarded as trustworthy and compatible. Fourth and finally, he urged correspondents to attend *sesshin* with the teacher at least once a year.

Aitken did not regard solo practice as a viable option for serious Zen practice in the long term. In his letters, he repeatedly stressed that Zen practice entails working with a qualified teacher. Nevertheless, some correspondents reported decades of more or less satisfactory practice as solo practitioners before writing to Aitken. One can only conclude that many such solo practitioners continue to practice in this manner. Their numbers may well far exceed the number of affiliated practitioners practicing at Zen centers throughout the Western world.

The present study represents a significant step toward extending the parameters of scholarly work on American Zen to include sympathizers and solo practitioners. Given the paucity of publicly available archival sources, as well as the growing shift toward electronic communications that are only rarely preserved in paper format, future studies of this type will necessarily be limited. Scholars will need to consider other innovative means to approach this nearly invisible segment of the American Zen community. The study raises several questions for future research: How widespread is the pattern of Distant Membership? Does it represent, for example, a large or significant proportion of affiliated Zen practitioners in the United States? Do other teachers and Zen communities encourage and support similar patterns of Distant Membership? Do other Zen teachers enter into epistolary relationships with potential students and solo practitioners? How does the internet contribute to the spread of solo Zen practice and how does it alter interaction between solo practitioners and Zen teachers?

Final Thoughts

My research on Aitken and his Distant Correspondents has transformed the way I think about Zen in the West. Like other scholars, I already had some idea who the Buddhist sympathizers are—they take my classes and attend the same public lectures, and sometimes they speak enthusiastically with me on airplanes when they learn my profession. Not a few are colleagues. I thought I could imagine them, but my imagination fell short of the vivid images that emerged from reading their words in the Aitken archive. I could never have imagined the deep sense of commitment and sincerity that underlies the efforts of these correspondents and untold numbers of other solo practitioners and sympathizers. To use a common Zen expression, I bow down to these correspondents and express my gratitude for what they taught me. It has been my honor to meet them, however vicariously.

Underlying some recent studies of Buddhism in America are assumptions about who counts as a real Buddhist and who does not. I admit that I wasn't sure myself if Buddhist sympathizers should count. They don't know as much about the Asian tradition as they could. Many have an overly romanticized view of Zen. Scholars may not be able to numerically count these individuals using any reliable demographic technique, but the Distant Correspondents have demonstrated to me that we must include them as Buddhists in our explorations of Zen in the West. In much the same way that unaffiliated Christians allow their faith to shape their lives and actions, these unaffiliated Buddhists allow their practice and understanding of the Buddhist teaching to shape their lives. They represent one of the methods through which Buddhism influences our culture and becomes an integrated part of the religious context of America.

Robert Aitken took these folks seriously throughout his career as a Zen teacher. He worked to make his Distant Correspondents feel included in the broader community of the Buddhist *sangha*, to validate their efforts to practice, and to invite them to affiliate with a practicing community. Among the many valuable lessons I have learned from Aitken Rōshi is that they are an important part of the American Buddhist community. I admired and respected him before I read through the archive. After reading through his uncensored private correspondence, including some less flattering items that he decided should remain in the archive, I respect him all the more. I hope that his commitment and sincerity shine through this work.

Notes

Introduction

1. Tweed suggests the inclusion and importance of this category for the study of Buddhism in America in "Night-Stand Buddhists and Other Creatures: Sympathizers, Adherents, and the Study of Religion," in *American Buddhism: Methods and Findings in Recent Scholarship*, Williams and Queen, eds., pp. 71–90.

2. The group now officially known as Honolulu Diamond Sangha has had several names throughout the years. Until 1992, it was named simply Diamond Sangha, although people often referred instead to one or the other of its primary sites of practice, Koko An Zendo, located in Honolulu, and Maui Zendo. Since 1992, Diamond Sangha refers to the whole network of affiliated Zen centers in the United States and abroad, while the name Honolulu Diamond Sangha was legally adopted for the sites on Oahu, including Koko An, before it closed, and the new temple in Palolo Valley.

3. Despite recognizing that many scholars regard the term Western Buddhism as problematic, I have elected to retain the term for this study. First, it was the accepted terminology for most of the time period under examination in the study, and it remains so for many of the practitioners who are its subject. Second, other terms are either inaccurate, infelicitous, or both. American Buddhism, for example, does not accurately reflect the identities of the Distant Correspondents, since a significant minority of them are European, Latin American, Australian, and New Zealanders. The term "Non-Asian Buddhism" not only sounds unpleasant to the ear, it would inaccurately suggest that Asian American Buddhists are somehow excluded from this study.

4. Designation as a Zen teacher is understood differently in the various Japanese denominations of Zen as well as in the various lineages established in the West. In Aitken's case, he received designation within the Sanbōkyōdan lineage, first as a Junshike, or Associate Zen Master, in 1974, and then later as a Shōshike, or Authentic Zen Master, in 1986. The latter permitted Aitken not only to teach independently, but also to designate his own Dharma heirs.

5. Kosmin and Mayer, p. 14.

6. Kosmin and Mayer, p. 16.

7. For translations of Tetsugen's letters, see Baroni.

8. For translations of some of Hakuin's letters, see Yampolsky.

9. Personal interview with the author, October 2003.

10. Gender was determined primarily based on the correspondent's name and, where the name was ambiguous to the researcher, by the content of the letter.

11. Emma McCloy Layman, *Buddhism in America* (Chicago: Nelson-Hall, 1976), p. 255.

12. Steven M. Tipton, *Getting Saved from the Sixties: Moral Meaning in Conversion and Cultural Change* (Berkeley: University of California Press, 1982), p. 103.

13. HDS routinely had a picture taken to commemorate *sesshin*. A review of these images shows that in many cases the balance between male and female is approximately fifty-fifty.

14. Stark and Bainbridge, especially pp. 190–195.

15. In *What Is Meditation?*, John White, ed., pp. 129–137.

16. Personal interview with the author, October 2003.

17. Robert A. Orsi, *Thank You, St. Jude: Women's Devotion to the Patron Saint of Hopeless Causes* (New Haven: Yale University Press, 1996). I am grateful that one of my readers reminded me of this insightful study. Indeed, Orsi's later work *Between Heaven and Earth: The Religious Worlds People Make and the Scholars Who Study Them* (Princeton: Princeton University Press, 2005) provided indirect inspiration for the present study.

18. Orsi, *Thank You, St. Jude*, p. xiii.

19. Gerber, "Epistolary Ethics: Personal Correspondence and the Culture of Emigration in the Nineteenth Century," *Journal of American Ethnic History* (Summer 2000), pp. 3–23. Gerber, "Acts of Deceiving and Withholding in Immigrant Letters: Personal Identity and Self-Presentation in Personal Correspondence," *Journal of Social History* (Winter 2005), pp. 315–330.

20. Gerber, "Acts of Deceiving," notes in his work that immigrants, who write letters to preserve relationships rather than to initiate them, have various motivations to present their life in America in glowing terms, rather than to reflect on the hardships they encountered.

21. Janet Maybin, "Death Row Penfriends: Some Effects of Letter Writing on Identity and Relationships," in *Letter Writing as Social Practice*, Davis Barton

and Nigel Hall, eds. (Philadelphia: John Benjamins Publishing Company, 2000), pp. 151–176.

22. Tweed, "Night-Stand Buddhists," pp. 71–90.

23. Philip Kapleau, *The Three Pillars of Zen: Teaching, Practice, and Enlightenment* (Boston: Beacon, 1967).

24. Philip Kapleau, *The Three Pillars of Zen: Teaching, Practice, and Enlightenment* (New York: Anchor Press, Doubleday, 1980).

25. John Daishin Buksbazen, *To Forget the Self: An Illustrated Guide to Zen Meditation* (Los Angeles: Zen Center of Los Angeles, 1977). Note that Aitken contributed the preface to this volume.

26. Gudō Nishijima, *How to Practice Zazen* (Tokorozawa, Japan: Bukkyosha, 1976).

Chapter 1. Setting the Stage

1. Aitken, *Taking the Path of Zen*, pp. 115–132.
2. Sharf, pp. 441–442.
3. http://libweb.hawaii.edu/libdept/speccoll/aitken/autobiography.html (accessed on October 30, 2009).
4. Tworkov, pp. 23–62.
5. Personal interview with the author, October 2003.
6. Aitken, *The Practice of Perfection* (New York: Pantheon Books, 1994), p. 21.
7. A new collection of Senzaki's teachings was recently published. See *Eloquent Silence: Nyogen Senzaki's Gateless Gate and Other Previously Unpublished Teachings and Letters*, Roko Sherry Chayat, ed. (Boston: Wisdom Publications, 2008).
8. A collection of Nakagawa Sōen's poetry was published posthumously. See *Endless Vow: The Zen Path of Sōen Nakagawa*, Kazuaki Tanahashi and Roko Sherry Chayat, trans. (Boston: Shambhala, 1996).
9. Sharf, p. 424.
10. http://www.thezensite.com/ZenEssays/CriticalZen/Aitken_Shimano_Letters.html (accessed on March 23, 2010).
11. http://www.shimanoarchive.com/ (accessed on May 26, 2011).
12. Letter to Barbara Spalding, dated December 14, 1988.
13. Personal interview with the author, September 2008.
14. Personal interview with the author, September 2008.
15. Personal interview with Michael Kieran, head teacher for HDS Palolo Zen Center, May 2, 2011.
16. Sharf, p. 433.
17. Personal interview with the author, September 2008.

18. Personal interview with Michael Kieran, May 2, 2011.

19. Maui Zendo has since reopened and functions as a Zen community within the Diamond Sangha tradition without a resident teacher.

20. Letter addressed to Michael Attie, dated January 27, 1993.

21. Sharf, pp. 448–451.

22. The best known of the traditional manuals for *zazen* is Dōgen's *Fukan zazengi*. Carl Bielefeldt provides an analysis of Dōgen's manuals as well as antecedent Chinese texts in *Dōgen's Manuals of Zen Meditation* (Berkeley: University of California Press, 1988).

23. In Japanese cultural contexts, the basic manner of instruction is learning by doing and imitating. When one is taught to bow, the instructor places her hand at the back of one's neck and places one in the appropriate posture. When learning to use the brush for calligraphy, the instructor takes one's hand and demonstrates the strokes. In my experience these situations involve little verbal instruction or discussion.

24. See, for example, Rick Fields, *How the Swans Came to the Lake*; James Ishmael Ford, *Zen Master Who?*; Charles Prebish, *Luminous Passage*; and Richard Hughes Seager, *Buddhism in America*.

25. See, for example, estimates of growth in Vietnamese temples reported by Nguyen and Barber, "Vietnamese Buddhism in North America: Tradition and Acculturation," in *Faces of Buddhism*, Prebish and Tanaka, eds. (Berkeley: University of California Press, 1999), p. 131.

26. Sharf, p. 424

27. Prebish provides information about the historical usage of the term *sangha* in *Luminous Passage*, pp. 203–206.

Chapter 2. Why People Write

1. Ford, p. 178.

2. Aitken assumed that the correspondent was a Catholic priest, but the correspondent never specifies his denomination. His close relationship working with the Catholic brothers from the Abbey of Gethsemani, the Trappist monastery in Kentucky made famous by Thomas Merton, supports the assumption that he was Roman Catholic. On the other hand, I find myself confounded by the correspondent's mention that he was "currently getting a divorce." Since the Roman Catholic Church does not allow clergy to marry, perhaps he was a former Catholic priest. Alternatively, he may have been an Episcopal priest.

3. "Ritual and Makyō," in *Original Dwelling Place: Zen Buddhist Essays* (Washington, D.C.: Counterpoint, 1996), pp. 97–102.

4. The correspondent did not explain how he came to hear the *teishō*, but it appears from the general context of the letter that he heard a tape recording

rather than a live performance. HDS routinely recorded and circulated copies of Aitken's sermons. Many of these tapes are preserved in the Aitken archive.

5. *The Mind of Clover*, pp. 5–6.

6. Sasaki Jōshū (b. 1907) is a Japanese Rinzai Zen teacher, who first came to the United States in 1962. He founded several Zen centers in the United States and Canada, including Rinzai-ji Zen Center in Los Angeles and Mount Baldy Zen Center.

7. The letter provides no reference for the interview, so there is no way to verify Aitken's actual remarks. Although Aitken did not name Eidō in published materials, on the advice of publishers, he wrote much more openly about Eidō's sexual misconduct at HDS in his private correspondence.

8. *The Mind of Clover*, pp. 59–60.

9. Aitken remarked on this difference in cultural awareness of alcoholism in the introduction to *The Mind of Clover*, pp. 13–14.

10. Personal interview, May 2, 2011.

Chapter 3. Patterns of Zen Practice among the Distant Correspondents

1. Aitken and his correspondent refer to Genpo as Gempo or Gempō. These are simply variant transliterations of the same Japanese name.

2. *The Mind of Clover*, pp. 175–176.

3. *Rohatsu sesshin* is typically held in early December to commemorate the Buddha's attainment of enlightenment, celebrated on December 8 using the Western calendar or the eighth day of the twelfth lunar month on the Chinese lunar calendar.

Chapter 4. Areas of Special Concern Raised by Distant Correspondents

1. Prebish, *Luminous Passage*, p. 85. Kenneth Kraft, "Recent Developments in North American Zen," in *Zen Tradition and Transition*, Kenneth Kraft, ed. (New York: Grove Press, 1988), pp. 178–198.

2. Tweed, *The American Encounter with Buddhism 1844–1912*, p. 44.

3. Aitken eventually discontinued the corresponding membership category, because, as he explained to a Distant Correspondent in 1982, he was writing to people regardless of whether or not they were paying members. Indeed, I found several cases before 1982 in which Aitken offers to correspond "as a friend" or "for free" when he sensed that financial constraints were a problem.

4. The U.S. Census Bureau estimated the white population of Hawaii to be 28.6 percent in 2006. See http://quickfacts.census.gov/qfd/states/15000.html (accessed on May 30, 2008).

5. Coleman, p. 20.

6. The correspondent refers here to two famous collections of kōan, the Mumonkan (Ch. Wumenguan) and the Biyanlu (J. Hekiganroku). They are not sutras, but classical texts from the Zen tradition in China.

7. Coleman, p. 20.

8. From the Buddhist Peace Fellowship mission statement, http://www.bpf.org/html/about_us/mission/mission.html (accessed February 16, 2009).

9. Donald Rothberg discusses the two aspects of the term "engaged Buddhism" in "Responding to the Cries of the World: Socially Engaged Buddhism in North America," in Prebish and Tanaka, eds., especially pp. 268–273.

10. I participated in one such discussion, having been invited by HDS to give a lecture on the history of the precepts in Japanese Buddhism, September 23, 2003.

11. Interview with Michael Kieran, March 30, 2005.

12. Osage Monastery, located in Sand Springs, Oklahoma, was founded in 1979 by the Benedictine Sisters of Perpetual Adoration. The community was modeled after monastic ashrams and was known for its openness to dialogue with other religious traditions. The Benedictine sisters no longer live at the monastery, although it continues to function as a contemplative center. It is now known as Osage Forest of Peace.

13. The earlier letter is not in the file.

14. Kapleau, pp. 269–291.

15. There are two nineteenth-century works with the title *In His Steps*. The correspondent almost certainly refers here to a novel written by the Congregational minister Charles M. Sheldon, subtitled *What Would Jesus Do?* Sheldon made frequent use of this question in his sermons and other writings. His work helped to inspire the Christian Social Gospel movement. The other book with the same title was written by James Russell Miller, a Presbyterian minister.

16. The one notable exception to this is the Jōdo Shin, or True Pure Land denominations, which had married clergy since their inception in the twelfth to thirteenth centuries.

17. See Richard Jaffe, *Neither Monk nor Layman*, for an excellent account of this transformation.

18. *Old Wisdom in the New World: Americanization in Two Immigrant Theravada Buddhist Temples* (Knoxville: University of Tennessee Press, 1999).

19. Dainin Katagiri (1928–1990) was a Sōtō Zen teacher, born in Osaka, Japan, who came to the United States in 1962 to serve the Zenshūji Sōtō Zen Mission in Los Angeles, California. He later moved to Minnesota in 1972 and founded the Minnesota Zen Meditation Center.

20. Taisen Deshimaru (1914–1982) was a Sōtō Zen priest who worked primarily in Europe.

21. Aikido is a modern Japanese form of martial art, created by Morihei Ueshiba. An Aikido website defines the term "suki" as "An opening or gap where one is vulnerable to attack or application of a technique, or where one's technique is otherwise flawed. SUKI may be either physical or psychological." http://www.aikiweb.com/language/vocab.html (accessed on June 6, 2008).

22. For similar comments, see Kapleau, *The Three Pillars of Zen*, p. 86.

23. For a discussion of the current scholarly understanding of the place of ritual within Zen practice, see Heine and Wright's *Zen Ritual: Studies of Zen Buddhist Theory in Practice* (Oxford: Oxford University Press, 2008).

24. Jeff Wilson, *Mourning the Unborn Dead: A Buddhist Ritual Comes to America* (New York: Oxford University Press, 2009), especially his chapter on rethinking American Buddhism, pp. 107–127.

25. Yvonne Rand continues to conduct an annual Ceremony for Children Who Have Died, a ritual "to acknowledge and mourn the death of children through abortion, miscarriage, stillbirth, and death after birth." The service is conducted without charge. See her website at http://www.goatintheroad.org/html/ceremony.html (accessed March 26, 2010).

26. Tworkov, pp. 34–35.

Chapter 5. Special Constituencies within the Distant Correspondents

1. The author can confirm that HDS remains quite open to alternative meditation postures. When I was experiencing serious back problems in 2006, a member of the HDS staff gave me instruction in alternative postures. She let me know that some members routinely make use of a small room attached to the main meditation hall when they assume postures that are inconvenient for others, such as lying down.

2. Other sources indicate that Maezumi entered the Betty Ford Center for treatment.

3. Aitken, "The Zen Buddhist Path," p. 137.

4. It seems likely that Aitken continued to use this style of distance teaching with his closest students while they were pursuing the later stages of the kōan curriculum. It is difficult to determine the extent of distance teaching with these students because the materials were carefully edited out of the collection before the archive came to the University of Hawaii.

5. Based on a letter written by Aitken to an inmate on Oahu, dated February 25, 1991.

6. A full description of Parker's final days and the campaign to save him can be found at http://www.engaged-zen.org/articles/Kobutsu-Death_Row_Practice.html (accessed on March 26, 2010).

Chapter 6. Robert Aitken's Zen Ministry by Mail

1. The article is published in John White's *What Is Meditation?*, pp. 129–137.

Chapter 7. These Words Are Your Words

1. The latter suggestion appears in *Taking the Path of Zen*, p. 32.
2. Personal interviews, October 2002.
3. *The Mind of Clover*, pp. 57–63.
4. The correspondent probably refers here to the "four aspirations" of a Zen practitioner, discussed in Kapleau, pp. 60–62.

Conclusion

1. Tipton, p. 104.
2. See David Voas and Alasdair Crockett, "Religion in Britain: Neither Believing nor Belonging," *Sociology* 39 (2005), pp. 11–27; Grace Davie, "Vicarious Religion: A Methodological Challenge," in *Everyday Religion: Observing Modern Religious Lives*, Nancy T. Ammerman, ed. (Oxford: Oxford University Press, 2007), pp. 21–35.
3. In my many discussions with members of HDS, I have found that a certain number of regular, active members will not self-identify as Buddhist when asked. They likewise reject the suggestion that they are "converts" to Buddhism. Self-identification thus appears to be more complicated even than Tweed, "Night-Stand Buddhists," suggests in his essay.
4. Tipton, pp. 104–105.
5. Tipton, pp. 103–104; Coleman, p. 20.

Bibliography

Aitken, Robert. "The Zen Buddhist Path of Self-realization." In *What Is Meditation?*, John White, ed. New York: Anchor Books, 1974.
———. *Taking the Path of Zen*. San Francisco, CA: North Point Press, 1982.
———. *The Mind of Clover: Essays in Zen Buddhist Ethics*. San Francisco: North Point Press, 1984.
———. *The Gateless Barrier: The Wu-men kuan (Mumonkan)*. San Francisco: North Point Press, 1990.
———. *The Dragon Who Never Sleeps: Verses for Zen Buddhist Practice*. Berkeley, CA: Parallax Press, 1992.
———. *Encouraging Words: Zen Buddhist Teachings for Western Students*. New York: Pantheon Books, 1993.
———. *The Practice of Perfection: The Paramitas from a Zen Buddhist Perspective*. New York: Pantheon Books, 1994.
———. *Original Dwelling Place: Zen Buddhist Essays*. Washington, D.C.: Counterpoint, 1996.
———. *The Morning Star: New and Selected Zen Writings*. Washington, D.C.: Shoemaker and Hoard, 2003.
———. Autobiographical Summary of Robert Baker Aitken's Career in Hawai'i (2003). Hamilton Library Special Collections: The Robert Baker Aitken Papers Website, http://libweb.hawaii.edu/libdept/speccoll/aitken/autobiography.html.
Ammerman, Nancy T. ed. *Everyday Religion: Observing Modern Religious Lives*. Oxford: Oxford University Press, 2007.
Baroni, Helen J. *Iron Eyes: The Life and Teachings of Obaku Master Tetsugen Dōkō*. Albany: State University of New York Press, 2006.

Barton, David, and Nigel Hall, eds. *Letter Writing as Social Practice*. Philadelphia: John Benjamins Publishing Company, 2000.
Bielefeldt, Carl. *Dōgen's Manuals of Zen Meditation*. Berkeley, CA: University of California Press, 1988.
Buksbazen, John Daishin. *To Forget the Self: An Illustrated Guide to Zen Meditation*. Los Angeles, CA: Zen Center of Los Angeles, 1977.
Coleman, James William. *The New Buddhism: The Western Transformation of an Ancient Tradition*. Oxford: Oxford University Press, 2001.
Davie, Grace. "Vicarious Religion: A Methodological Challenge." In *Everyday Religion: Observing Modern Religious Lives*, Nancy T. Ammerman, ed. (Oxford: Oxford University Press, 2007). 21–35.
Fields, Rick. *How the Swans Came to the Lake: A Narrative History of Buddhism in America*, 3rd ed. Boston: Shambhala Publications, 1992.
Ford, James Ishmael. *Zen Master Who? A Guide to the People and Stories of Zen*. Boston: Wisdom Publications, 2006.
Gerber, David A. "Epistolary Ethics: Personal Correspondence and the Culture of Emigration in the Nineteenth Century." *Journal of American Ethnic History* (Summer 2000), pp. 3–23.
———. "Acts of Deceiving and Withholding in Immigrant Letters: Personal Identity and Self-Presentation in Personal Correspondence." *Journal of Social History* (Winter 2005), pp. 315–330.
Heine, Steven, and Dale S. Wright. *Zen Ritual: Studies of Zen Buddhist Theory in Practice*. Oxford: Oxford University Press, 2008.
Jaffe, Richard. *Neither Monk nor Layman: Clerical Marriage in Modern Japanese Buddhism*. Princeton, NJ: Princeton University Press, 2001.
Kapleau, Philip. *The Three Pillars of Zen: Teaching, Practice, and Enlightenment*. Boston: Beacon Press, 1967.
Keremidschieff, Vladimir, and Stuart Lachs. "The Aitken-Shimano Letters" at http://www.thezensite.com/ZenEssays/CriticalZen/Aitken_Shimano_Letters.html (accessed on March 23, 2010).
Kosmin, Barry A., and Egon Mayer. *American Religious Identification Survey 2001*. The Graduate Center of the City University of New York, 2001.
Kraft, Kenneth. "Recent Developments in North American Zen." In *Zen Tradition and Transition: A Sourcebook by Contemporary Zen Masters and Scholars*, Kenneth Kraft, ed. New York: Grove Press, 1988. 178–198.
Layman, Emma McCloy. *Buddhism in America*. Chicago: Nelson-Hall Publishers, 1976.
Maybin, Janet. "Death Row Penfriends: Some Effects of Letter Writing on Identity and Relationships." In *Letter Writing as Social Practice*, David Barton and Nigel Hall, eds. Philadelphia: John Benjamins Publishing Company, 2000. 151–176.
McMahan, David L. *The Making of Buddhist Modernism*. New York, NY: Oxford University Press, 2008.

Morreale, Don. *The Complete Guide to Buddhist America*. Boston: Shambhala, 1998.

Nakagawa Sōen. *Endless Vow: The Zen Path of Sōen Nakagawa*. Kazuaki Tanahashi and Roko Sherry Chayat, translators. Boston: Shambhala, 1996.

Nguyen, Cuong Tu, and A. W. Barber. "Vietnamese Buddhism in North America: Tradition and Acculturation." In *The Faces of Buddhism*, Charles S. Prebish and Kenneth K. Tanaka, eds. Berkeley: University of California Press, 1998. 129–146.

Nishijima Gudō. *How to Practice Zazen*. Tokorozawa, Japan: Bukkyosha, 1976.

Numrich, Paul David. *Old Wisdom in the New World: Americanization in Two Immigrant Theravada Buddhist Temples*. Knoxville: University of Tennessee Press, 1996.

Orsi, Robert A. *Thank You, St. Jude: Women's Devotion to the Patron Saints of Hopeless Causes*. New Haven, CT: Yale University Press, 1996.

———. *Between Heaven and Earth: The Religious Worlds People Make and the Scholars Who Study Them*. Princeton, NJ: Princeton University Press, 2005.

Prebish, Charles S. *American Buddhism*. North Scituate, MA: Duxbury Press, 1979.

———. *Luminous Passage: The Practice and Study of Buddhism in America*. Berkeley: University of California Press, 1999.

Prebish Charles S., and Kenneth K. Tanaka, eds. *The Faces of Buddhism in America*. Berkeley: University of California Press, 1998.

Rothberg, Donald. "Responding to the Cries of the World: Socially Engaged Buddhism in North America." In *The Faces of Buddhism in America*, Charles S. Prebish and Kenneth K. Tanaka, eds. Berkeley: University of California Press, 1998. 266–286.

Seager, Richard Hughes. *Buddhism in America*. New York: Columbia University Press, 1999.

Senzaki Nyogen. *Eloquent Silence: Nyogen Senzaki's Gateless Gate and Other Previously Unpublished Teachings and Letters*. Roko Sherry Chayat, ed. Boston: Wisdom Publications, 2008.

Sharf, Robert. "Sanbōkyōdan Zen and the Way of the New Religions." *Japanese Journal of Religious Studies* 22, 3–4 (1995), pp. 417–458.

Stark, Rodney, and William Sims Bainbridge. *The Future of Religion: Secularization, Revival, and Cult Formation*. Berkeley: University of California Press, 1985.

Tipton, Steven M. *Getting Saved from the Sixties: Moral Meaning in Conversion and Cultural Change*. Berkeley: University of California Press, 1982.

Tweed, Thomas. *The American Encounter with Buddhism 1844–1912: Victorian Culture and the Limits of Dissent*. Bloomington, IN: Indiana University Press, 1992.

———. "Night-Stand Buddhists and Other Creatures: Sympathizers, Adherents, and the Study of Religion." In *American Buddhism: Methods and Findings in*

Recent Scholarship, Duncan Ryūken Williams and Christopher S. Queen, eds. Surrey, England: Curzon Press, 1999. 71–90.

Tworkov, Helen. *Zen in America: Profiles of Five Teachers*. San Francisco: North Point Press, 1989.

Voas, David, and Alasdair Crockett. "Religion in Britain: Neither Believing nor Belonging." *Sociology* 39 (2005), 11–27.

White, John, ed. *What Is Meditation?* Garden City, NY: Anchor Press, 1974.

Williams, Duncan Ryūken, and Christopher S. Queen, eds. *American Buddhism: Methods and Findings in Recent Scholarship*. Surrey, England: Curzon Press, 1999.

Wilson, Jeff. *Mourning the Unborn Dead: A Buddhist Ritual Comes to America*. New York, NY: Oxford University Press, 2009.

Yampolsky, Philip B. *The Zen Master Hakuin: Selected Writings*. New York: Columbia University Press, 1971.

Index

abortion, 75, 108, 109, 185n25
abusive behavior, 29, 62, 76, 100, 117, 119, 122, 132
affiliation: Buddhist, 5, 174; in alternative religions, 12; and Distant Correspondents, 74, 99–100, 110, 116, 149; encouraged by Aitken, 99, 150–52, 175–77
Aikido, 77, 105, 185n21
Aitken, Anne (née Hopkins), 8, 11, 27, 32; assisting with correspondence, 143, 144, 145; cofounder of HDS, 23, 28–29, 32–33, 39; death, 32–33; and Maui Zendo, 30, 31; and social justice, 88, 91, 93–94; Zen practice, 28
Aitken, Mary (née Laune), 26–27
Aitken, Robert: archive (*see* Robert Baker Aitken Papers); Dharma heirs, 32, 33–34, 51–52, 57, 76, 102, 106, 140; *Dragon Who Never Sleeps, The*, 98; *Encouraging Words*, 50, 125; internment camp experience, 4, 25–26; in Japan, 4, 23, 25–28, 29, 31, 63, 66, 111, 118, 176; living at Maui Zendo, 11, 30, 31–32, 128, 143, 162, 164, 179n2, 182n19; living in Kaimu, xiii–xv, 33, 140, 160; *Mind of Clover, The* (*see Mind of Clover, The*); *Taking the Path of Zen* (see *Taking the Path of Zen*); writing program, xiv, 140; Willy-Nilly Zen, 24; *Zen Buddhist Path of Self-realization, The*, 12, 49, 115, 139, 141, 185n3; *Zen Wave, A*, 26, 50
Aitken, Thomas, xiv, 26–27, 28, 33, 162
Alcalde, Augusto, 33
alcoholism, 63–64, 85, 118, 122, 158, 163, 183n9
ango, 43
ARIS (American Religious Identification Survey), 5
Asahina Beppō Sōgen, 27

Baby Boomer generation, 19, 79, 172
Baker, Richard Zentatsu, 53, 62, 92, 105, 121
Barzaghi, Subhana, 34
Beat poets, 106
Beck, Charlotte Joko, 156
Betsuin Shōbōji, 38
Bielefeldt, Carl, 182n22
Biyanlu, 87, 184n6
Blind Donkey, 92
Blyth, R. H., 4, 26; *Zen in English Literature and Oriental Classics*, 4, 26
Bobrow, Joseph, 34
bodhicitta, 102, 165

Index

bodhisattva, 24, 101
Bolleter, Ross, 43
breath counting: in Aitken's letter's, 60, 78, 103, 163; in Aitken's writings, 35, 36; and distant correspondents, 52, 53, 69, 70, 86, 91; and Kwan Um Zen, 100
Buddhism: American, 5, 37–41, 82, 112, 178, 179n1; ethnic, 38, 39; Japanese, 5–6, 43, 95–97, 184n10; Japanese American, 39, 97; nonethnic, 42, 85, 95, 96, 106–07; Theravada, 18, 19, 97; Tibetan, 57, 74, 75, 116, 124, 164; Vajrayana, 19; Western, 4, 81, 87, 171–72, 179n3
Buddhist: adherents, 5, 19, 133; affiliation (*see* affiliation); ethics, 10, 37, 53–54, 88–94, 120–21, 174; ethnic temples, 38–39, 97; meditation (*see* meditation); practice, 17, 96, 139, 172; precepts (*see* precepts); self- identification, 3, 16, 17, 186n3 (Concl.); solo practitioners (*see* solo practitioners); sympathizers (*see* sympathizers); teachers (*see* *individual names*); unaffiliated, 4, 5, 17–18, 98–102, 172–73, 177, 178
Buddhist Peace Fellowship, 88–89, 90, 91–92, 94, 184n8
Buksbazen, John Daishin, 19; *To Forget the Self*, 19

California Diamond Sangha, 57
Catholicism, 58, 90, 95, 156, 182n2
Chan Buddhism, 5, 41–42, 59–60, 106
checking questions, 58, 155–56
Chicago Zen Center, 75
Chogyam Trungpa, 116
Christianity, 86; and Aitken, 62, 123, 130, 178, 184n15; and Distant Correspondents, 90, 104, 158; and social justice, 90; and Zen, 93, 104
Coleman, James, 85, 87
Complete Guide to Buddhist America, The (Morreale), 38
conventional mail, 13, 127, 138, 146, 156, 163, 172, 176
corresponding membership, 83, 87–88, 141–42, 161, 165, 176, 183n3 (chap. 4)
counseling, 20, 48, 51, 56, 75, 128, 141

Dai Bosatsu Zendo, 99, 121
Dainin Katagiri, 99, 184n19
Dharma, 3, 6, 7, 15, 99, 137–38, 151, 155, 168
Dharma heirs, 40, 180n4; Aitken's, 12, 33–34, 76, 140, 151; Aitken's designation as, 32, 143, 180n4
distant correspondents: definition, 4; demographic information, 9–13; sub-categories, (*see* long-term correspondents; prison inmates; Seekers and Dabblers; Walking Wounded)
distant membership, 17, 152–54, 175–77, 169
Dōgen Kigen, 96, 102, 182n22
dokusan, 31, 43, 105, 138, 156, 167; and checking questions, 58; confidentiality, 7, 118, 143; by mail, 83, 104, 127, 143, 163, 176
Dragon Who Never Sleeps, The (Aitken), 98
Drosten, Rolf, 34
drugs, 36, 63–64, 163–64
Duffy, Jack, 34, 157

Eidō Shimano, 97, 121; abusive behavior, 29–30, 62, 119–20, 152; in Aitken's letters, 92, 122; in Aitken's writings, 62, 183n7; and distant correspondents, 100, 116, 119–20, 122; at Koko An, 29–30
email, 13, 33, 80, 112, 126, 146, 172
emptiness, 92
Encouraging Words (Aitken), 50, 125
Engaged Buddhism, 81, 88–89, 184n9
Engakuji, 27
enlightenment experience, 54, 63, 92, 95; confirmation of, 7, 20, 48, 57–59, 130; initial, 7, 130; as a goal, 65, 130. See also *kenshō*; *satori*
ethics: Aitken's concern for, 34, 37, 49,

120–21; concern of distant correspondents, 20, 53–54, 79, 81, 88–94, 118, 121, 174; and Mind of Clover, 34, 53, 118, 121
ethnic temples, 38–39

family responsibilities, 43, 54, 56, 112, 150, 162, 174–75, 176
Fellowship of Reconciliation, 94
financial concerns: concern of Aitken, 87–88, 150, 161–62, 176, 183n3 (chap.4); concern of distant correspondents, 56, 83, 87, 94; factor in isolation, 83, 87, 112, 174; in scholarship, 87, 112, 175
Foster, Nelson, 33, 88, 102, 140, 157, 165

General Letters, 9, 143, 144–45
Gerber, David A., 15, 180n20
Glassman, Tetsugen Bernard, 59, 117, 157, 158
Gudō Nishijima, 19; *How to Practice Zazen*, 19
Gyger, Pia, 34

Hakuin Ekaku, 5–6, 96
Happy Valley School, 27, 28, 167
Harada Daiun Sogaku, 27–28, 34–35, 66, 92, 96
Harada-Yasutani lineage, 39, 96, 97
Hawaii: and Aitken, 9, 24–26, 31, 176; demographics, 184n4; and distant correspondents, 12, 56, 98, 161–62; high cost, 161–62; prison ministry in 128–29; and transmission of Zen, 38, 39
Hawk, Patrick, 33, 57, 73, 130, 140, 151–52, 157, 158
HDS (Honolulu Diamond Sangha), 4, 23, 24, 108, 138, 150, 154, 162; affiliated groups, 40, 57, 73, 129, 151, 158; corresponding membership, 83, 87–88, 141, 176; distant correspondents later affiliate, 9, 50, 95, 110, 122; distant correspondents wish to join, 48, 56, 62, 99; early history, 28–31; and Eidō Shimano,

29–30, 119, 152, 183n7; membership, 10–11, 13, 85, 144; orientation, 34, 70, 177; practice at, 36, 63, 66, 67, 89–90, 97–98, 107, 111, 118, 185n1; prison ministry, 128; procedures, 11, 42, 98, 109, 143, 144, 146, 180n13, 182–83n4; publications, 92, 126, 142, 161; and Robert Baker Aitken Papers, xiii–xv, 4; sabbatical requests, 90; and Sanbōkyōdan, 32, 96; teachers, 29–33, 39, 146; terminology, 42, 43, 186n3
Honolulu Diamond Sangha (*see* HDS)
Hōsen Isobe, 38
How to Practice Zazen (Gudō), 19

immigrant letters, 18–19, 180n20
In His Steps (Sheldon), 93, 184n15
Insight Meditation, 124, 166
internment camp, 4, 25–26
internet, 79, 112, 138, 146, 175, 177
Islam, 51, 123
isolation, 16, 146, 168; concern of Aitken, 151, 160; concern of distant correspondents, 81, 82–88, 112, 174; and long-term correspondents, 126–27; and ritual, 108; and solo practitioners, 174, 175
Iwasaki Yaeko, 92–93

Jager, Willigis, 58, 157, 158
Japan: Aitken in, 4, 23, 25–28, 29, 31, 63, 66, 111, 118, 176; Buddhism in, 95, 96–97, 100, 171, 172; culture, 64, 182n23; and distant correspondents, 51, 55, 56, 77, 96, 99, 162; and religion, 173; and Zen 34–35, 38, 40, 41, 106–07, 137; and Zen denominations, 27–28; and Zen teachers, 3–6, 180n4
Japanese Buddhism, 43, 95, 96–97, 100, 171, 172, 184n10
Jizo, 75, 110
Jude, Saint, 14, 122
jukai: and distant correspondents, 62, 92, 108, 154, 158; with HDS, 43, 73–74; as initiation, 43; via mail, 109, 128

Kapleau, Philip, 52, 71, 74, 124–25; *Three Pillars of Zen, The*, 18, 56, 70, 71, 77, 92, 160
Kennedy, Robert Jinsen, 157, 158
Kennet, Jiyu, 116, 117
kenshō, 7, 24, 31, 57, 101–02. See also *satori*
kenshōki, 24
Keremidschieff, Vladimir, 29
Kieran, Michael, 33, 42, 66, 137, 146
kōan, 57, 63, 69, 118; curriculum, 7, 31, 43, 185n4; and distant correspondents, 69, 93, 101, 155, 166; literature, 65, 184n6; Mu (see Mu kōan); practice with, 52, 58, 70, 104, 130; versus *shikan taza*, 19, 28, 42, 153; via correspondence, 7, 127–28, 143
Koko An Zendo, 31, 32, 78, 98, 124, 138, 151, 179n2; and Eidō, 29, 30, 62; and distant correspondents, 50, 99, 143
Kornfield, Jack, 166
Krishnamurti, 124, 125, 166–67
Kwan Um Zen School, 100–01, 111, 158
kyōsaku, 66

Lachs, Stuart, 29
Laune, Mary, 26–27
lay practice, 20, 54–55, 95–96, 112, 118, 161,
Layman, Emma McCloy, 10
literature, 59, 65, 79, 130, 138; and Aitken, , 7, 26, 139; as basis for practice, 9, 69, 173; as introduction to Zen, 4, 7, 98, 173
long-term correspondents, 21, 29, 47, 115, 126–28
Lotus Sutra, 6

Maezumi Taizan: and Aitken, 31, 164; alcoholism, 64, 92, 117, 118, 122, 185n2; and distant correspondents, 62, 118; and monastic practice, 97–98; recommended by Aitken, 78, 157, 158, 166
makyō, 52–53, 59, 71, 80, 175
Malone, Kobutsu, 132

martial arts, 61, 77, 105, 185n21
master, 63, 85, 115, 159, 180n4; image of, 4, 57, 60, 65, 145; within Sanbōkyōdan, 31, 32, 180n4. See also teacher
Maui Zendo, 124, 138, 162, 179n2, 182n19; Aitken living at, 11, 30, 31–32, 128, 143; closure, 36; and distant correspondents, 50, 53, 164; prison ministry, 128–29; residential program, 11, 78, 164
meditation: and Aitken, 18, 27, 65; Aitken's advice, 10, 49, 53, 84, 177; and alcohol, 163; benefits, 78, 168; and distant correspondents, 68, 69–70, 76–77, 116, 128; experiences during, 52, 58, 121, 168; groups, 38, 42, 72–73, 82, 85, 150–51, 152, 177; and kōan, 28, 42–43; and martial arts, 77; monastic, 96–97; in prison, 128–32; postures, 118, 185n1; requesting advice, 51–53; self-taught, 18, 79, 173; and sesshin, 27, 43; styles, 28, 65, 124, 150, 153; in *Taking the Path*, 35–36, 107, 160; in Western Zen, 43. See also *zazen*
Merzel, Dennis Genpo, 74–75, 89, 183n1 (chap. 3)
Mind of Clover, The (Aitken), 4, 12, 81, 91, 160; and distant correspondents, 16, 34, 36–37, 49–50, 53, 58, 60–61, 62, 63, 118; and drugs, 163; and *mizuko kuyo*, 75, 109–10; and precepts, 19, 61, 62, 65,n 118, 163; and social justice, 19, 88–89; and Zen scandals, 120, 121
Mindfulness groups, 40
Ministry, 8, 21, 139
Ministry by mail, 137–39, 146, 156, 157, 176
mizuko kuyo, 108–10, 158
monastic celibacy, 95–96
monastic practice, 42, 43, 112, 174, 184n12; Aitken's experience, 27, 66; and distant correspondents, 54–55, 70; and Sanbōkyōdan, 28; versus lay practice, 20, 28, 54–55, 81, 94–98
mondo, 59
Moonspring Hermitage, 104–05

Morgan, Marian, 157
Morreale, Don, 38; *Complete Guide to Buddhist America, The*, 38
Mourning the Unborn Dead (Wilson), 107
Mu kōan, 59, 91; and distant correspondents, 52, 71, 74, 104, 127, 130, 156; at HDS, 36; and Sanbōkyōdan, 28; and solo practice, 71; in *Taking the Path*, 36, 103; via mail, 127, 156
Mumonkan, 87, 184n6

Nakagawa Kyudo, 110, 116, 118, 158
Nakagawa Sōen, 23, 27, 29, 31, 181n8
New Religious Movements, 79, 171
Nowick, Walter, 104, 116
Numrich, Paul, 97

Ōbaku Zen, 5, 28, 96–97
ordination, 43, 55, 92
orientation talks, 34–35, 177
Orsi, Robert, 14, 180n17
Osage Monastery, 90, 184n12

Palolo Zen Center, 32, 33, 138, 179n2
Parker, Frankie, 131–32, 186n6
precepts: and American Zen, 89–90, 174; and distant correspondents, 112, 120–21; and HDS, 89–90, 184n10; and *jukai*, 43, 73–74, 108, 109; in Mind of Clover, 36–37, 49–50, 61, 65
prison inmates, 21, 98, 133; as a category, 115, 128–32; and isolation, 83, 86; and long-term correspondents, 126; and reading, 129, 160, 161 and social justice, 91; and therapeutic practice, 78, 130; and Walking Wounded, 117
prison ministry, 73, 126, 128–29, 133
prisoner of war camp, 4, 25–26

Quakers, 72, 90, 111

rakusu, 74, 109
Rand, Yvonne, 75, 110, 158, 185n25
reading: Aitken's concern for, 21, 76–77, 131, 139, 147, 149, 152, 159–61; Aitken's early exposure, 4, 26; Aitken's recommendations for, 160; and communal practice, 73, 108–09; as primary form of practice, 18; and prison inmates, 129–30, 131, 160; requests for suggestions, 51, 129; and self-taught practice, 69–70; and solo practice, 152, 160; Zen introduced through, 4, 18–19, 26, 131
Rieck, Joan, 58, 157, 158
Right Action, 92
Right Effort, 92, 93
Right Livelihood, 54, 61, 92
Ring of Bone Zendo, 33, 57, 157
Rinzai Zen, 5, 27–28, 40, 42–43, 61, 96–97, 183n6
ritual, 106–12, 171; bowing, 27, 111; and distant correspondents, 20, 48, 73, 81, 108–12, 124; *jukai*, 43, 75, 109; *mizuko kuyo*, 109–10, 158, 185n25; and Zen, 106–07
Robert Baker Aitken Papers, xiii-xvi, 141, 173; letters, 4, 6–8, 24, 139, 144; and Shimano Archive, 29
Rochester Zen Center, 40, 74, 116
Rohatsu sesshin, 62, 76, 183n3 (chap. 3)
rōshi: challenging, 20, 59–64; faith in, 92; form of address, 42, 142; role of, 109, 137, 139; in Sanbōkyōdan, 96. *See also* teacher
Rural Southern Voice for Peace, 90
Ryūtakuji, 27, 29

San Diego Zen Center, 156
San Francisco Zen Center. *See* SFZC
Sanbōkyōdan: and Aitken, 12, 31, 32, 96, 164, 180n4; and American Zen, 39–40; lineage, 27–28, 39–40, 97, 157, 180n4; procedures, 24, 35, 42–43, 96, 97
sangha: and abusive teachers, 120, 121, 168; affiliation with, 80; as Buddha Dharma, 99–100, 151, 155; and communal practice, 36, 72–73, 150, 169; definition, 42, 182n27; and distant membership, 17; and ethics, 37; hindrances to joining, 87, 157 isolation from, 82–88, 112, 128, 160, 168, 174,

sangha (continued)
176; resistance to joining, 81, 112–13, 133; and ritual, 108, 110–11; sought by distant correspondents, 20, 48, 56–57, 83, 99, 116, 158; and scandals, 118, 121, 168; and women, 54; in Western Buddhism, 42, 81, 85, 98;
sanzen, 43, 105, 154. See also *dokusan*
Sasaki Jōshū, 6, 61–62, 183n6
satori, 57, 64–65, 129
Seekers and Dabblers, 18, 21, 115, 123–26, 133
Sekida Katsuki, 30
sensei, 42
Senzaki Nyogen, 26, 27, 181n7
sesshin: Aitken's advice, 98, 151–52, 154, 160; Aitken extends invitation, 53, 57; Aitken recommends, 52, 60, 71, 125–26; and checking an experience, 58, 156; and distant membership, 87, 105, 109, 151–52, 177; and family concerns, 54, 85, 162–63; financial limitations, 88, 75; at HDS, 9, 23, 29, 31–32, 36, 63, 138, 154, 180n13; in Japan, 27, 111; participation by distant correspondents, 62–63, 70, 85, 95, 119, 127, 154, 156; *rohatsu*, 62, 76, 183n3 (chap. 3); and solo practice, 69, 105; in Western Zen, 43, 172
Seing Sahn, 100–01, 157, 158
SFZC (San Francisco Zen Center), 150, 161; and distant correspondents, 53, 62, 95, 110, 116, 121; membership, 10, 174; scandal, 53, 118
Shakyamuni Buddha, 35, 55, 100
shikan taza, 19, 28, 42–43, 62, 69, 70, 98, 153
Shimano Archive, The, 29
Snyder, Gary, 73, 90
social activism, 36, 37, 39
social justice, xv, 19, 20, 34, 79, 81, 88–94, 174
Sōkōji, 38, 39
solo practitioners: Aitken's understanding of, 151–52, 157, 160, 166, 176–77; as a category, 16, 18, 69–72, 79–80, 173–76; hindrances to affiliating, 112–13, 174; and isolation, 82–88, 174–75; and long-term correspondents, 126–28; and need for a teacher, 103–06; and reading, 159–60; regard Aitken as teacher, 50; 59–60; and ritual, 111–12; and scholarship, 13, 178; and *Taking the Path*, 36; view of the teacher, 56; and Western Buddhism, 4, 10, 19, 81, 172, 173–76, 178
Sōtō Mission, 38
Sōtō Zen, 101, 110, 173, 184n19, 185n20; and American Zen, 38, 39, 40, 97; in Japan, 96–97, 102; and Sanbōkyōdan, 27–28; and *shikan taza*, 42, 43, 98
Stuart, Maurine, 92, 116
student-teacher relationship: and abusive teachers, 100, 118, 120, 152; with Aitken, 15–17, 48, 71, 99, 138, 156; Aitken's understanding, 64, 74, 100, 105, 153; and distant membership, 152, 177; establishing, 15–17, 68; and ethics, 64, 120; with prisoners, 128;
suki, 105, 185n21
Suzuki, D.T., 66, 106, 125
Suzuki Shunryu, 62
Sydney Zen Center, 34, 129, 165
sympathizer, 37, 113, 125; and Aitken, 33, 34, 50, 83, 139; as a category, 4, 17–18, 19, 79, 125, 133; and Dabblers, 125, 133; and isolation, 86, 112; knowledge of Zen, 56, 107; and scholarship, xv, 13, 20, 115, 172, 177, 178; and Tweed, 3, 17–18, 82, 179n1; view of Zen, 10, 56, 64, 106, 173

Taisen Deshimaru, 104, 184n20
Taking the Path of Zen (Aitken), 23, 47, 67, 125, 149, 171; advice from, 36, 72, 78, 149, 150 appeal of, 4, 12; as basis for practice, 52, 69–70, 79, 84, 100, 124, 130; commented on by distant correspondent, 16, 92, 122; gratitude

for, 47; and HDS 36, 67, 177; as a manual, 18, 34–36, 103; read by distant correspondents, 49–50, 58, 65, 82, 92, 153; recommended by Aitken, 77, 111, 160; requested by distant correspondent, 91, 131; and ritual, 107; and Willy-Nilly Zen, 24
Takuan Sōhō, 61
Tarrant, John, 33, 34, 157
teacher: abusive behavior, 76, 116–23, 132; and alcoholism, 64, 92; Aitken's recommendations, 52, 127, 150–51, 153, 157–59, 168–69; and celibacy, 96–97; challenging, 59–64; designation as, 180n4; finding a new, 56–57, 117, 120; need for, 70–71, 102, 106, 137, 154; perceptions of, 36–37, 56, 65, 145; practice without, 71, 102–06, 118, 155; student's interaction with, 43, 58, 67–68, 74, 156, 163; terminology, 42, 180n4; trusting, 99, 100, 118, 120, 153; unethical, 116–23, 153. *See also* master
teishō: Aitken's style, 137–38; as a pillar of Zen, 105; on the precepts, 36, 89, 121; on tape, 51, 60, 121, 141, 161, 182–83n4
Tetsugen Dōkō, 5–6
Theravada Buddhism, 18, 19, 97
Three Pillars of Zen, The (Kapleau), 18, 56, 70, 71, 77, 92, 160
Three Treasures, 36, 100
Tibetan Buddhism, 57, 74, 75, 116, 124, 164
Thich Nhat Hanh, 40
Tipton, Steven M., 10, 174
To Forget the Self (Buksbazen), 19
Turning Wheel, 88
Tweed, Thomas, 3, 17–18, 82, 179n1, 186n3 (concl.)
Tworkov, Helen, 24, 111; *Zen in America: Profiles of Five Teachers*, 24

University of Hawaii, xiii, 4, 24, 25, 26, 31, 185n4

Vajrayana Buddhism, 19
Vipassana, 24, 166

Walking Wounded, xv, 115, 116–23, 127, 133, 160
warning staff, 66
Watts, Alan, 125
What Is Meditation (White), 49, 142
White, John, 49; *What Is Meditation*, 49, 142
White Plum lineage, 40
Wilson, Jeff, 107; *Mourning the Unborn Dead*, 107

Yamada Kōun: as Aitken's teacher, 12, 23, 24, 31, 138; and correspondence, 143; and Sanbōkyōdan, 32, 164; and Zen for Catholics, 58
Yamamoto Genpō, 27
Yasutani Hakuun, 27–28, 29, 31, 35, 39, 66, 96, 97, 164

zafu, 18, 27
zazen: Aitken's practical advice, 51–52, 108, 118, 162, 17; and disabilities, 77–78, 84, 1104, 128; and distant membership, 152; encouraged by Aitken, 36, 72, 123, 146, 155; as focus of Zen, 49, 79, 105, 106, 138, 168; forms of, 42, 65; goals for, 67, 164; at HDS, 63, 98; introduction to, 34, 71; at Japanese temples, 27, 97; and *makyō*, 52–53, 59, 71, 74, 163; manuals, 18–19, 34, 36, 182n22; practiced by distant correspondents, 20, 69–70, 124, 125, 159; in prison, 128, 130; requires a teacher, 154; and ritual, 107; and Sanbōkyōdan, 26, 28; solo practice, 18, 69, 82, 103, 151; therapeutic, 77–78;
zazenkai, 78, 83, 84, 175; and distant correspondents, 69, 72; at ethnic temples, 97; for prisoners, 128, 129; suggestions for, 73, 108
ZCLA (Zen Center of Los Angeles), 150, 158; Aitken recommends, 78, 98, 154,

ZCLA (*continued*)
166; and distant correspondents, 57, 62, 74–75, 89, 116, 117–18, 123, 154, 167; and ethics, 121–22; and Genpo Merzel, 74–75, 89; and Maezumi, 62, 64, 78, 97, 98, 117–18, 122, 154

Zen: American, 5, 37–41, 82, 112, 178, 179n1; and alcoholism, 63–64, 85, 118, 122, 158, 163, 183n9; in Australia, 9, 12, 32, 33, 34, 71, 129, 165; centers (*see individual names*); communal practice, 36, 72–73, 147, 150–52, 161, 169, 177; communities (*see* sangha); and drugs, 36, 63–64, 163–64; and family responsibilities, 43, 54, 56, 112, 150, 162, 174–75, 176; and the internet, 79, 112, 138, 146, 175, 177; literature (*see* literature); and martial arts, 61, 77, 105, 185n21; master (*see* master); meditation (*see* meditation; zazen); and mental illness, 77–78, 104; Ōbaku Zen, 5, 28, 96–97; orientation talks, 34–35, 177; and physical disabilities, 77–78, 84, 104, 128; and reading (*see* reading); residential programs, 31, 32, 43, 78, 95, 97, 98, 143; Rinzai Zen, 5, 27–28, 40, 42–43, 61, 96–97, 183n6; ritual (*see* ritual); scandals, 19, 53, 100, 116, 118, 120, 121, 132, 168; solo practitioners (*see* solo practitioners); Sōtō (*see* Sōtō Zen); sympathizers (*see* sympathizers); talk (*see teishō*); teacher (*see* teacher); as therapy, 77–78, 130

Zen Buddhist Path of Self-realization, The, 12, 115, 139

Zen Center of Los Angeles. *See* ZCLA

Zen Desert Sangha, 33, 73

Zen in America: Profiles of Five Teachers (Tworkov), 24

Zen in English Literature and Oriental Classics (Blyth), 4, 26

Zen Wave, A (Aitken), 26, 50

zendo, 36, 72, 106

Zenshūji, 38, 39, 184n19

www.ingramcontent.com/pod-product-compliance
Lightning Source LLC
Chambersburg PA
CBHW020332240426
43665CB00043B/443